GODZILLA
RULERS OF EARTH

VOLUME **2**

STORY BY **CHRIS MOWRY** AND **MATT FRANK**

WRITTEN BY
CHRIS MOWRY

ART BY
MATT FRANK AND JEFF ZORNOW

INK ASSIST BY
MOSTAFA MOUSSA (CHAPTER THREE)

COLORS BY
PRISCILLA TRAMONTANO

LETTERS BY
SHAWN LEE

SERIES EDITS BY
BOBBY CURNOW

COVER ART BY **MATT FRANK**

COLLECTION EDITS BY **JUSTIN EISINGER** AND **ALONZO SIMON**
COLLECTION DESIGN BY **CHRIS MOWRY**

ISBN: 978-1-61377-933-0
18 17 16 15   3 4 5 6

Special thanks to Yoshiko Fukuda and everyone at Toho for their invaluable assistance.

Ted Adams, CEO & Publisher
Greg Goldstein, President & COO
Robbie Robbins, EVP/Sr. Graphic Artist
Chris Ryall, Chief Creative Officer/Editor-in-Chief
Matthew Ruzicka, CPA, Chief Financial Officer
Alan Payne, VP of Sales
Dirk Wood, VP of Marketing
Lorelei Bunjes, VP of Digital Services
Jeff Webber, VP of Digital Publishing & Business Development

Facebook: facebook.com/idwpublishing
Twitter: @idwpublishing
YouTube: youtube.com/idwpublishing
Instagram: instagram.com/idwpublishing
deviantART: idwpublishing.deviantart.com
Pinterest: pinterest.com/idwpublishing/idw-staff-faves

www.IDWPUBLISHING.com
IDW founded by Ted Adams, Alex Garner, Kris Oprisko, and Robbie Robbins

THE STORY SO FAR

Humanity has come to terms with the arrival of giant monsters across the globe. After an attack from space that nearly destroyed the planet, Godzilla reappeared in Hawaii and nearly killed budding scientist Lucy Casprell and her Kaiju Watcher research team. Saved by Commander Steven Woods of the Counter-Kaiju Reactionary forces (CKR, "Seekers"), Lucy joins her group as they depart for China in search of a mysterious giant monster.

The CKR team discovers a new species called Destoroyah and a piece of Godzilla's flesh, and take both to their facility in San Diego for analysis. An attack at sea which destroyed an aircraft carrier and supporting fleet signals the invasion of downtown San Diego by a swarm of Destoroyah crabs. Leaving the facility to engage the crabs, the CKR forces are unaware that an alien race known as the Cryog have stolen the Godzilla specimen, leaving a sole survivor.

Turning the Godzilla specimen over to their undersea cohorts, the Devonians, the Cryog are confident that Godzilla will soon be destroyed, easing their conquest of the planet. When Godzilla faces the mighty Destoroyah, he nearly falls in defeat. Only with the intervention of Mothra do the two defeat Destoroyah, and thwart the Cryog/Devonian plans.

CHAPTER ONE:
CAPTIVE

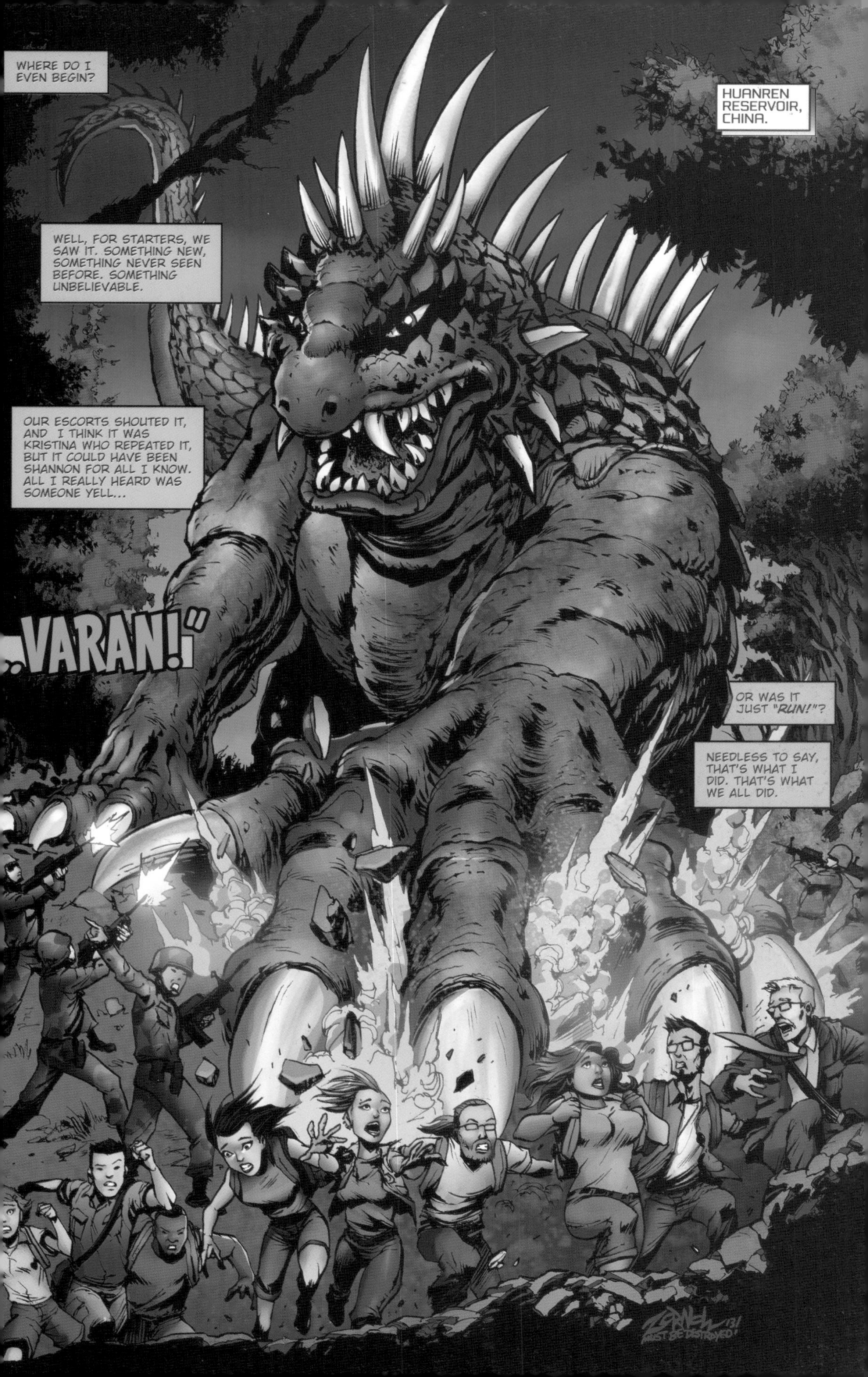
WHERE DO I EVEN BEGIN?
HUANREN RESERVOIR, CHINA.
WELL, FOR STARTERS, WE SAW IT. SOMETHING NEW, SOMETHING NEVER SEEN BEFORE. SOMETHING UNBELIEVABLE.
OUR ESCORTS SHOUTED IT, AND I THINK IT WAS KRISTINA WHO REPEATED IT, BUT IT COULD HAVE BEEN SHANNON FOR ALL I KNOW. ALL I REALLY HEARD WAS SOMEONE YELL...
"VARAN!"
OR WAS IT JUST "RUN!"?
NEEDLESS TO SAY, THAT'S WHAT I DID. THAT'S WHAT WE ALL DID.

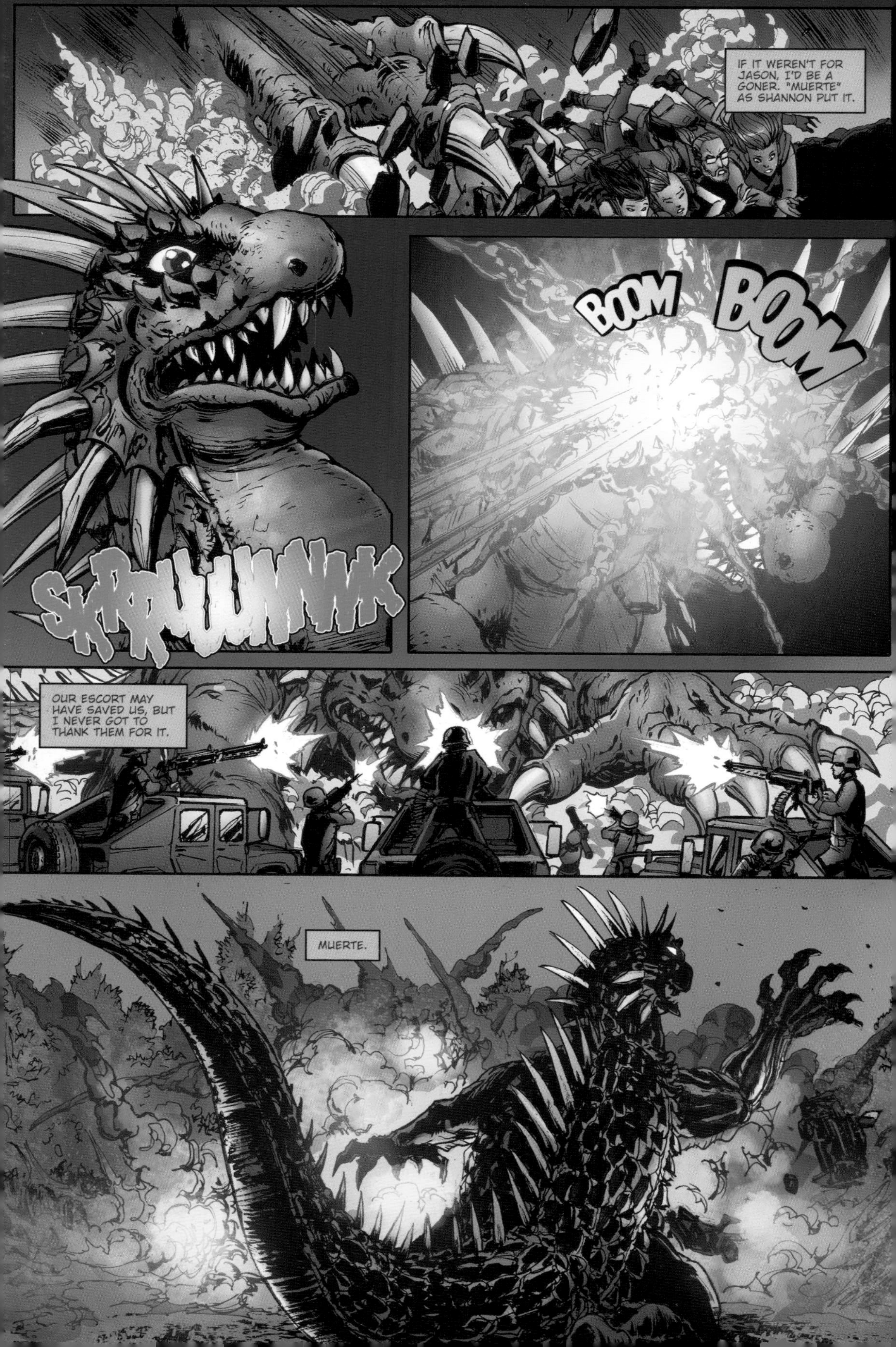
IF IT WEREN'T FOR JASON, I'D BE A GONER. "MUERTE" AS SHANNON PUT IT.
SKRRUUUNNWK
BOOM BOOM
OUR ESCORT MAY HAVE SAVED US, BUT I NEVER GOT TO THANK THEM FOR IT.
MUERTE.

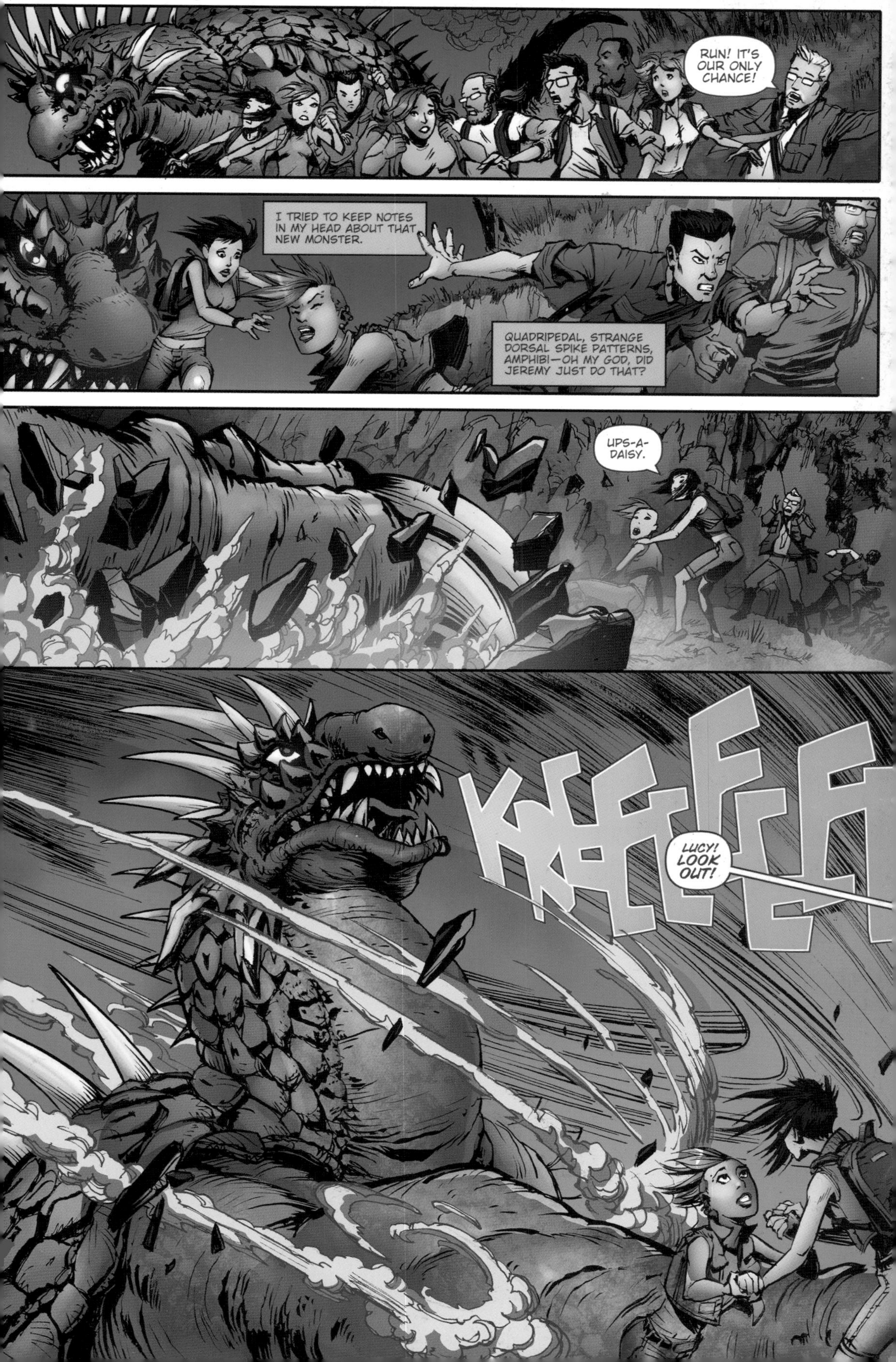
RUN! IT'S OUR ONLY CHANCE!
I TRIED TO KEEP NOTES IN MY HEAD ABOUT THAT NEW MONSTER.
QUADRIPEDAL, STRANGE DORSAL SPIKE PATTERNS, AMPHIBI—OH MY GOD, DID JEREMY JUST DO THAT?
UPS-A-DAISY.
KREEEEEE
LUCY! LOOK OUT!

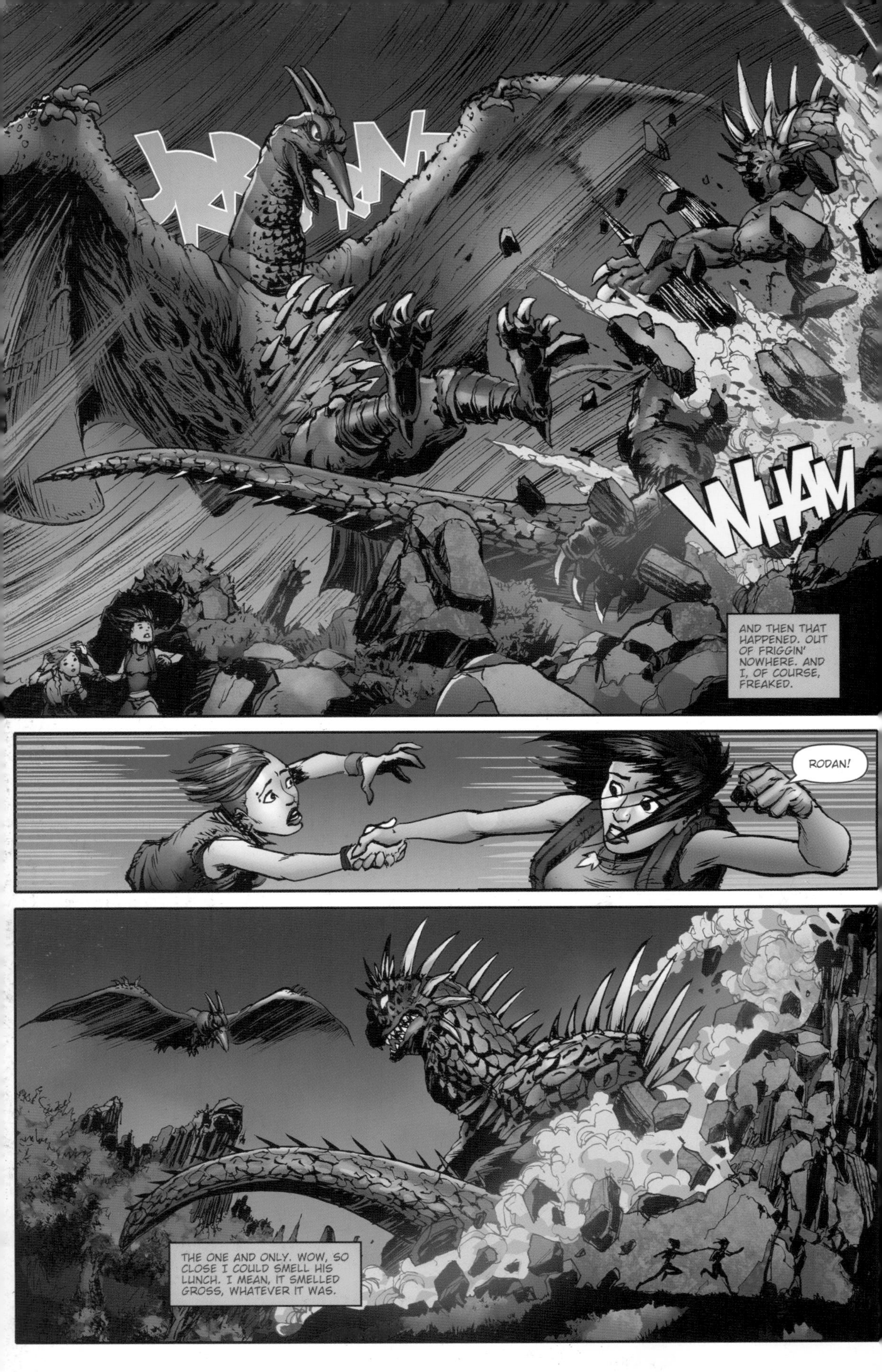
WHAM
AND THEN THAT HAPPENED. OUT OF FRIGGIN' NOWHERE. AND I, OF COURSE, FREAKED.
RODAN!
THE ONE AND ONLY. WOW, SO CLOSE I COULD SMELL HIS LUNCH. I MEAN, IT SMELLED GROSS, WHATEVER IT WAS.

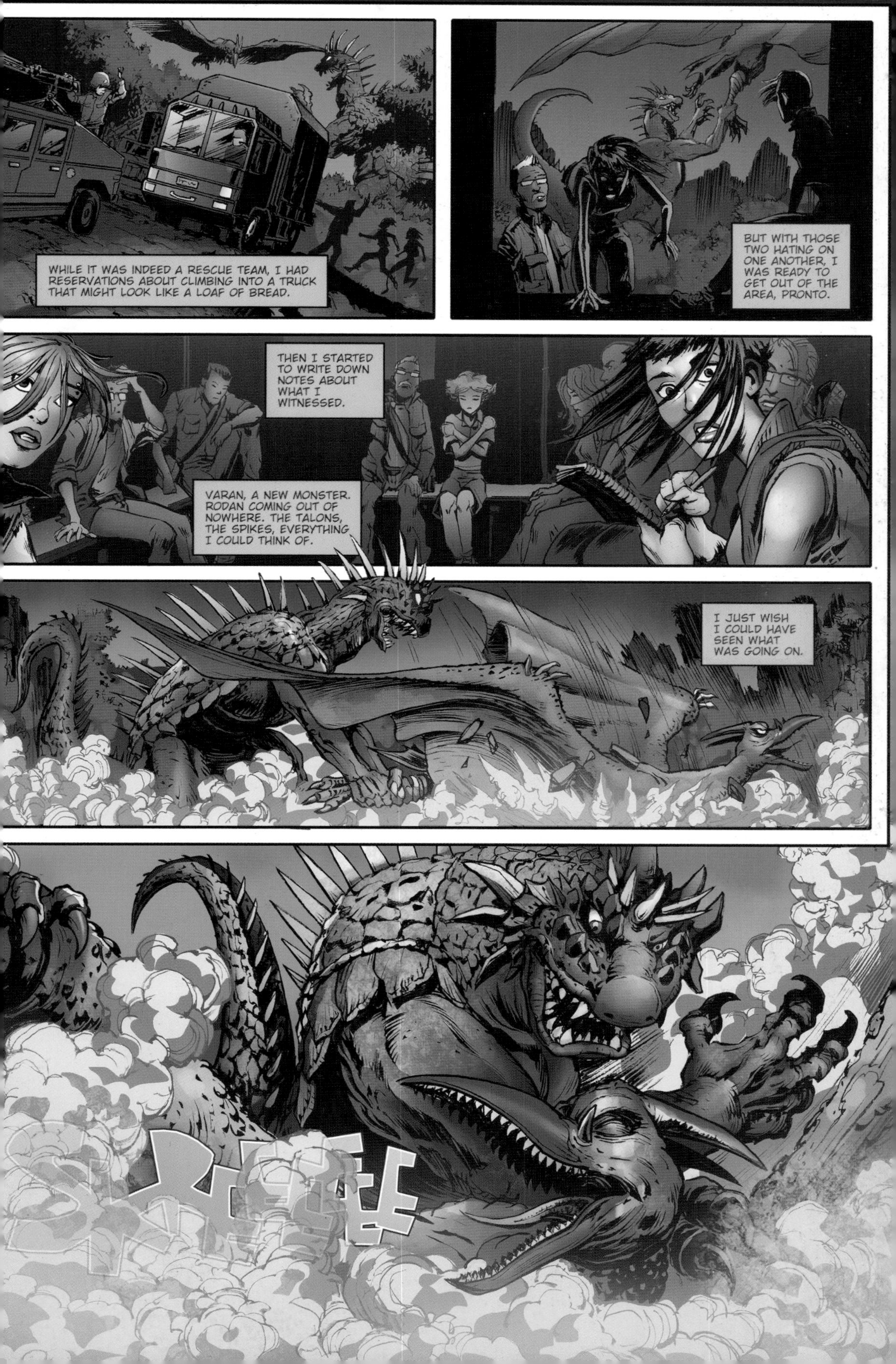
WHILE IT WAS INDEED A RESCUE TEAM, I HAD RESERVATIONS ABOUT CLIMBING INTO A TRUCK THAT MIGHT LOOK LIKE A LOAF OF BREAD.
BUT WITH THOSE TWO HATING ON ONE ANOTHER, I WAS READY TO GET OUT OF THE AREA, PRONTO.
THEN I STARTED TO WRITE DOWN NOTES ABOUT WHAT I WITNESSED.
VARAN, A NEW MONSTER. RODAN COMING OUT OF NOWHERE. THE TALONS, THE SPIKES, EVERYTHING I COULD THINK OF.
I JUST WISH I COULD HAVE SEEN WHAT WAS GOING ON.

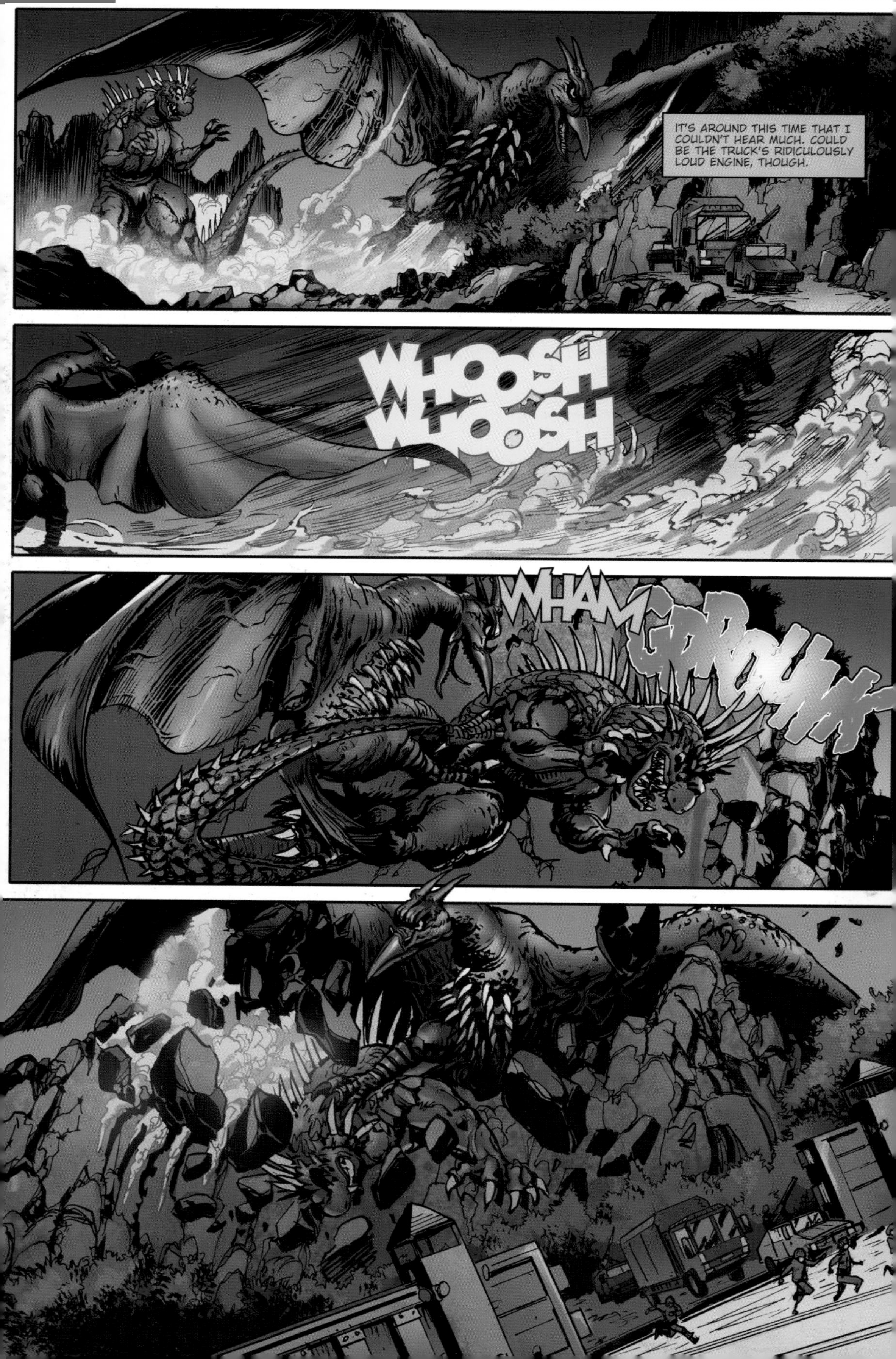
IT'S AROUND THIS TIME THAT I COULDN'T HEAR MUCH. COULD BE THE TRUCK'S RIDICULOUSLY LOUD ENGINE, THOUGH.
WHOOSH
WHOOSH
WHAM
GROWK

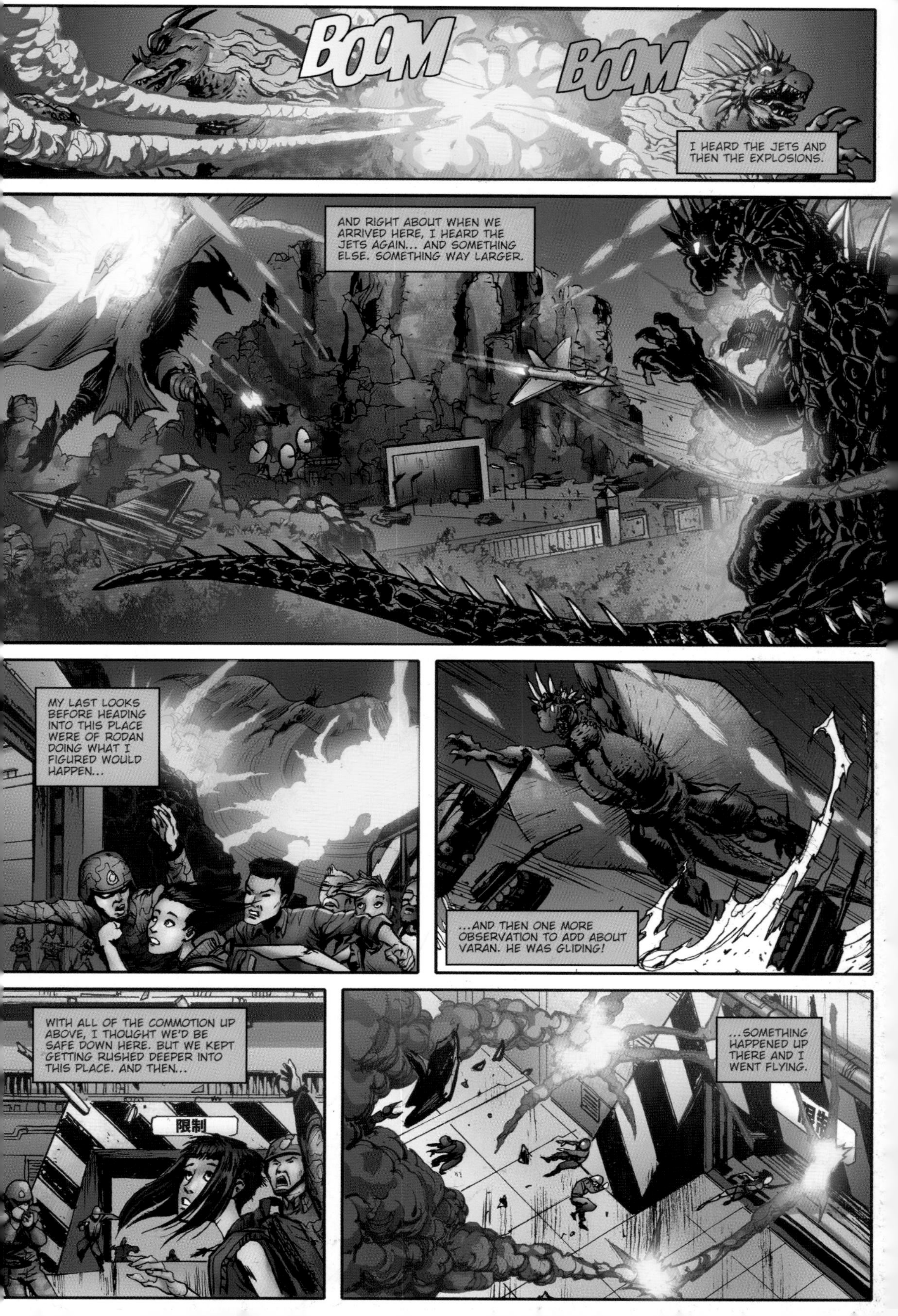
BOOM
BOOM
I HEARD THE JETS AND THEN THE EXPLOSIONS.
AND RIGHT ABOUT WHEN WE ARRIVED HERE, I HEARD THE JETS AGAIN... AND SOMETHING ELSE. SOMETHING WAY LARGER.
MY LAST LOOKS BEFORE HEADING INTO THIS PLACE WERE OF RODAN DOING WHAT I FIGURED WOULD HAPPEN...
...AND THEN ONE MORE OBSERVATION TO ADD ABOUT VARAN. HE WAS GLIDING!
WITH ALL OF THE COMMOTION UP ABOVE, I THOUGHT WE'D BE SAFE DOWN HERE. BUT WE KEPT GETTING RUSHED DEEPER INTO THIS PLACE. AND THEN...
限制
...SOMETHING HAPPENED UP THERE AND I WENT FLYING.

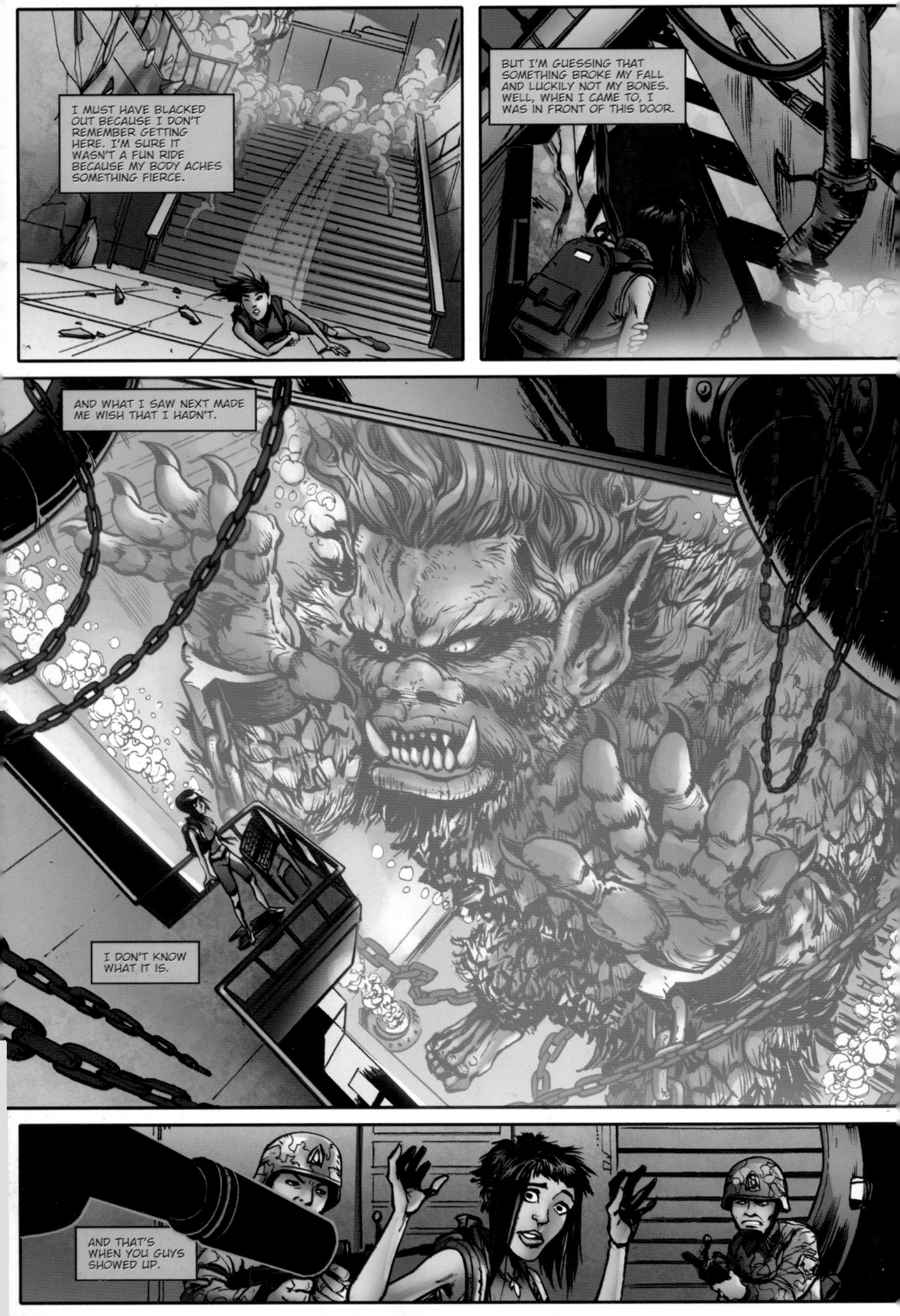
I MUST HAVE BLACKED OUT BECAUSE I DON'T REMEMBER GETTING HERE. I'M SURE IT WASN'T A FUN RIDE BECAUSE MY BODY ACHES SOMETHING FIERCE.
BUT I'M GUESSING THAT SOMETHING BROKE MY FALL AND LUCKILY NOT MY BONES. WELL, WHEN I CAME TO, I WAS IN FRONT OF THIS DOOR.
AND WHAT I SAW NEXT MADE ME WISH THAT I HADN'T.
I DON'T KNOW WHAT IT IS.
AND THAT'S WHEN YOU GUYS SHOWED UP.

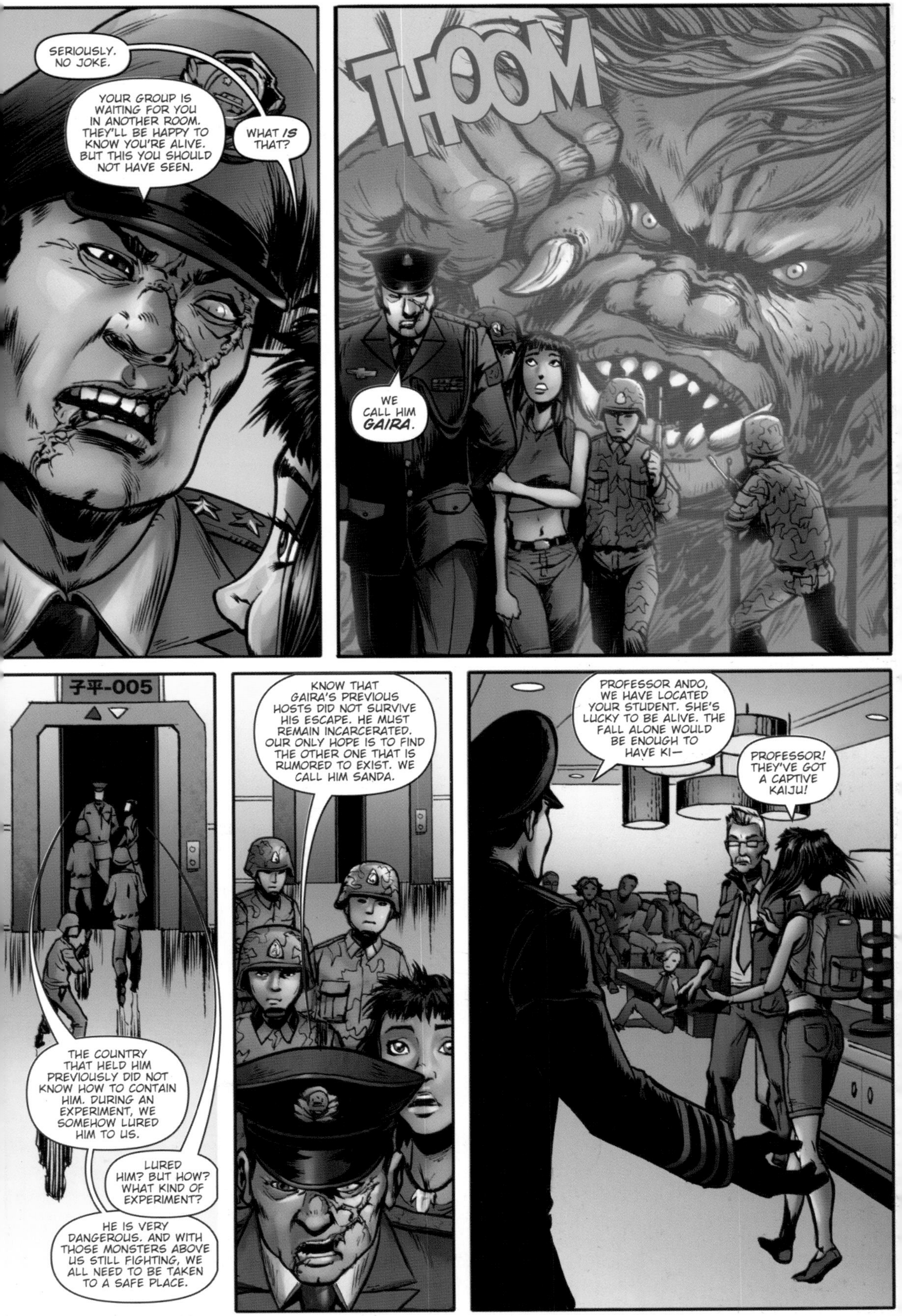

SERIOUSLY. NO JOKE.
YOUR GROUP IS WAITING FOR YOU IN ANOTHER ROOM. THEY'LL BE HAPPY TO KNOW YOU'RE ALIVE. BUT THIS YOU SHOULD NOT HAVE SEEN.
WHAT *IS* THAT?
THOOM
WE CALL HIM **GAIRA**.
子平-005
THE COUNTRY THAT HELD HIM PREVIOUSLY DID NOT KNOW HOW TO CONTAIN HIM. DURING AN EXPERIMENT, WE SOMEHOW LURED HIM TO US.
LURED HIM? BUT HOW? WHAT KIND OF EXPERIMENT?
HE IS VERY DANGEROUS. AND WITH THOSE MONSTERS ABOVE US STILL FIGHTING, WE ALL NEED TO BE TAKEN TO A SAFE PLACE.
KNOW THAT GAIRA'S PREVIOUS HOSTS DID NOT SURVIVE HIS ESCAPE. HE MUST REMAIN INCARCERATED. OUR ONLY HOPE IS TO FIND THE OTHER ONE THAT IS RUMORED TO EXIST. WE CALL HIM SANDA.
PROFESSOR ANDO, WE HAVE LOCATED YOUR STUDENT. SHE'S LUCKY TO BE ALIVE. THE FALL ALONE WOULD BE ENOUGH TO HAVE KI—
PROFESSOR! THEY'VE GOT A CAPTIVE KAIJU!

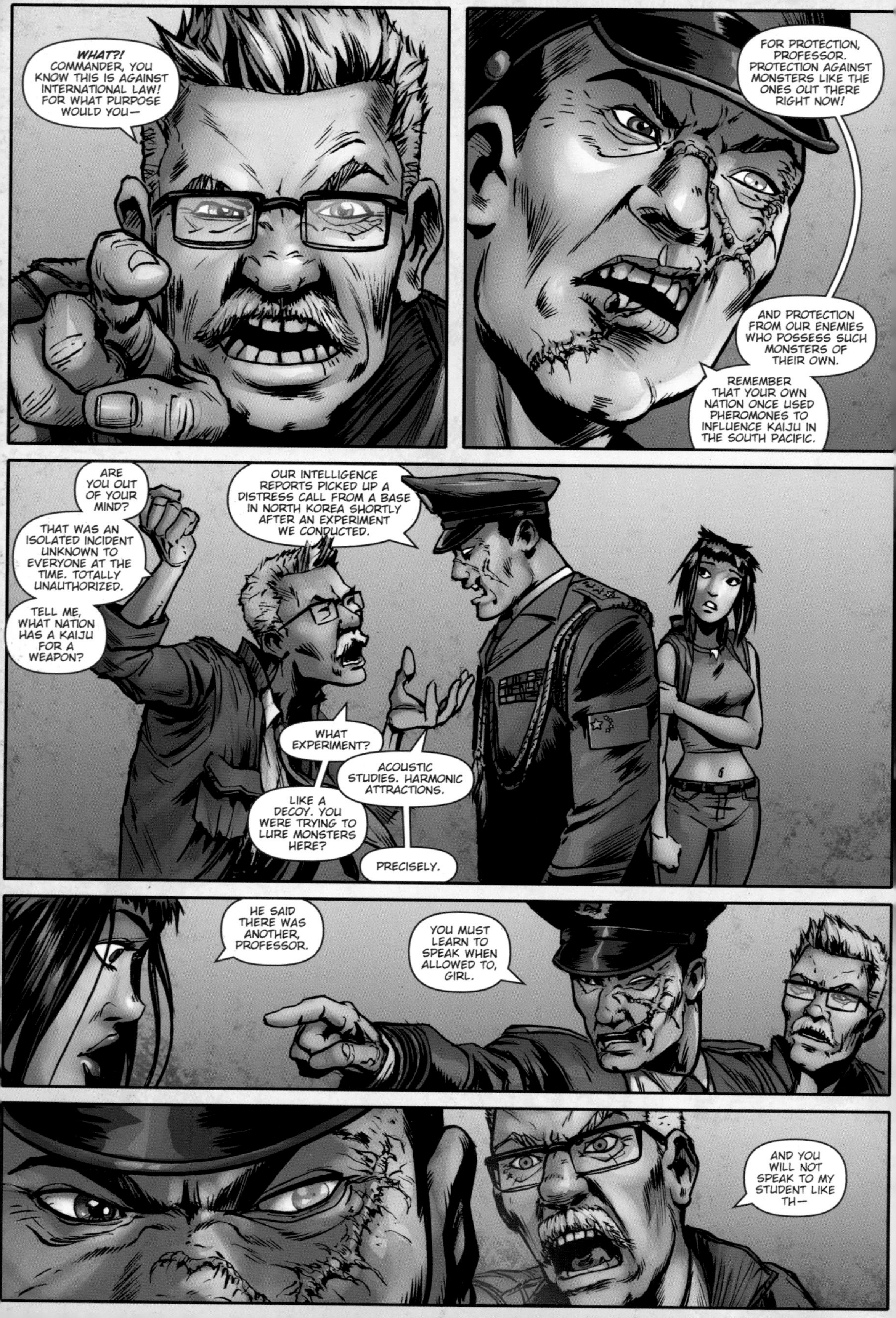
WHAT?! COMMANDER, YOU KNOW THIS IS AGAINST INTERNATIONAL LAW! FOR WHAT PURPOSE WOULD YOU—
FOR PROTECTION, PROFESSOR. PROTECTION AGAINST MONSTERS LIKE THE ONES OUT THERE RIGHT NOW!
AND PROTECTION FROM OUR ENEMIES WHO POSSESS SUCH MONSTERS OF THEIR OWN.
REMEMBER THAT YOUR OWN NATION ONCE USED PHEROMONES TO INFLUENCE KAIJU IN THE SOUTH PACIFIC.
ARE YOU OUT OF YOUR MIND?
THAT WAS AN ISOLATED INCIDENT UNKNOWN TO EVERYONE AT THE TIME. TOTALLY UNAUTHORIZED.
TELL ME, WHAT NATION HAS A KAIJU FOR A WEAPON?
OUR INTELLIGENCE REPORTS PICKED UP A DISTRESS CALL FROM A BASE IN NORTH KOREA SHORTLY AFTER AN EXPERIMENT WE CONDUCTED.
WHAT EXPERIMENT?
ACOUSTIC STUDIES. HARMONIC ATTRACTIONS.
LIKE A DECOY. YOU WERE TRYING TO LURE MONSTERS HERE?
PRECISELY.
HE SAID THERE WAS ANOTHER, PROFESSOR.
YOU MUST LEARN TO SPEAK WHEN ALLOWED TO, GIRL.
AND YOU WILL NOT SPEAK TO MY STUDENT LIKE TH—

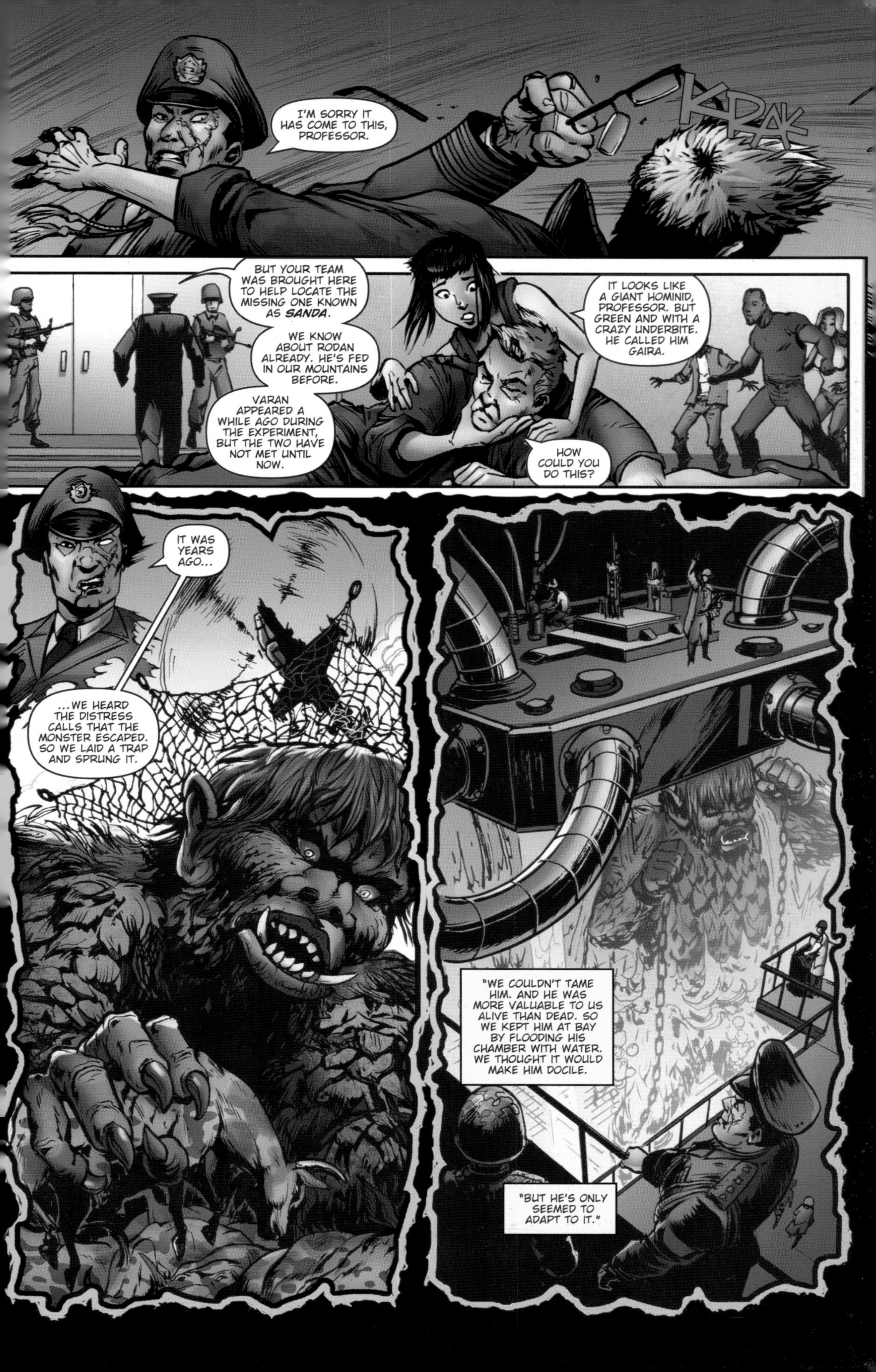
I'M SORRY IT HAS COME TO THIS, PROFESSOR.
KRAK
BUT YOUR TEAM WAS BROUGHT HERE TO HELP LOCATE THE MISSING ONE KNOWN AS SANDA.
WE KNOW ABOUT RODAN ALREADY. HE'S FED IN OUR MOUNTAINS BEFORE.
VARAN APPEARED A WHILE AGO DURING THE EXPERIMENT, BUT THE TWO HAVE NOT MET UNTIL NOW.
HOW COULD YOU DO THIS?
IT LOOKS LIKE A GIANT HOMINID, PROFESSOR. BUT GREEN AND WITH A CRAZY UNDERBITE. HE CALLED HIM GAIRA.
IT WAS YEARS AGO...
...WE HEARD THE DISTRESS CALLS THAT THE MONSTER ESCAPED. SO WE LAID A TRAP AND SPRUNG IT.
"WE COULDN'T TAME HIM. AND HE WAS MORE VALUABLE TO US ALIVE THAN DEAD. SO WE KEPT HIM AT BAY BY FLOODING HIS CHAMBER WITH WATER. WE THOUGHT IT WOULD MAKE HIM DOCILE.
"BUT HE'S ONLY SEEMED TO ADAPT TO IT."

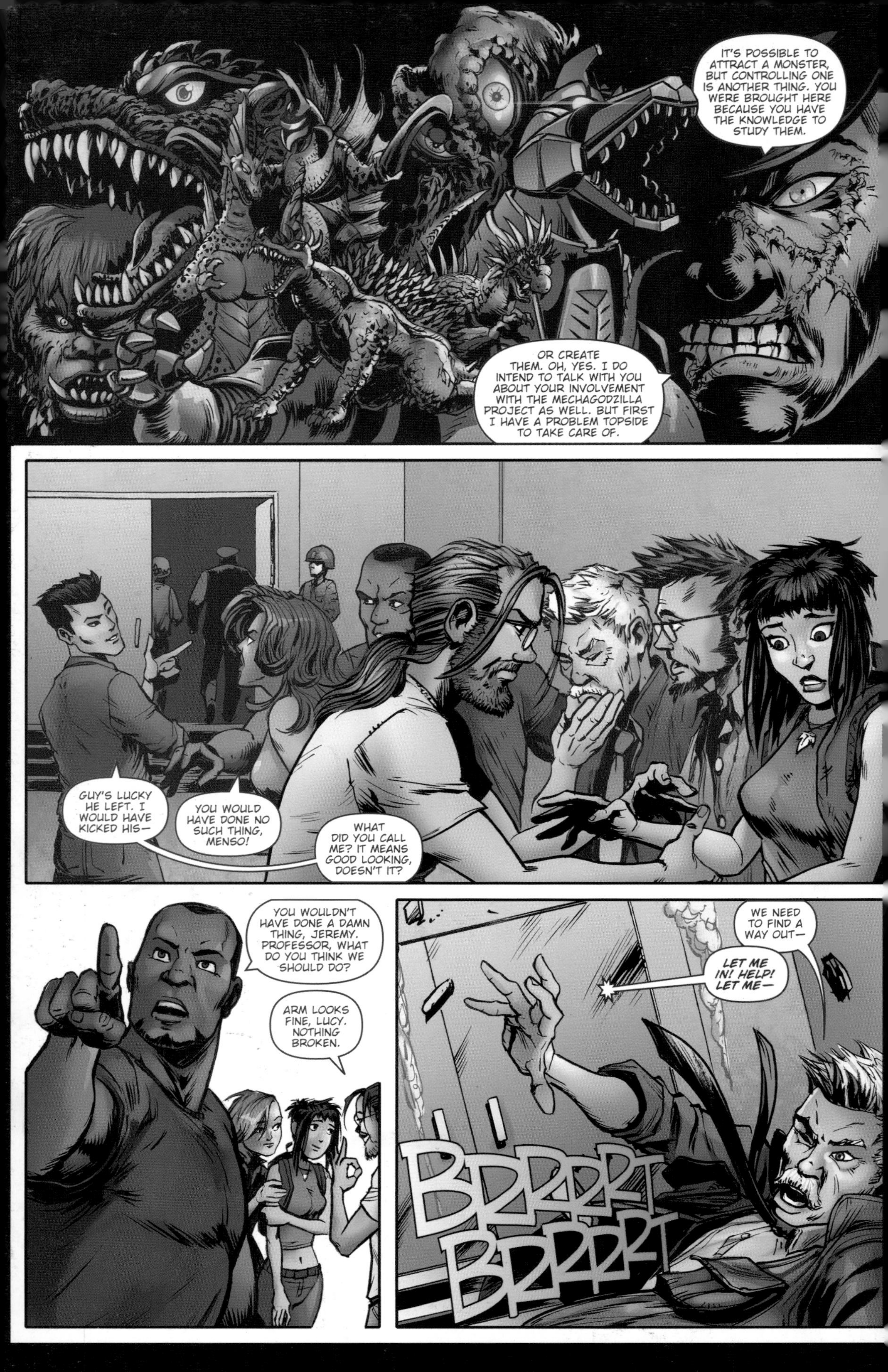
IT'S POSSIBLE TO ATTRACT A MONSTER, BUT CONTROLLING ONE IS ANOTHER THING. YOU WERE BROUGHT HERE BECAUSE YOU HAVE THE KNOWLEDGE TO STUDY THEM.
OR CREATE THEM. OH, YES. I DO INTEND TO TALK WITH YOU ABOUT YOUR INVOLVEMENT WITH THE MECHAGODZILLA PROJECT AS WELL. BUT FIRST I HAVE A PROBLEM TOPSIDE TO TAKE CARE OF.
GUY'S LUCKY HE LEFT. I WOULD HAVE KICKED HIS—
YOU WOULD HAVE DONE NO SUCH THING, MENSO!
WHAT DID YOU CALL ME? IT MEANS GOOD LOOKING, DOESN'T IT?
YOU WOULDN'T HAVE DONE A DAMN THING, JEREMY. PROFESSOR, WHAT DO YOU THINK WE SHOULD DO?
ARM LOOKS FINE, LUCY. NOTHING BROKEN.
WE NEED TO FIND A WAY OUT—
LET ME IN! HELP! LET ME—
BRRRRT
BRRRRT

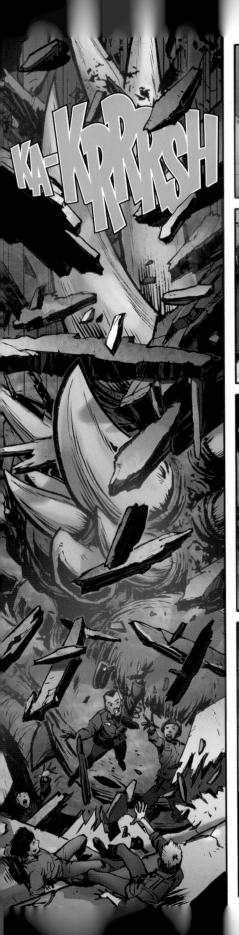

KA-KRRRKSH

KREEEUURRNT

SKRREEET

SKRRUKK

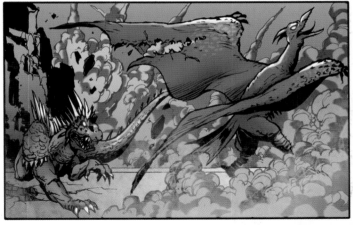

AS RODAN TRIES TO ESCAPE, SO DOES EVERYONE ELSE.

CLASS, WE NEED TO LEAVE. NOW.

EVERYONE BE CAREFUL. IF YOU'RE TOO HURT TO MOVE WE CAN HELP YOU.

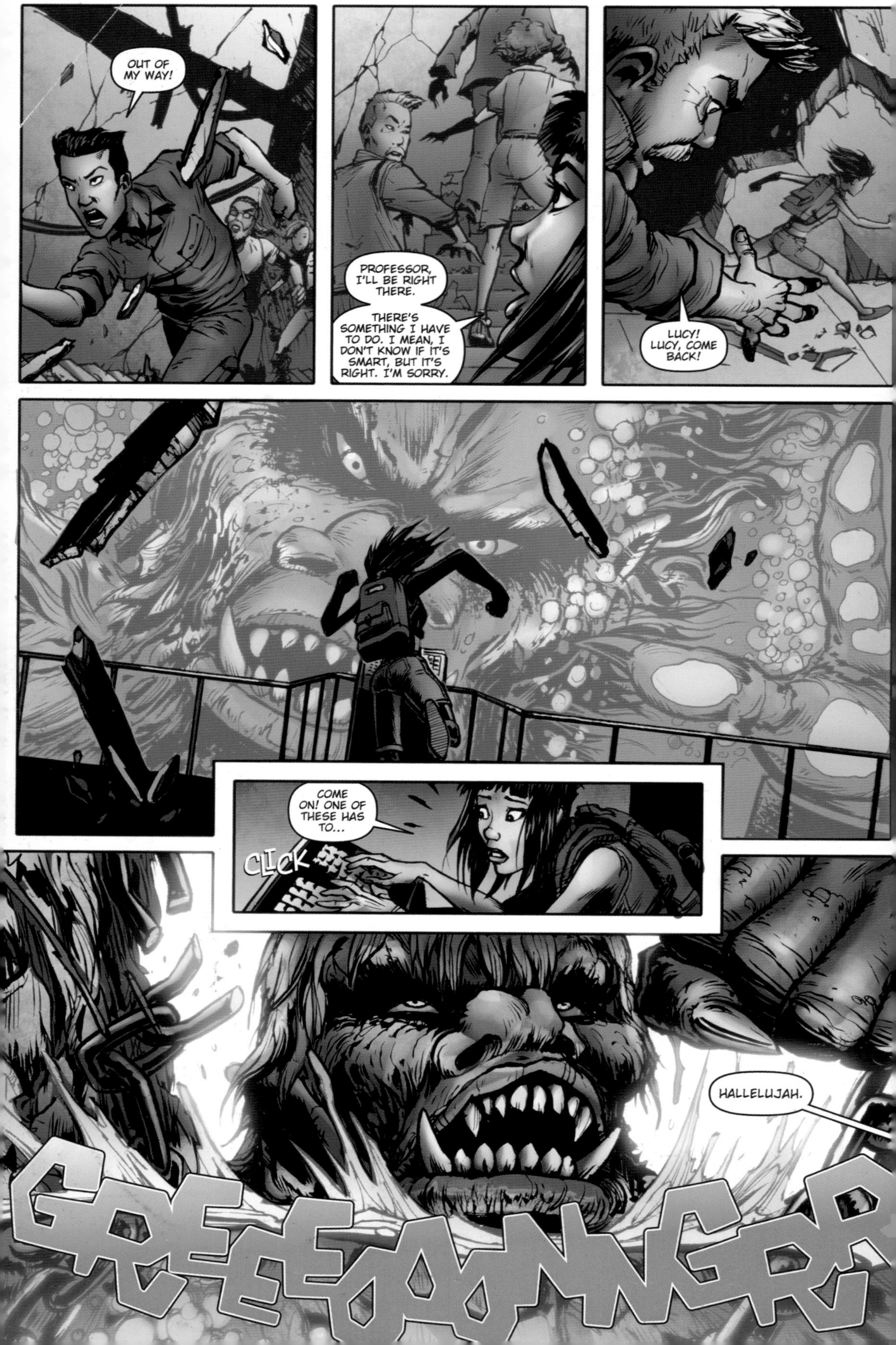
OUT OF MY WAY!
PROFESSOR, I'LL BE RIGHT THERE.
THERE'S SOMETHING I HAVE TO DO. I MEAN, I DON'T KNOW IF IT'S SMART, BUT IT'S RIGHT. I'M SORRY.
LUCY! LUCY, COME BACK!
COME ON! ONE OF THESE HAS TO...
CLICK
HALLELUJAH.
GREEEOOONNGRR

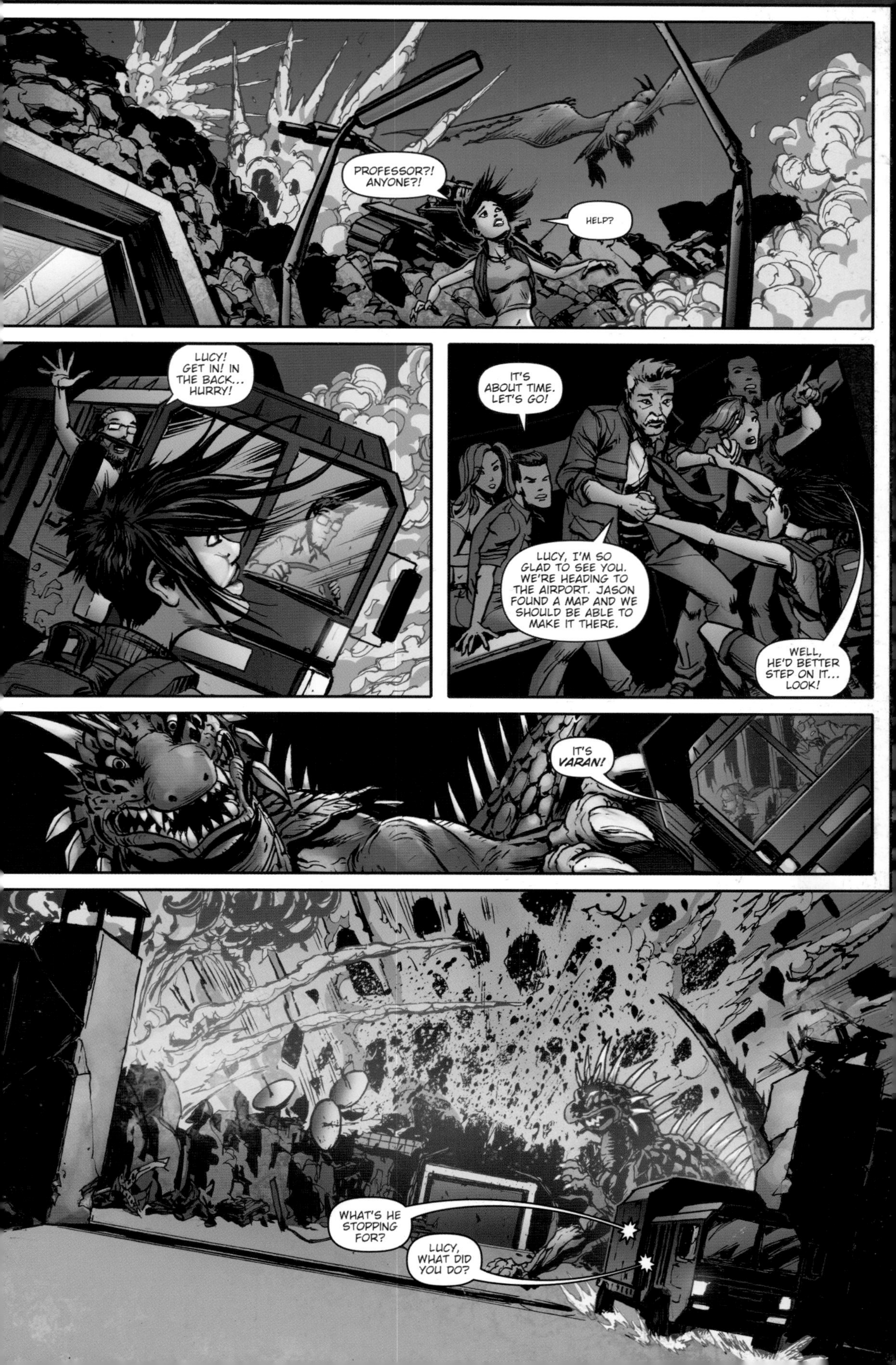
PROFESSOR?! ANYONE?!
HELP?
LUCY! GET IN! IN THE BACK... HURRY!
IT'S ABOUT TIME. LET'S GO!
LUCY, I'M SO GLAD TO SEE YOU. WE'RE HEADING TO THE AIRPORT. JASON FOUND A MAP AND WE SHOULD BE ABLE TO MAKE IT THERE.
WELL, HE'D BETTER STEP ON IT... LOOK!
IT'S VARAN!
WHAT'S HE STOPPING FOR?
LUCY, WHAT DID YOU DO?

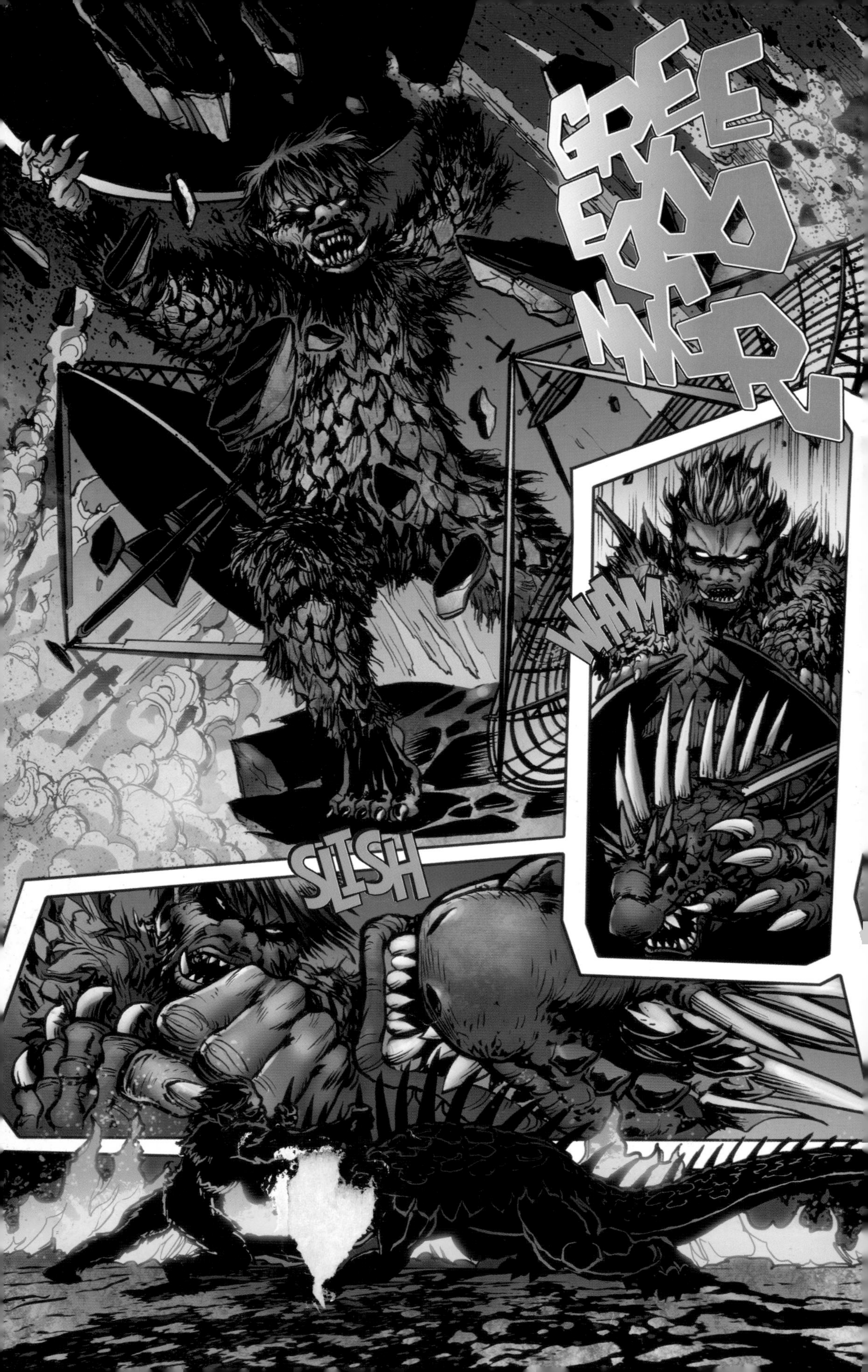
WHAM
SLISH

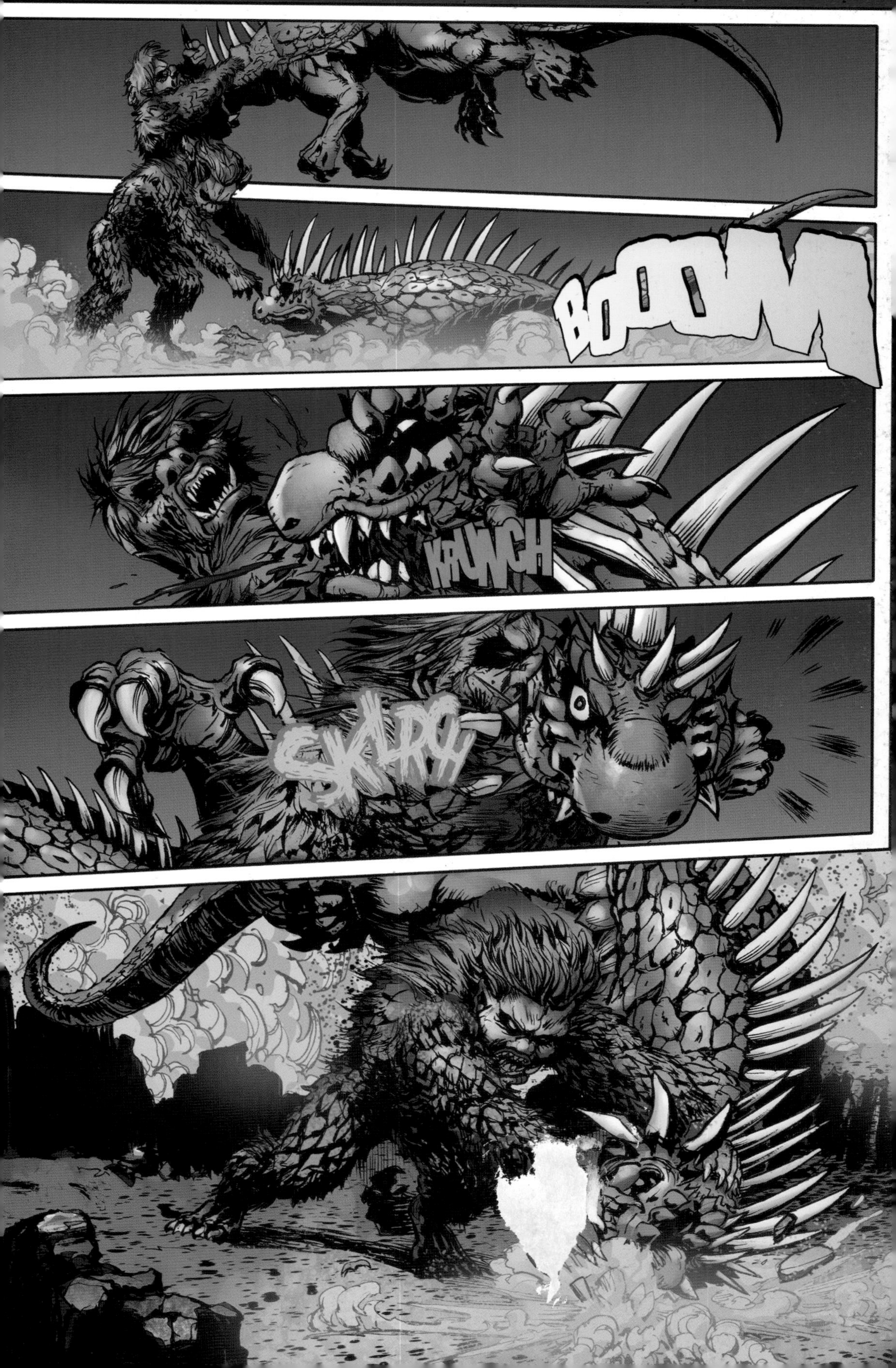
BOOOM
KRUNCH
SKLRCH

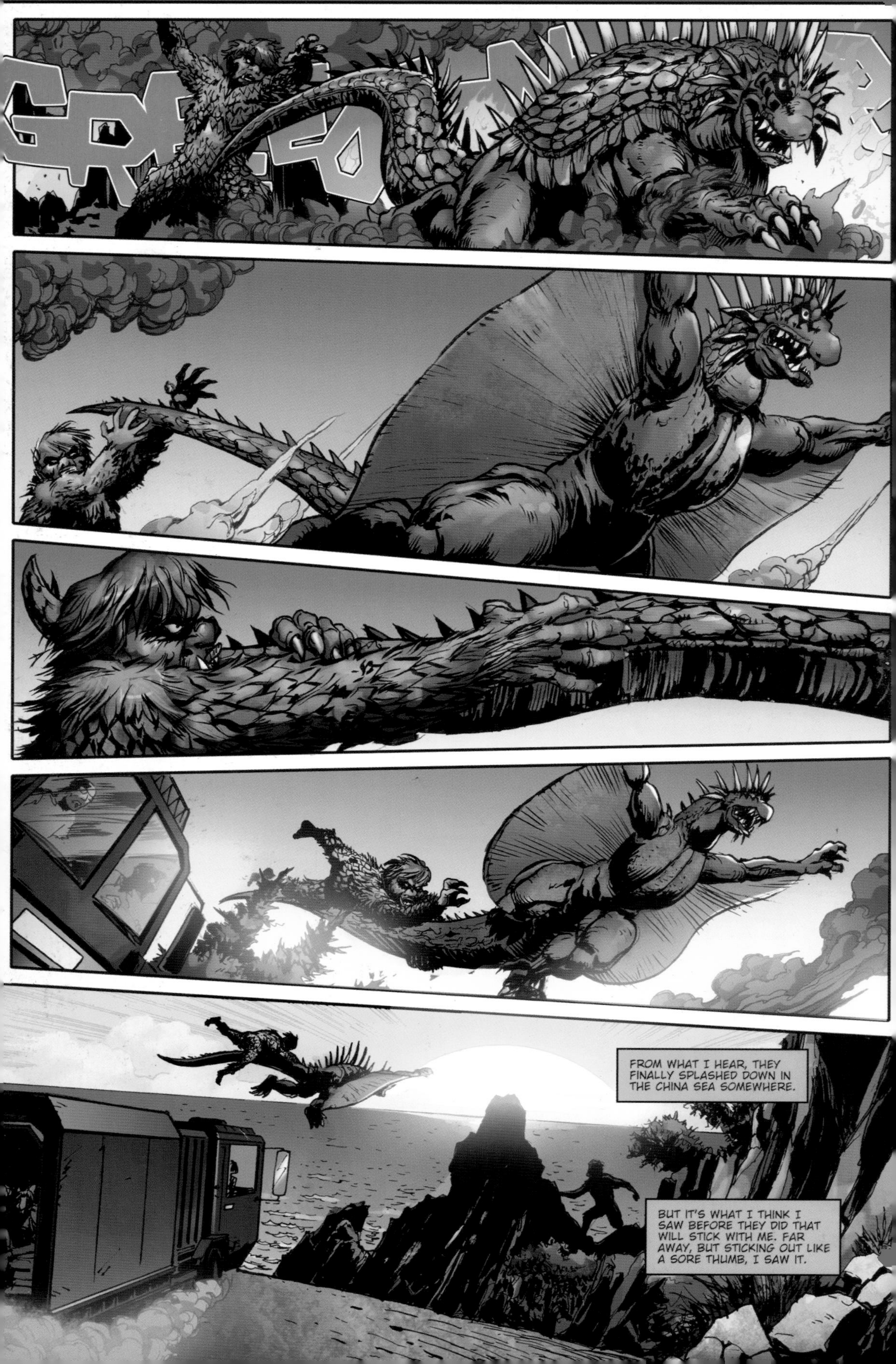
FROM WHAT I HEAR, THEY FINALLY SPLASHED DOWN IN THE CHINA SEA SOMEWHERE.
BUT IT'S WHAT I THINK I SAW BEFORE THEY DID THAT WILL STICK WITH ME. FAR AWAY, BUT STICKING OUT LIKE A SORE THUMB, I SAW IT.

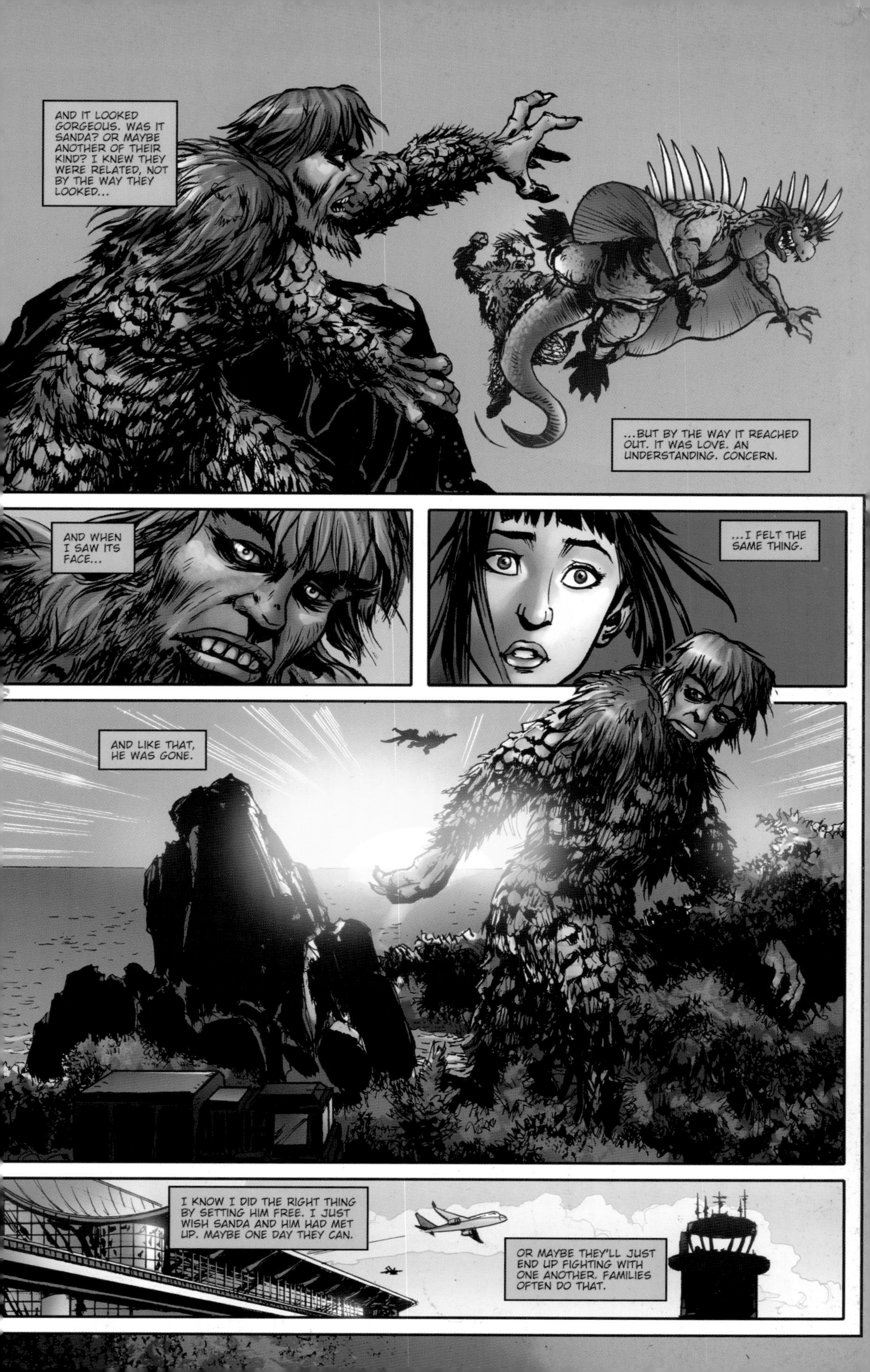
AND IT LOOKED GORGEOUS. WAS IT SANDA? OR MAYBE ANOTHER OF THEIR KIND? I KNEW THEY WERE RELATED, NOT BY THE WAY THEY LOOKED...
...BUT BY THE WAY IT REACHED OUT. IT WAS LOVE. AN UNDERSTANDING. CONCERN.
AND WHEN I SAW ITS FACE...
...I FELT THE SAME THING.
AND LIKE THAT, HE WAS GONE.
I KNOW I DID THE RIGHT THING BY SETTING HIM FREE. I JUST WISH SANDA AND HIM HAD MET UP. MAYBE ONE DAY THEY CAN.
OR MAYBE THEY'LL JUST END UP FIGHTING WITH ONE ANOTHER. FAMILIES OFTEN DO THAT.

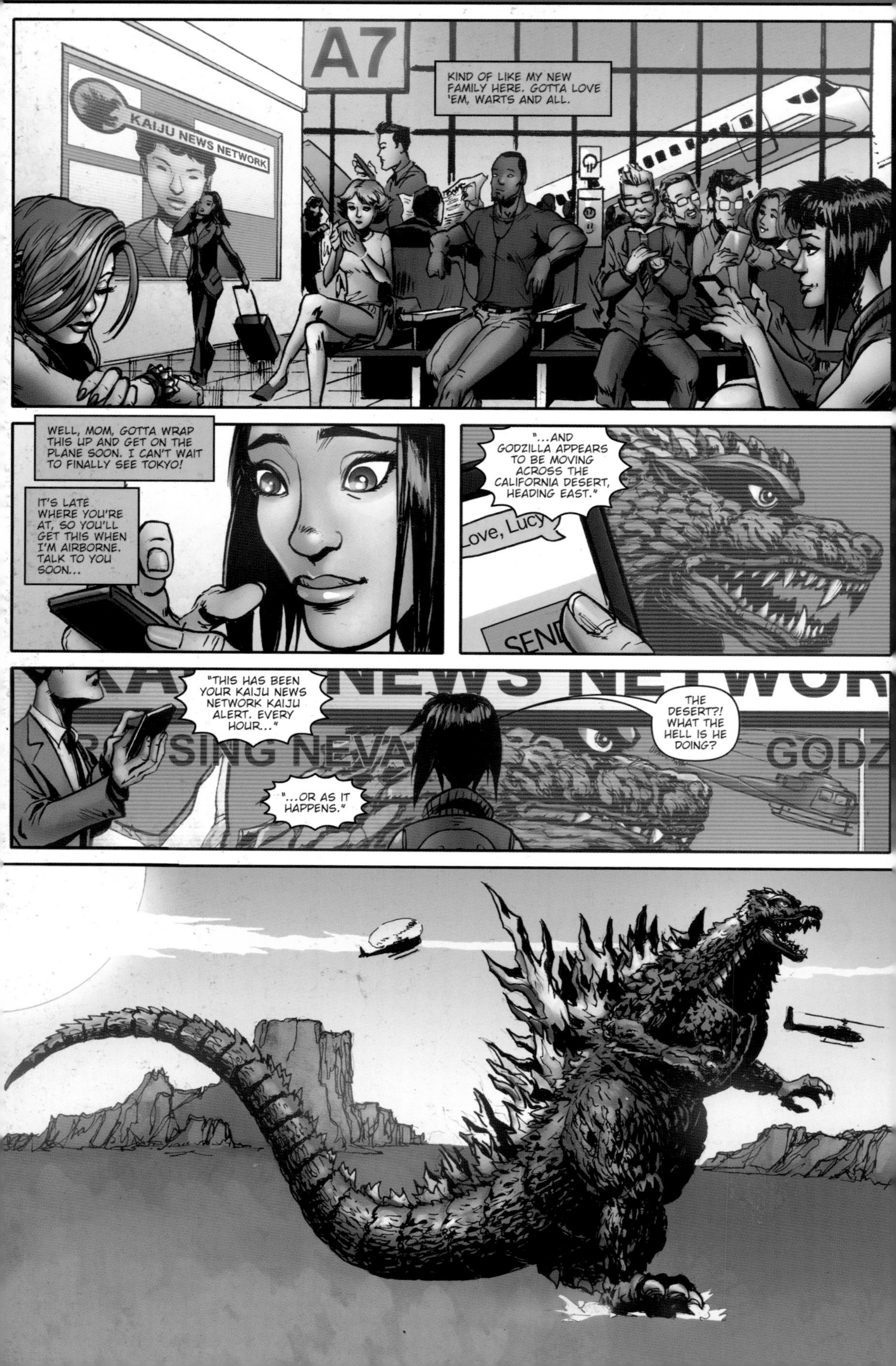
A7
KAIJU NEWS NETWORK
KIND OF LIKE MY NEW FAMILY HERE. GOTTA LOVE 'EM, WARTS AND ALL.
WELL, MOM, GOTTA WRAP THIS UP AND GET ON THE PLANE SOON. I CAN'T WAIT TO FINALLY SEE TOKYO!
IT'S LATE WHERE YOU'RE AT, SO YOU'LL GET THIS WHEN I'M AIRBORNE. TALK TO YOU SOON...
"...AND GODZILLA APPEARS TO BE MOVING ACROSS THE CALIFORNIA DESERT, HEADING EAST."
Love, Lucy
SEND
"THIS HAS BEEN YOUR KAIJU NEWS NETWORK KAIJU ALERT. EVERY HOUR..."
THE DESERT?! WHAT THE HELL IS HE DOING?
"...OR AS IT HAPPENS."

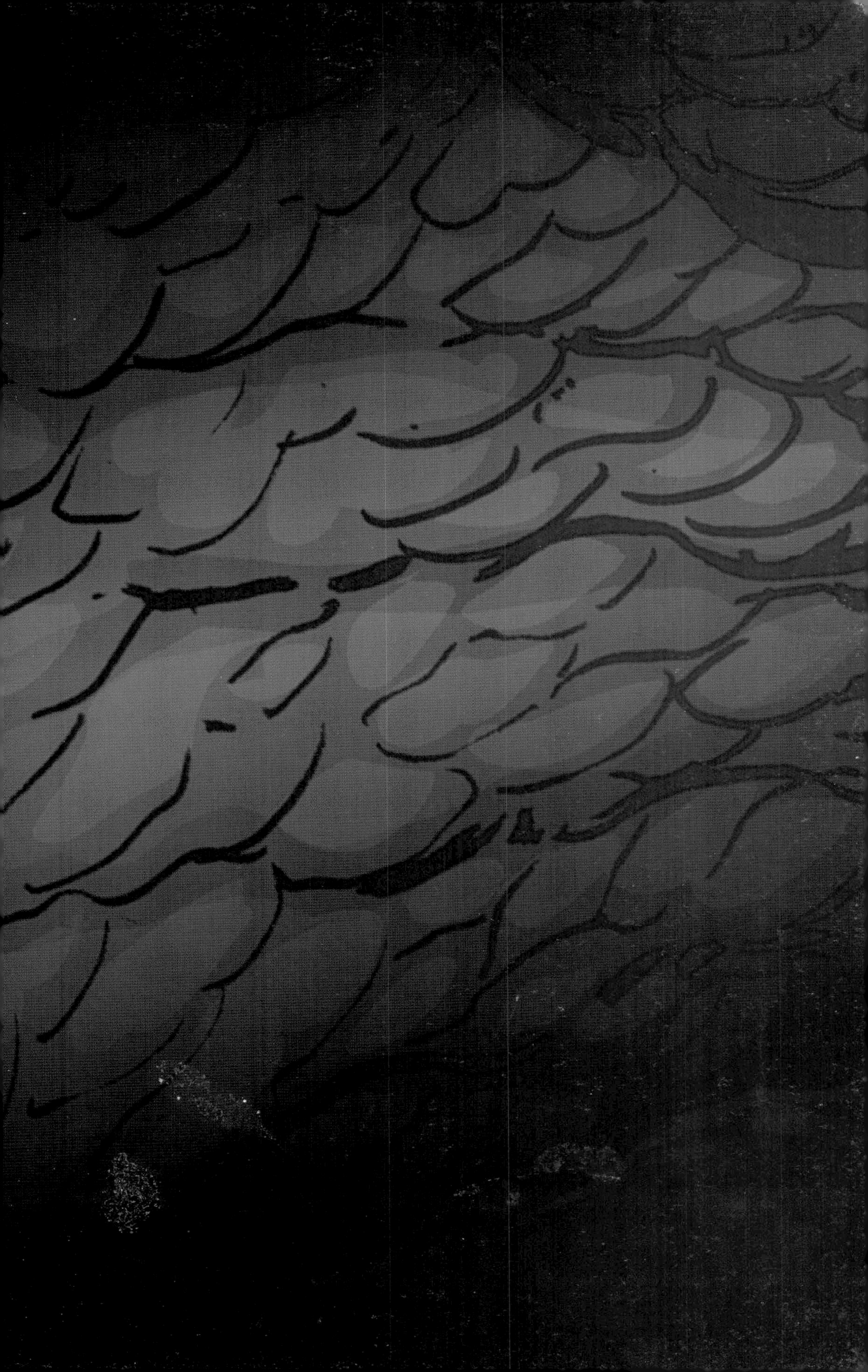

CHAPTER TWO:
TWO OF A KIND

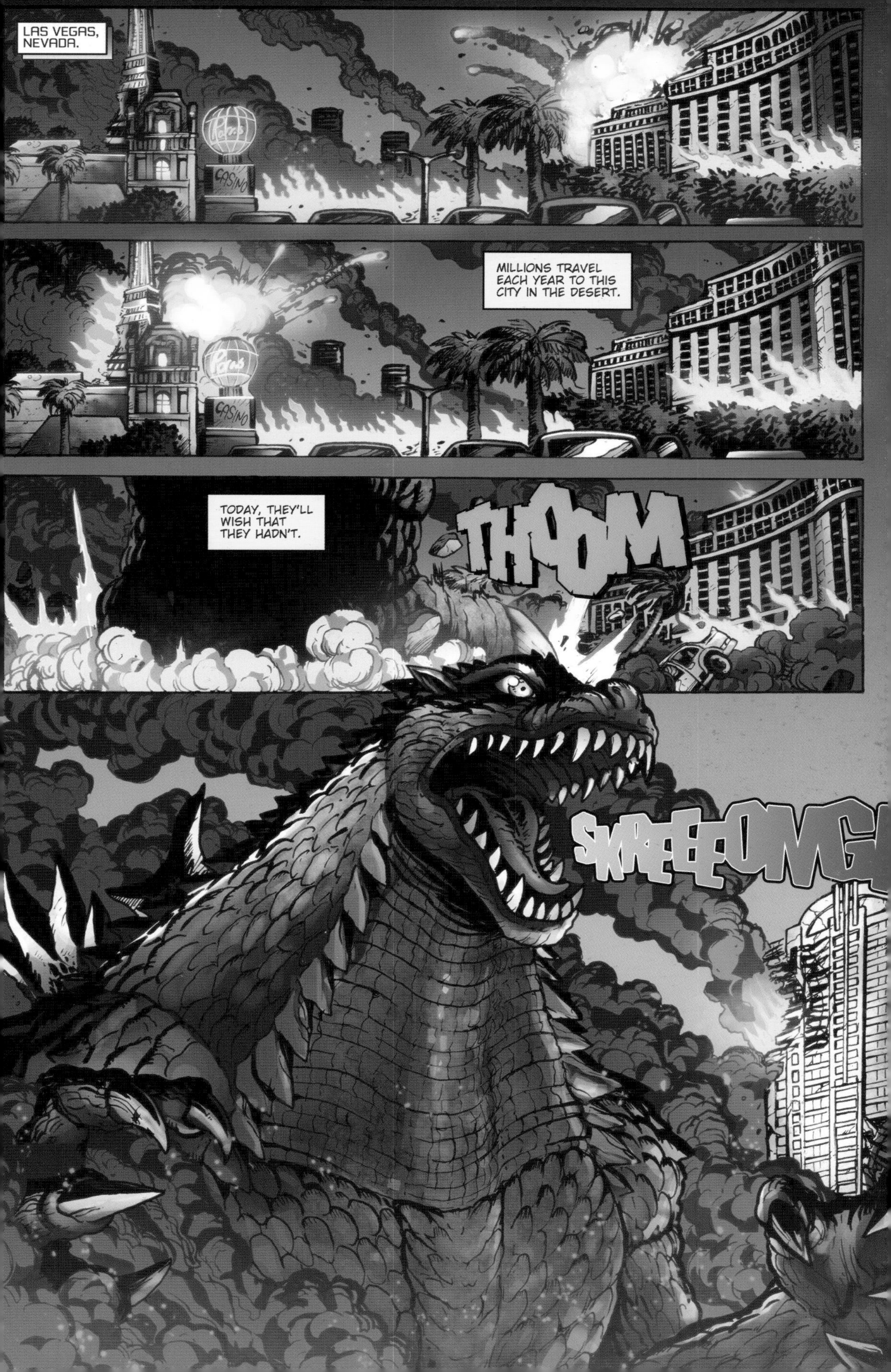

LAS VEGAS, NEVADA.
CASINO
MILLIONS TRAVEL EACH YEAR TO THIS CITY IN THE DESERT.
CASINO
TODAY, THEY'LL WISH THAT THEY HADN'T.
THOOM
SKREEEEONG

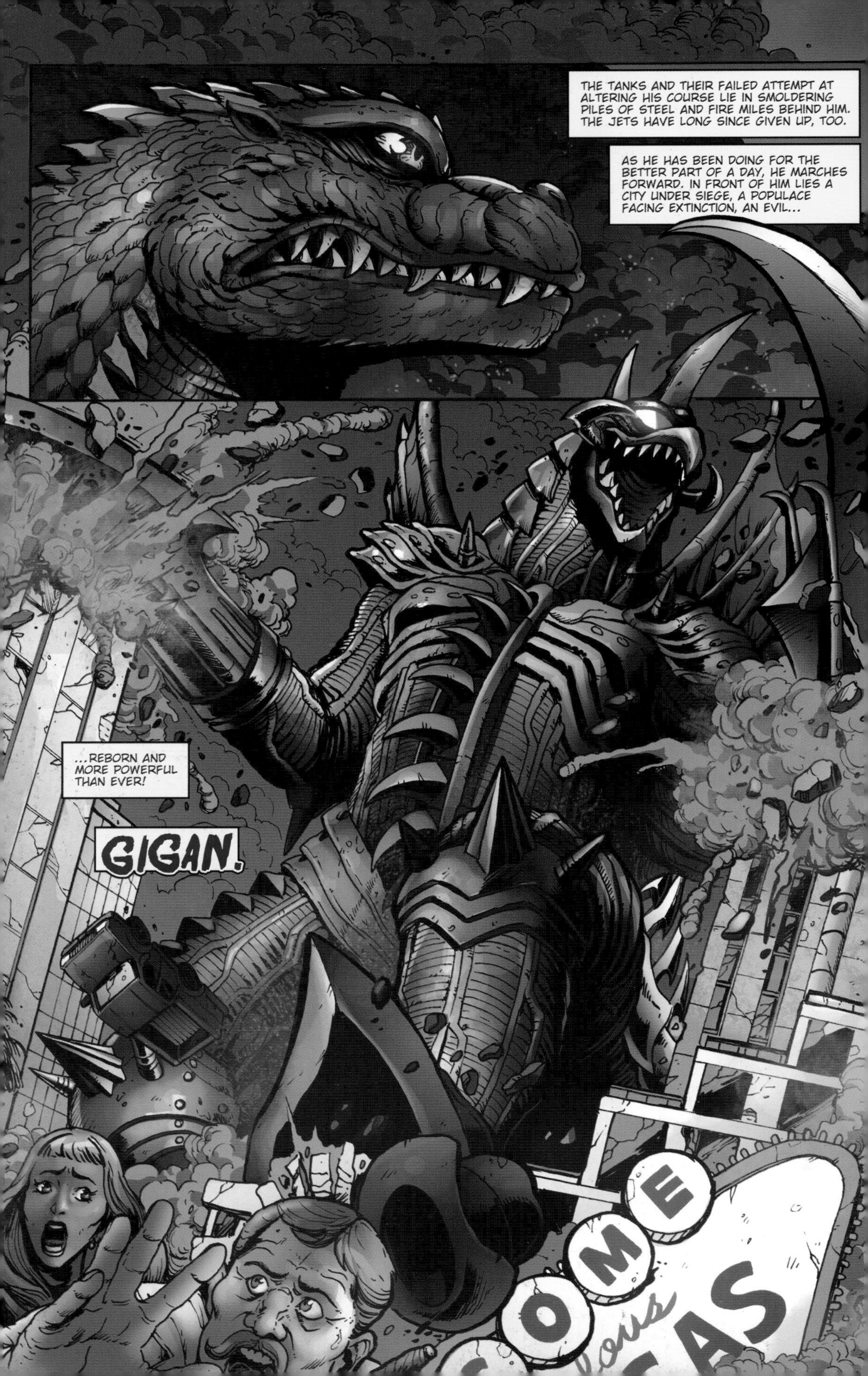
THE TANKS AND THEIR FAILED ATTEMPT AT ALTERING HIS COURSE LIE IN SMOLDERING PILES OF STEEL AND FIRE MILES BEHIND HIM. THE JETS HAVE LONG SINCE GIVEN UP, TOO.
AS HE HAS BEEN DOING FOR THE BETTER PART OF A DAY, HE MARCHES FORWARD. IN FRONT OF HIM LIES A CITY UNDER SIEGE, A POPULACE FACING EXTINCTION, AN EVIL...
...REBORN AND MORE POWERFUL THAN EVER!
GIGAN.

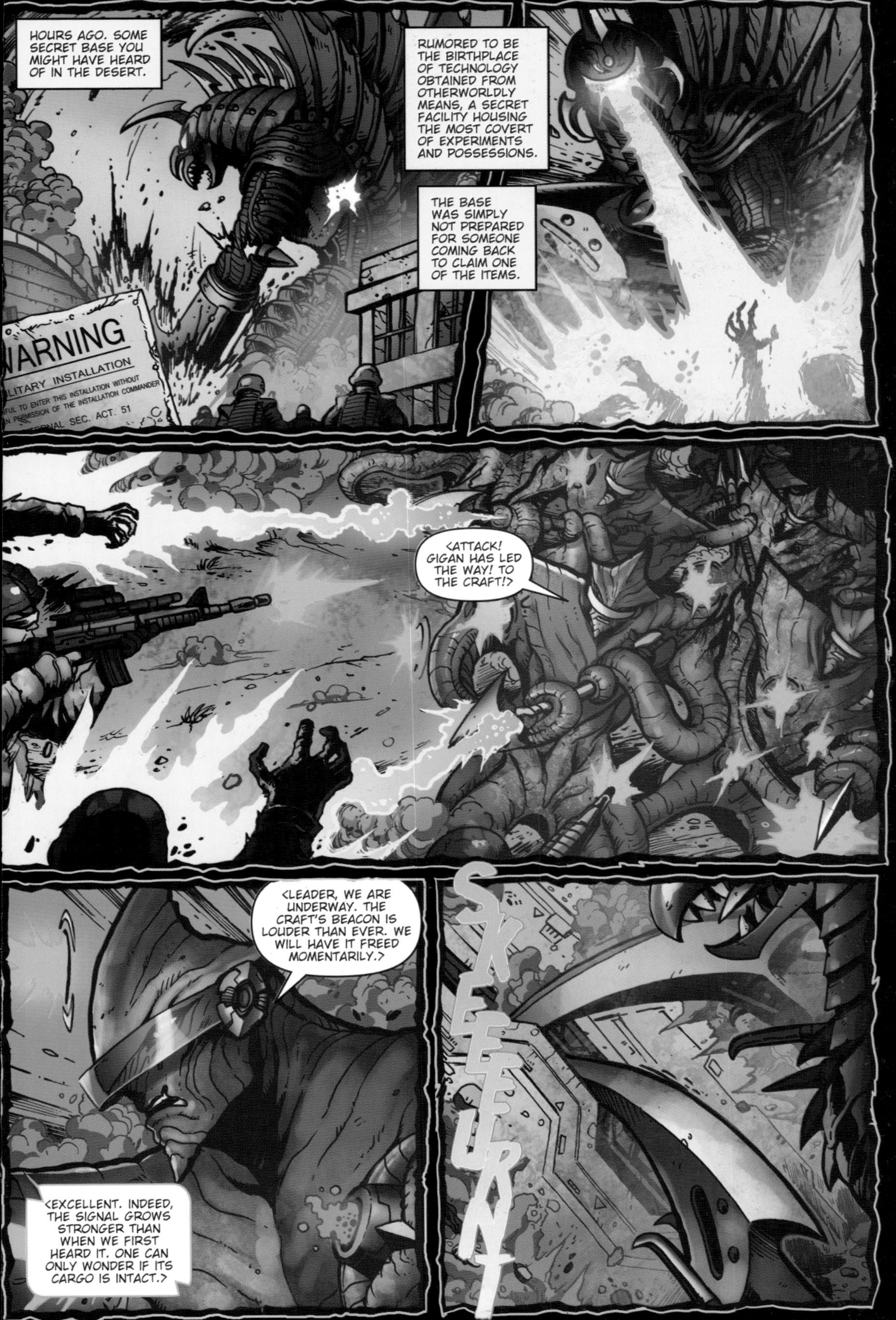
HOURS AGO. SOME SECRET BASE YOU MIGHT HAVE HEARD OF IN THE DESERT.
WARNING
RUMORED TO BE THE BIRTHPLACE OF TECHNOLOGY OBTAINED FROM OTHERWORLDLY MEANS, A SECRET FACILITY HOUSING THE MOST COVERT OF EXPERIMENTS AND POSSESSIONS.
THE BASE WAS SIMPLY NOT PREPARED FOR SOMEONE COMING BACK TO CLAIM ONE OF THE ITEMS.
<ATTACK! GIGAN HAS LED THE WAY! TO THE CRAFT!>
<LEADER, WE ARE UNDERWAY. THE CRAFT'S BEACON IS LOUDER THAN EVER. WE WILL HAVE IT FREED MOMENTARILY.>
<EXCELLENT. INDEED, THE SIGNAL GROWS STRONGER THAN WHEN WE FIRST HEARD IT. ONE CAN ONLY WONDER IF ITS CARGO IS INTACT.>
SKEEEURNT

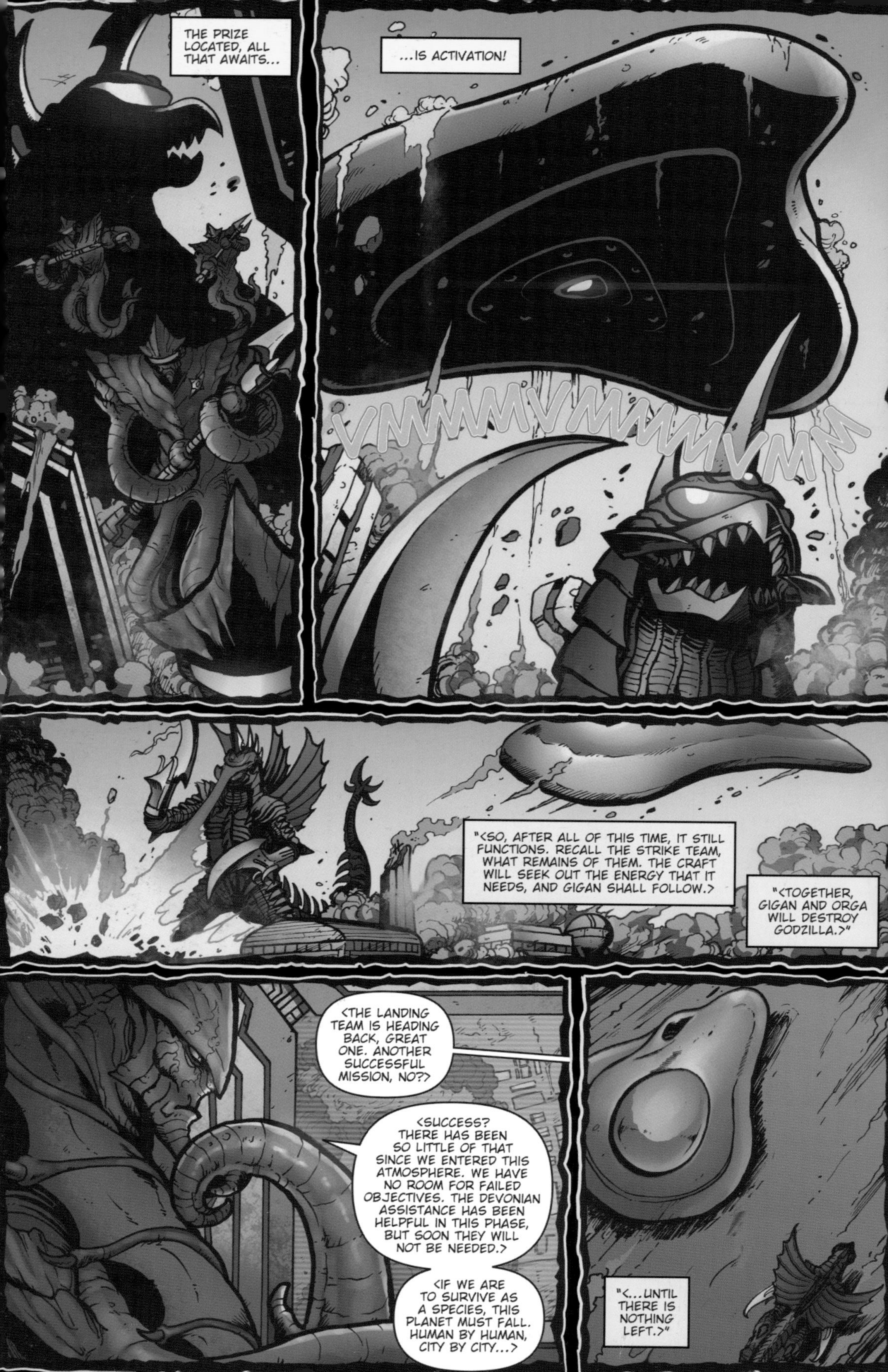
THE PRIZE LOCATED, ALL THAT AWAITS...
...IS ACTIVATION!
VMMMVMMMMVMM
"<SO, AFTER ALL OF THIS TIME, IT STILL FUNCTIONS. RECALL THE STRIKE TEAM, WHAT REMAINS OF THEM. THE CRAFT WILL SEEK OUT THE ENERGY THAT IT NEEDS, AND GIGAN SHALL FOLLOW.>
"<TOGETHER, GIGAN AND ORGA WILL DESTROY GODZILLA.>"
<THE LANDING TEAM IS HEADING BACK, GREAT ONE. ANOTHER SUCCESSFUL MISSION, NO?>
<SUCCESS? THERE HAS BEEN SO LITTLE OF THAT SINCE WE ENTERED THIS ATMOSPHERE. WE HAVE NO ROOM FOR FAILED OBJECTIVES. THE DEVONIAN ASSISTANCE HAS BEEN HELPFUL IN THIS PHASE, BUT SOON THEY WILL NOT BE NEEDED.>
<IF WE ARE TO SURVIVE AS A SPECIES, THIS PLANET MUST FALL. HUMAN BY HUMAN, CITY BY CITY...>
"<...UNTIL THERE IS NOTHING LEFT.>"

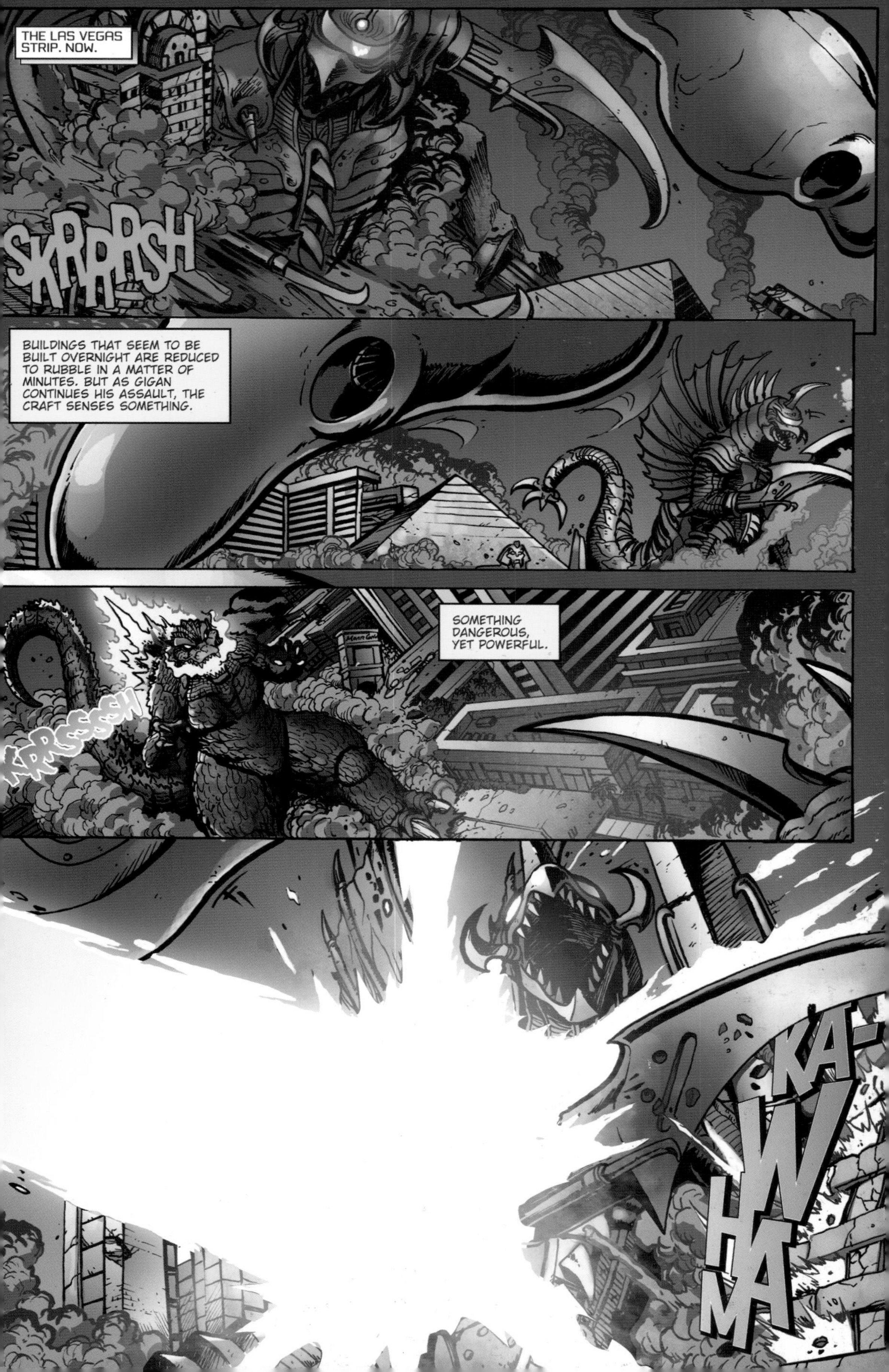
THE LAS VEGAS STRIP. NOW.
SKRRRSH
BUILDINGS THAT SEEM TO BE BUILT OVERNIGHT ARE REDUCED TO RUBBLE IN A MATTER OF MINUTES. BUT AS GIGAN CONTINUES HIS ASSAULT, THE CRAFT SENSES SOMETHING.
SOMETHING DANGEROUS, YET POWERFUL.
KRRSSSSH
KA-WHAM

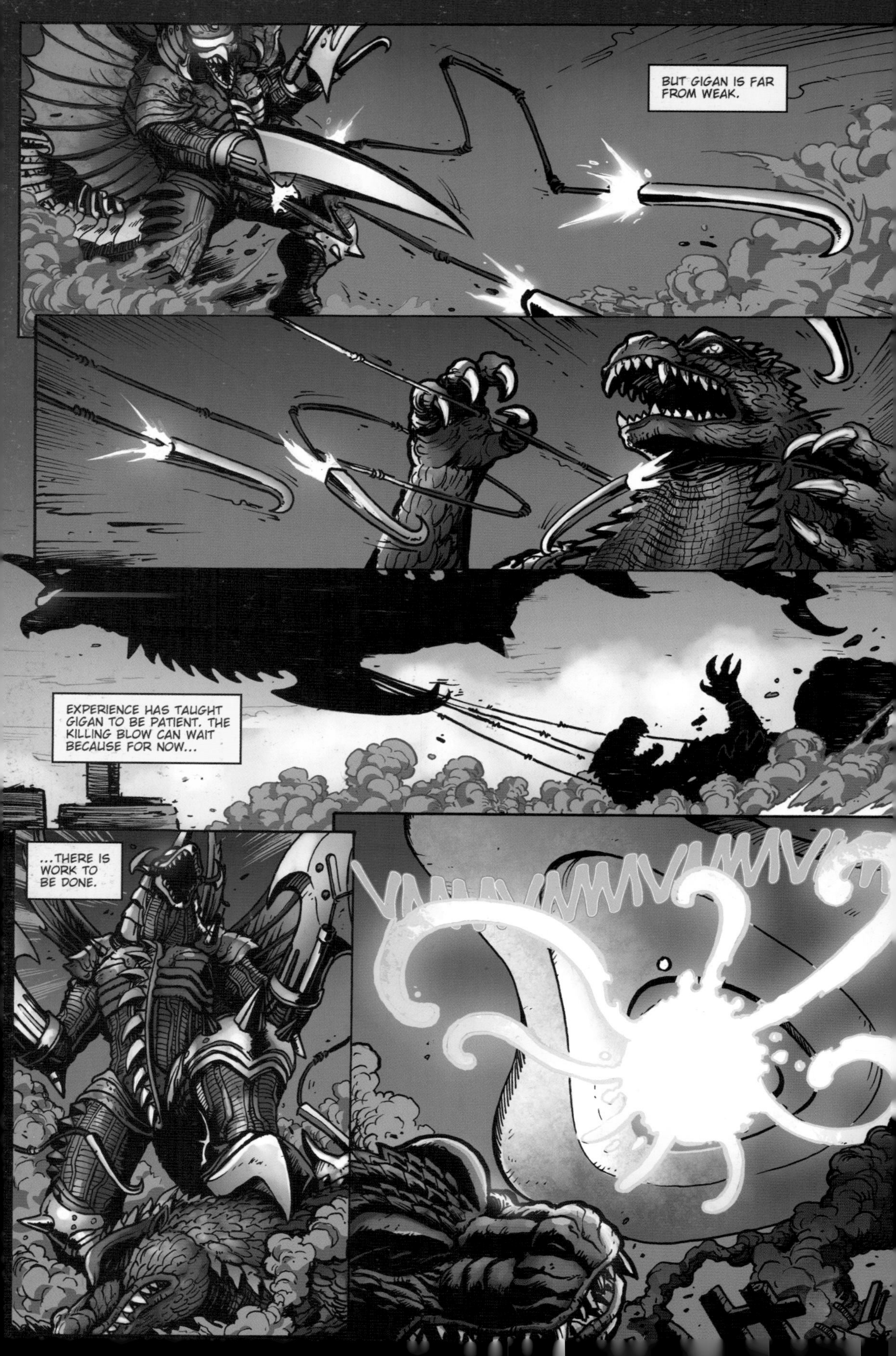
BUT GIGAN IS FAR FROM WEAK.
EXPERIENCE HAS TAUGHT GIGAN TO BE PATIENT. THE KILLING BLOW CAN WAIT BECAUSE FOR NOW...
...THERE IS WORK TO BE DONE.

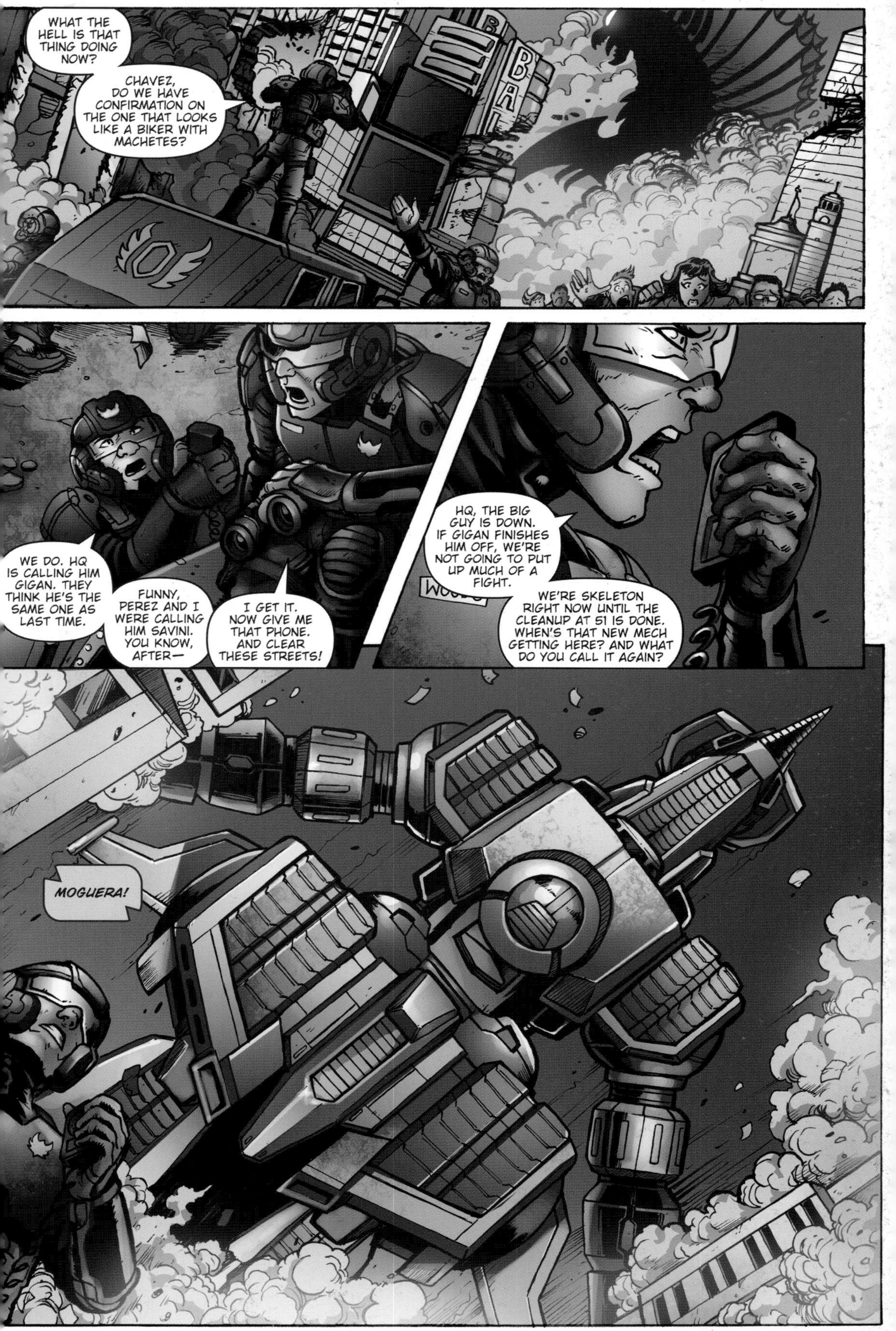
WHAT THE HELL IS THAT THING DOING NOW?
CHAVEZ, DO WE HAVE CONFIRMATION ON THE ONE THAT LOOKS LIKE A BIKER WITH MACHETES?
WE DO. HQ IS CALLING HIM GIGAN. THEY THINK HE'S THE SAME ONE AS LAST TIME.
FUNNY, PEREZ AND I WERE CALLING HIM SAVINI. YOU KNOW, AFTER—
I GET IT. NOW GIVE ME THAT PHONE. AND CLEAR THESE STREETS!
HQ, THE BIG GUY IS DOWN. IF GIGAN FINISHES HIM OFF, WE'RE NOT GOING TO PUT UP MUCH OF A FIGHT.
WE'RE SKELETON RIGHT NOW UNTIL THE CLEANUP AT 51 IS DONE. WHEN'S THAT NEW MECH GETTING HERE? AND WHAT DO YOU CALL IT AGAIN?
MOGUERA!

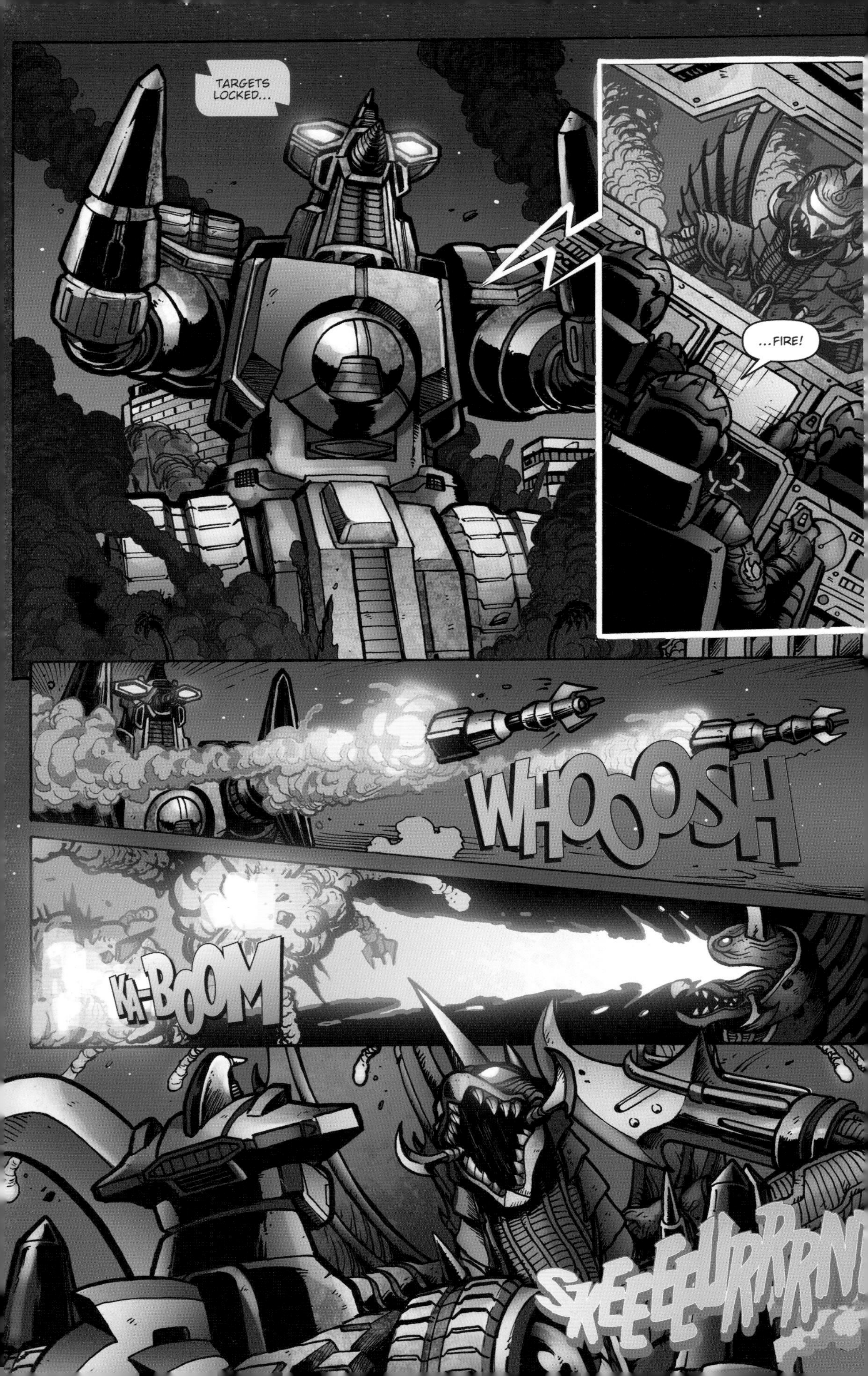
TARGETS LOCKED...
...FIRE!
WHOOOOSH
KA-BOOM
SKEEEEURRRRN

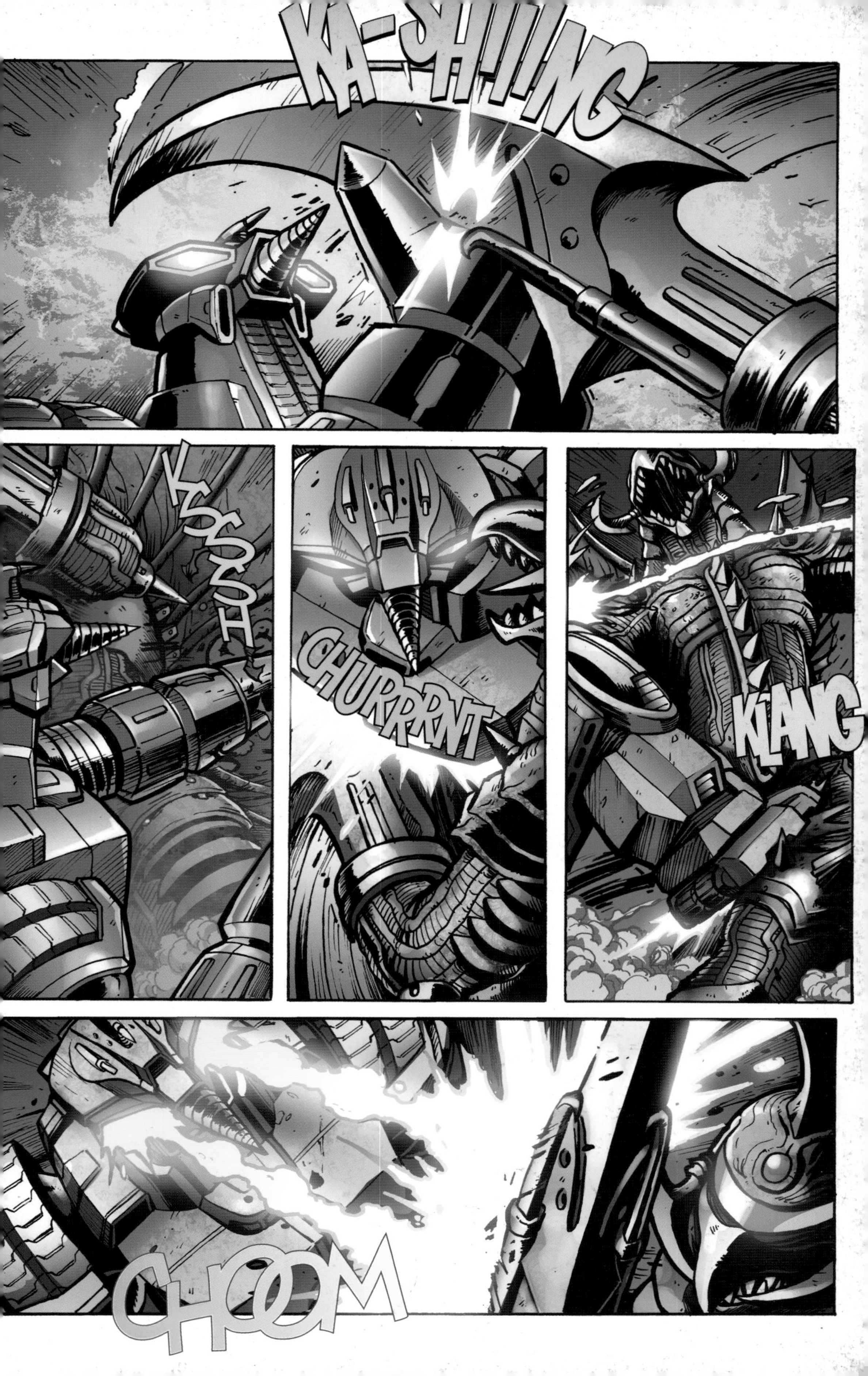
KA-SHIING
KSSSSH
CHURRRNT
KLANG
CHOOM

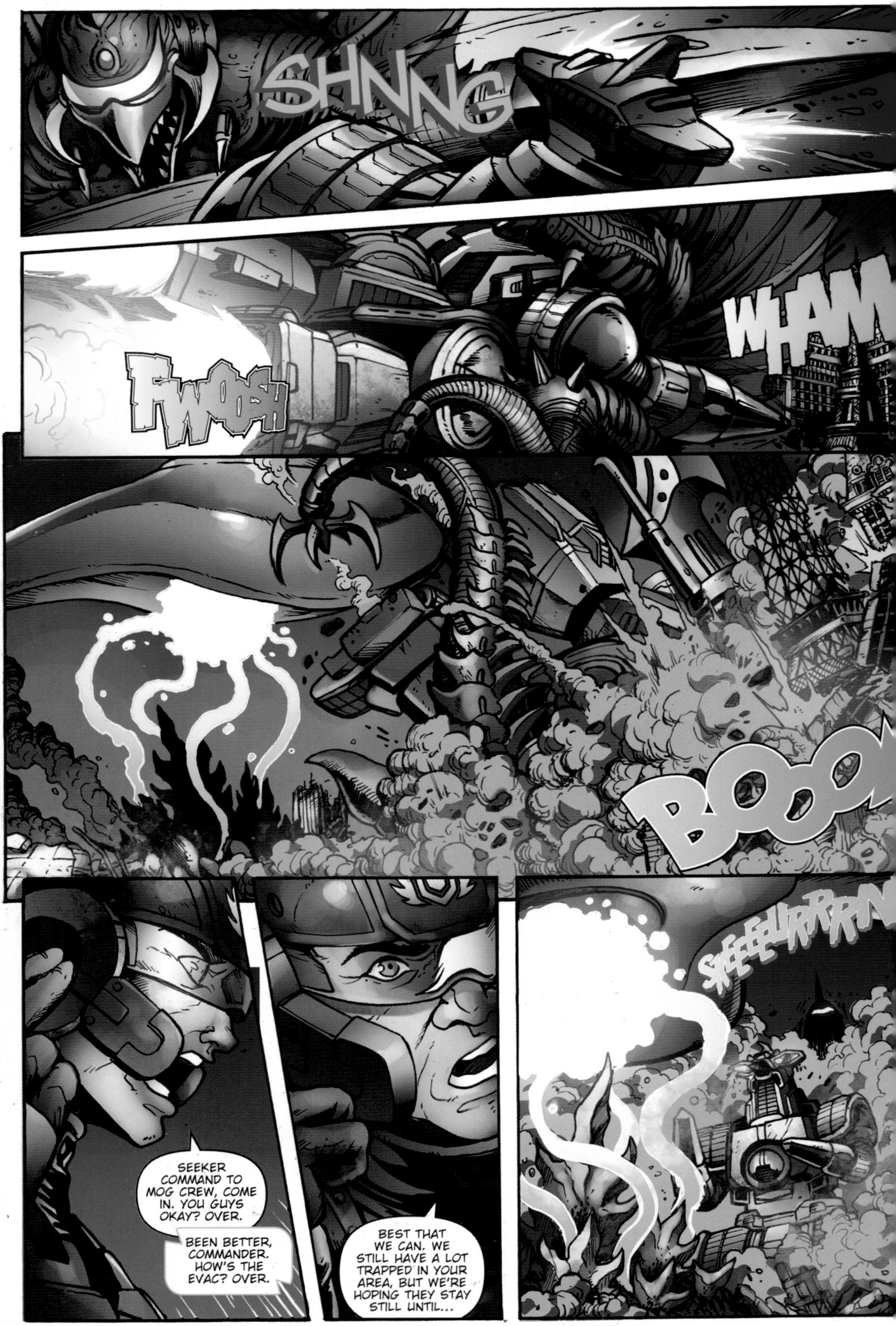
SHNNG
FWOOSH
WHAM
BOO
SKEEEURRRRN
SEEKER COMMAND TO MOG CREW, COME IN. YOU GUYS OKAY? OVER.
BEEN BETTER, COMMANDER. HOW'S THE EVAC? OVER.
BEST THAT WE CAN. WE STILL HAVE A LOT TRAPPED IN YOUR AREA, BUT WE'RE HOPING THEY STAY STILL UNTIL...

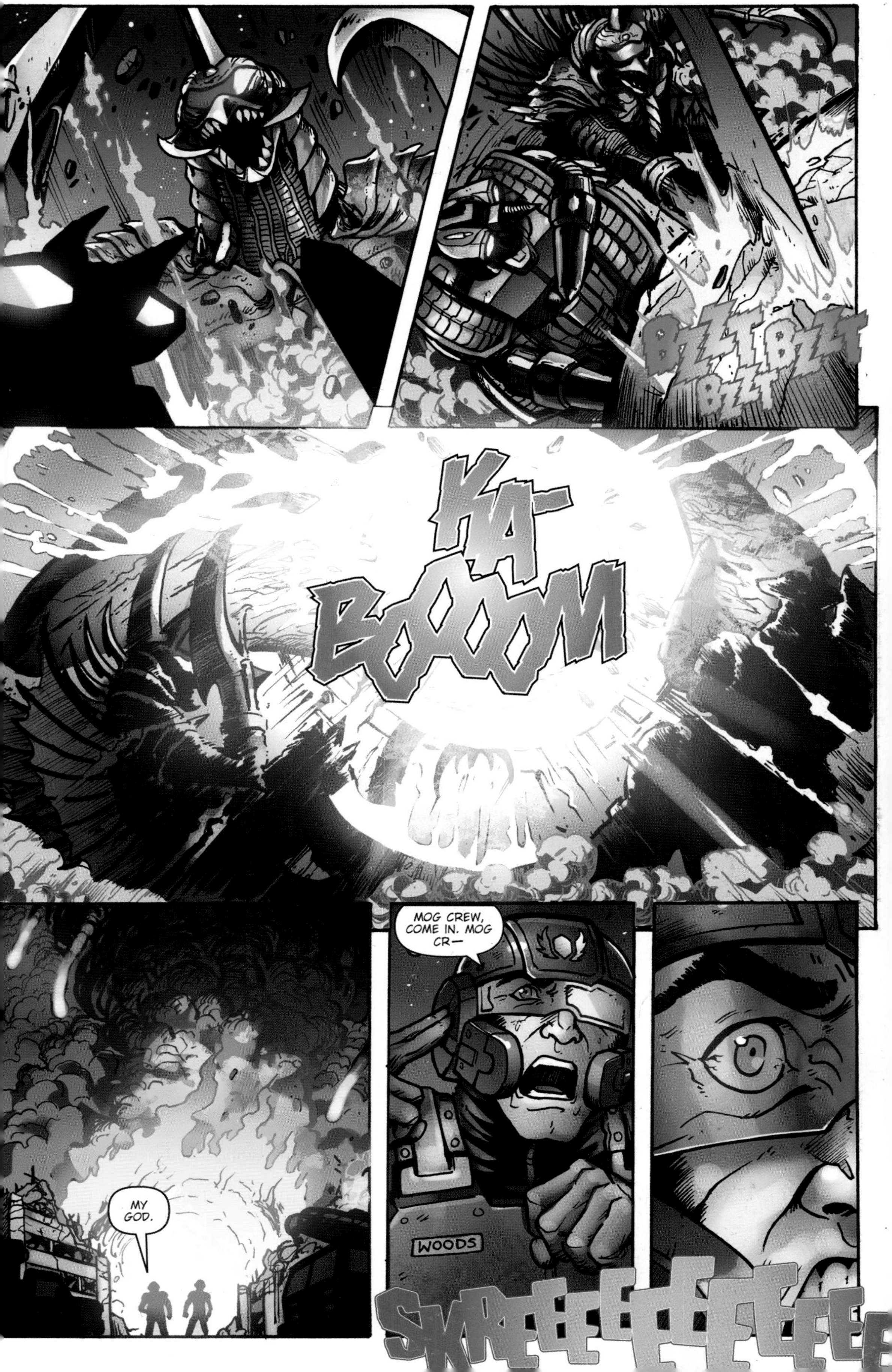
BZZT BZZT
BZZT
KA-BOOOM
MY GOD.
MOG CREW, COME IN. MOG CR—
WOODS
SKREEEEEEEEEEEE

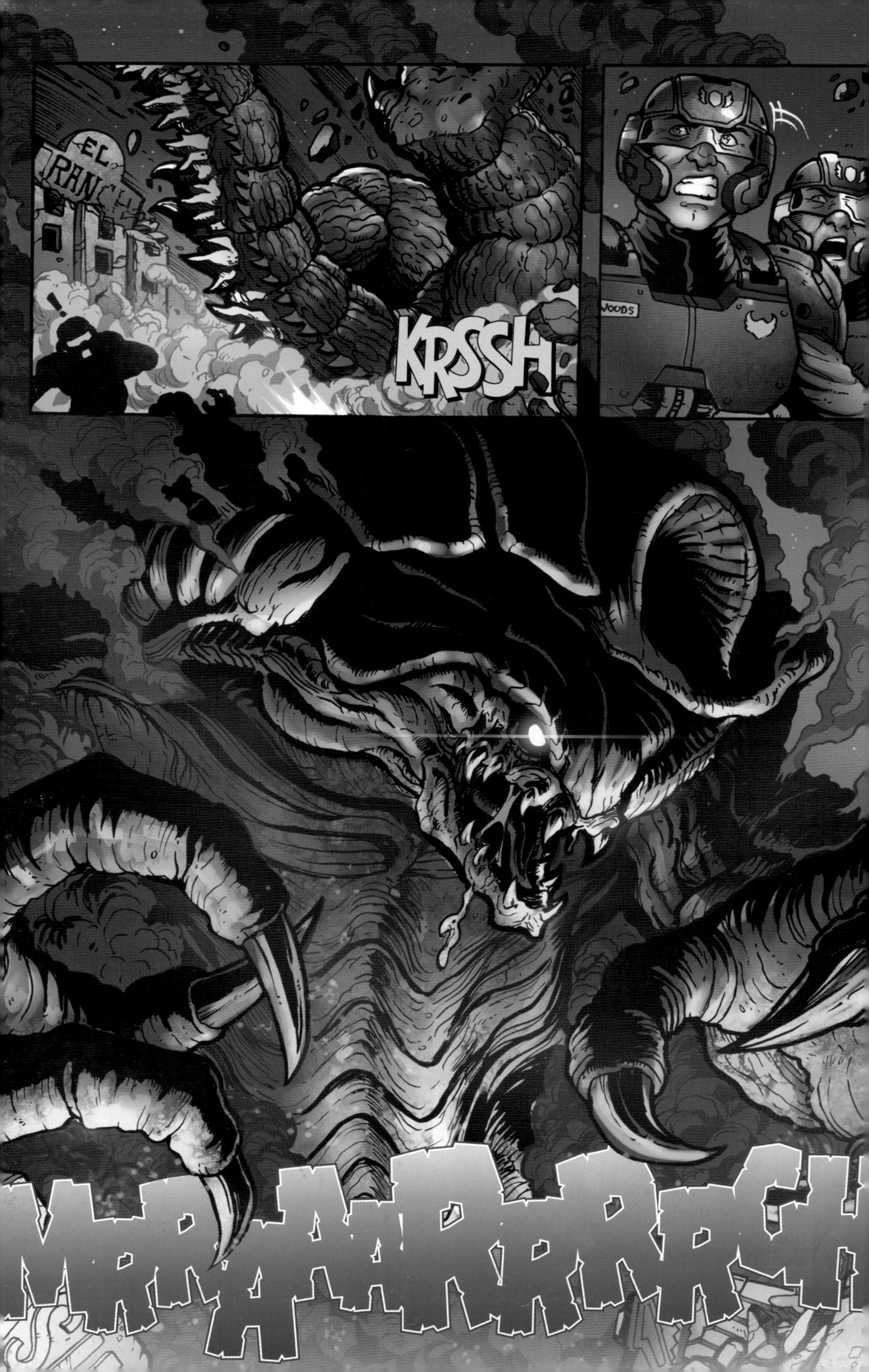
EL RAN
KRSSH
WOODS
WRRAAARRRGH

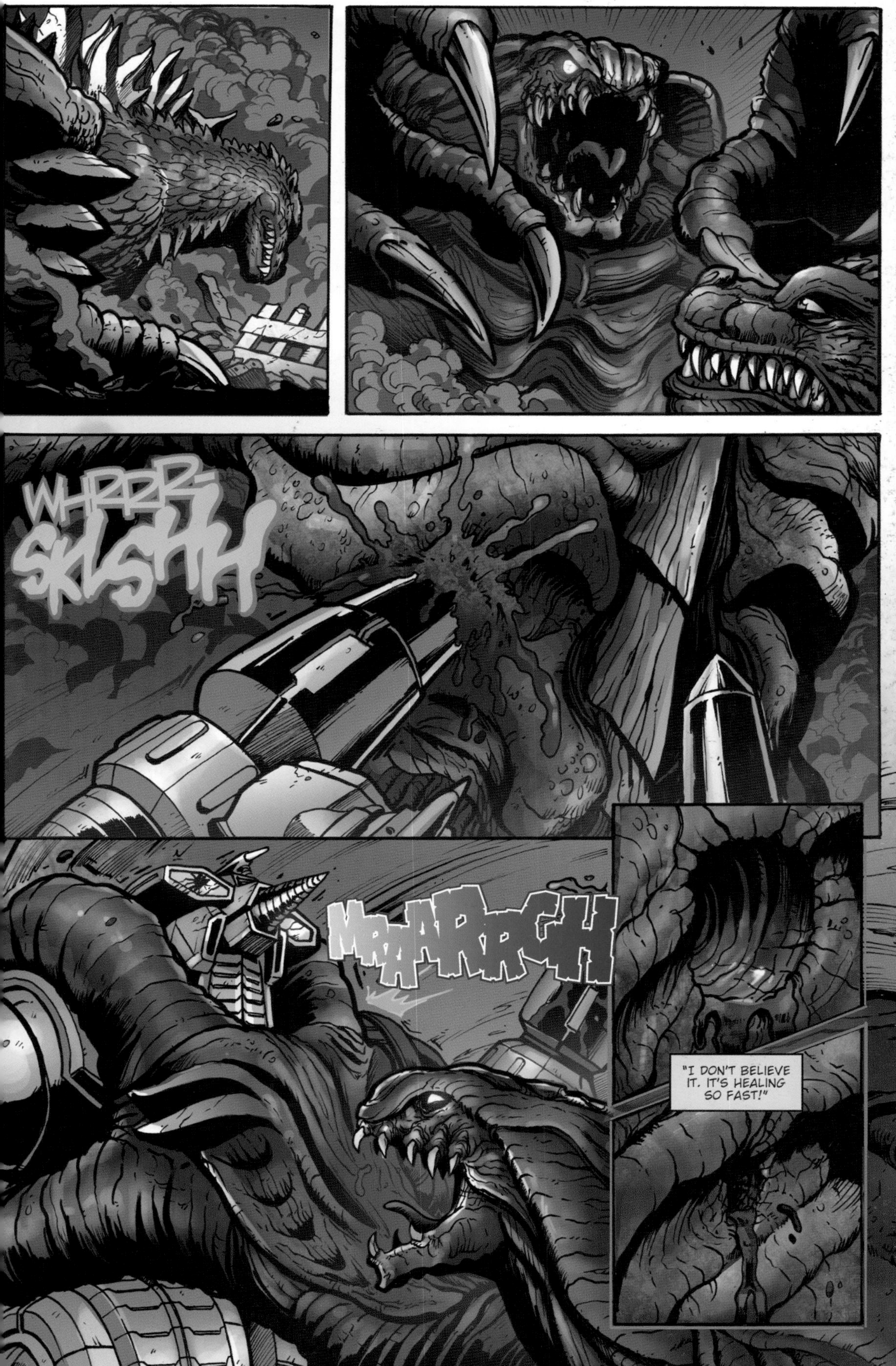

WHRRR-SKLSHH
MRAAARRRGH
"I DON'T BELIEVE IT. IT'S HEALING SO FAST!"

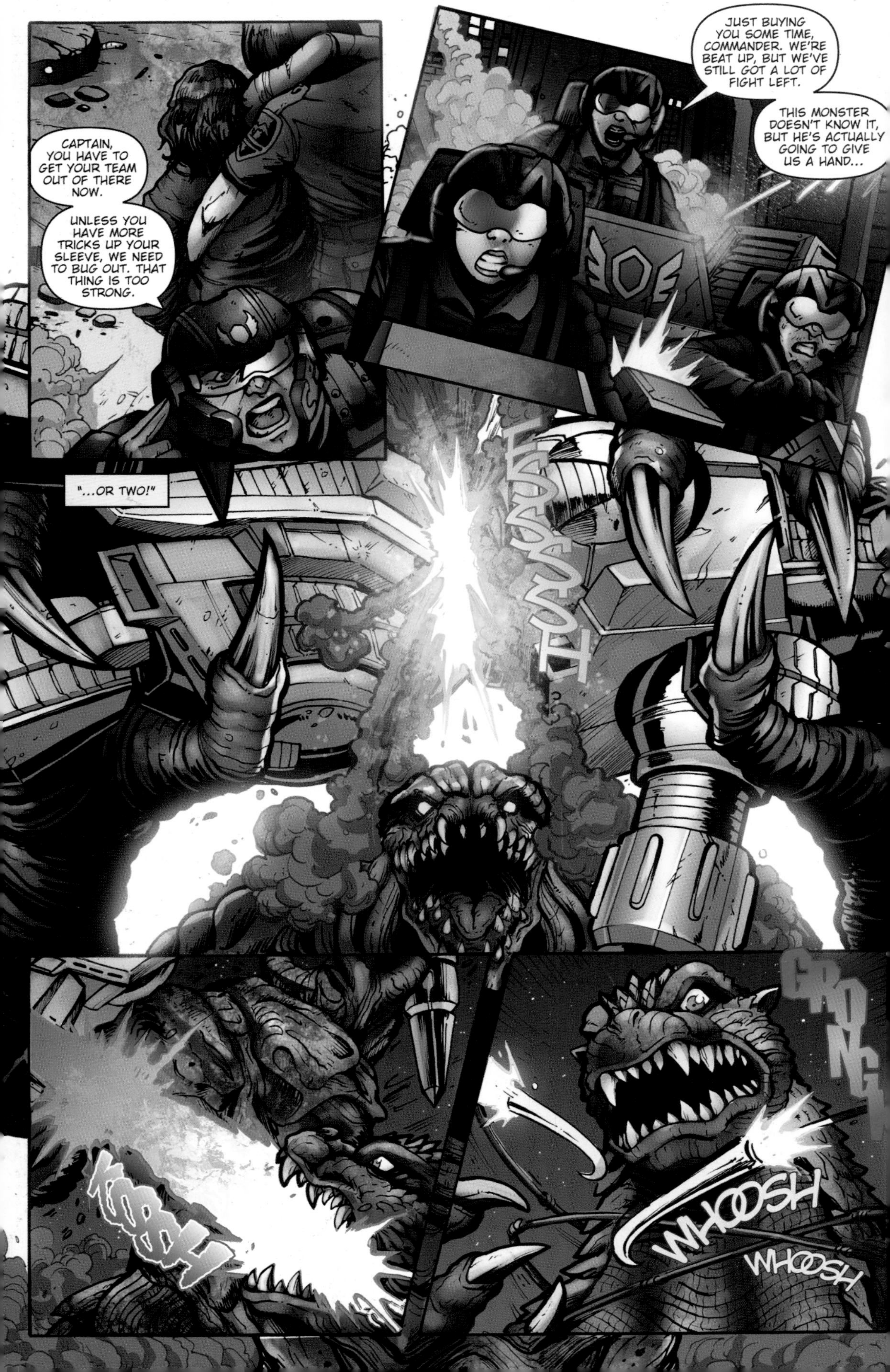
CAPTAIN, YOU HAVE TO GET YOUR TEAM OUT OF THERE NOW.
UNLESS YOU HAVE MORE TRICKS UP YOUR SLEEVE, WE NEED TO BUG OUT. THAT THING IS TOO STRONG.
JUST BUYING YOU SOME TIME, COMMANDER. WE'RE BEAT UP, BUT WE'VE STILL GOT A LOT OF FIGHT LEFT.
THIS MONSTER DOESN'T KNOW IT, BUT HE'S ACTUALLY GOING TO GIVE US A HAND...
"...OR TWO!"
KSSSSHH
KSSSSHH
GRONNGH
WHOOSH
WHOOSH

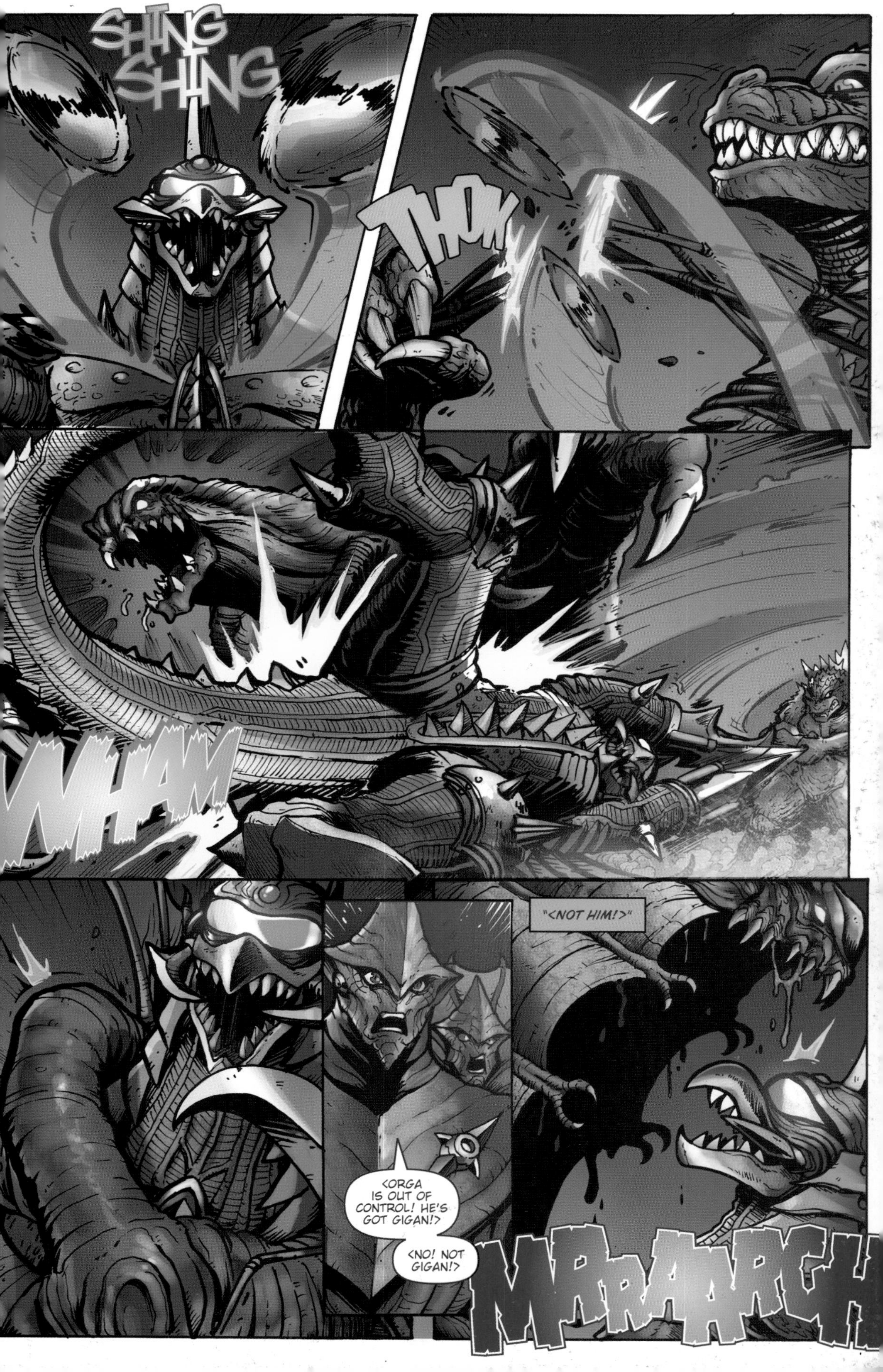
SHING SHING
THOK
WHAM
"<NOT HIM!>"
<ORGA IS OUT OF CONTROL! HE'S GOT GIGAN!>
<NO! NOT GIGAN!>
MRRAARGH

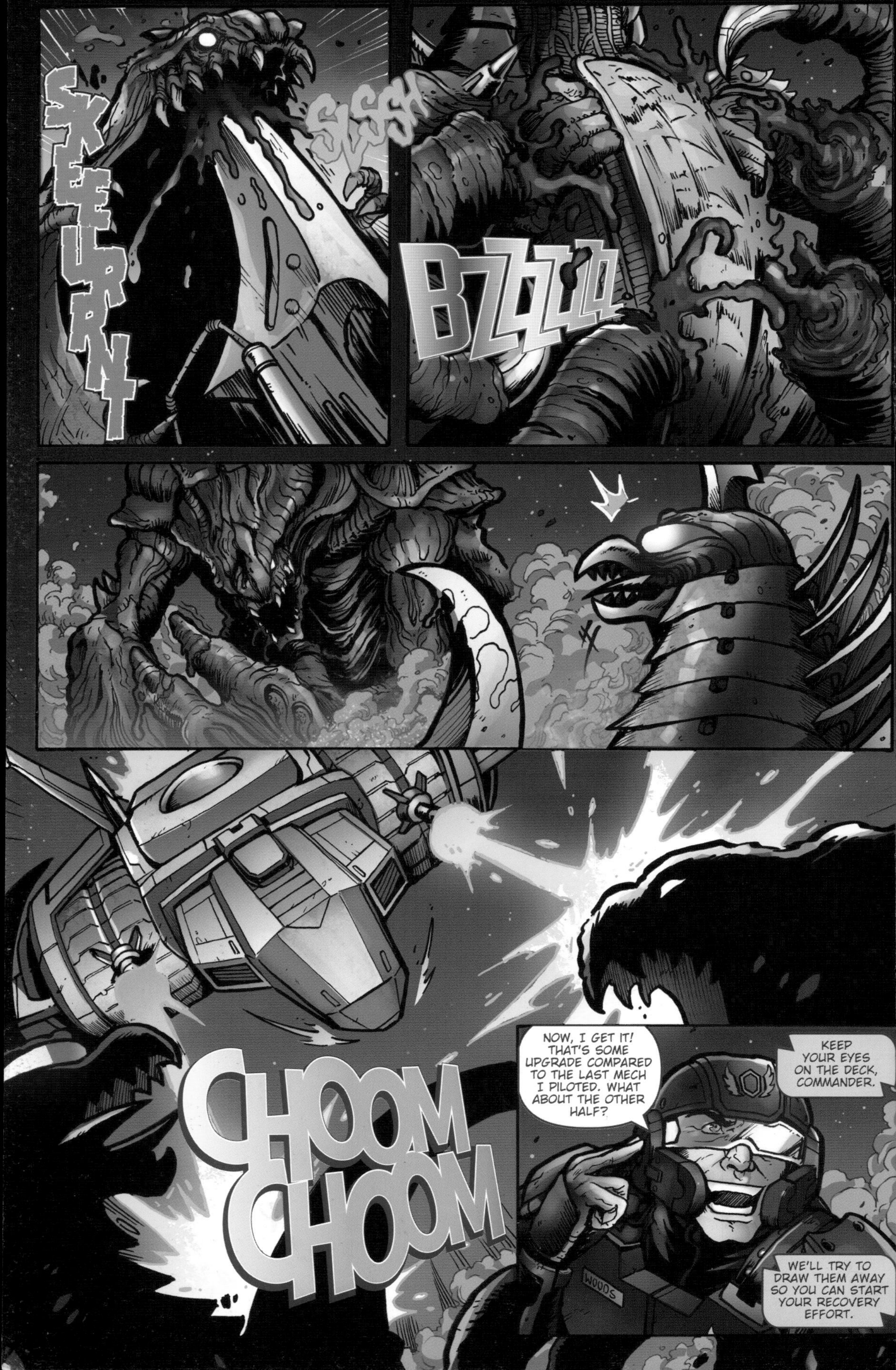
SKEEURRNT
SLSSH
BZZZZZZ
CHOOM CHOOM
NOW, I GET IT! THAT'S SOME UPGRADE COMPARED TO THE LAST MECH I PILOTED. WHAT ABOUT THE OTHER HALF?
KEEP YOUR EYES ON THE DECK, COMMANDER.
WE'LL TRY TO DRAW THEM AWAY SO YOU CAN START YOUR RECOVERY EFFORT.
WOODS

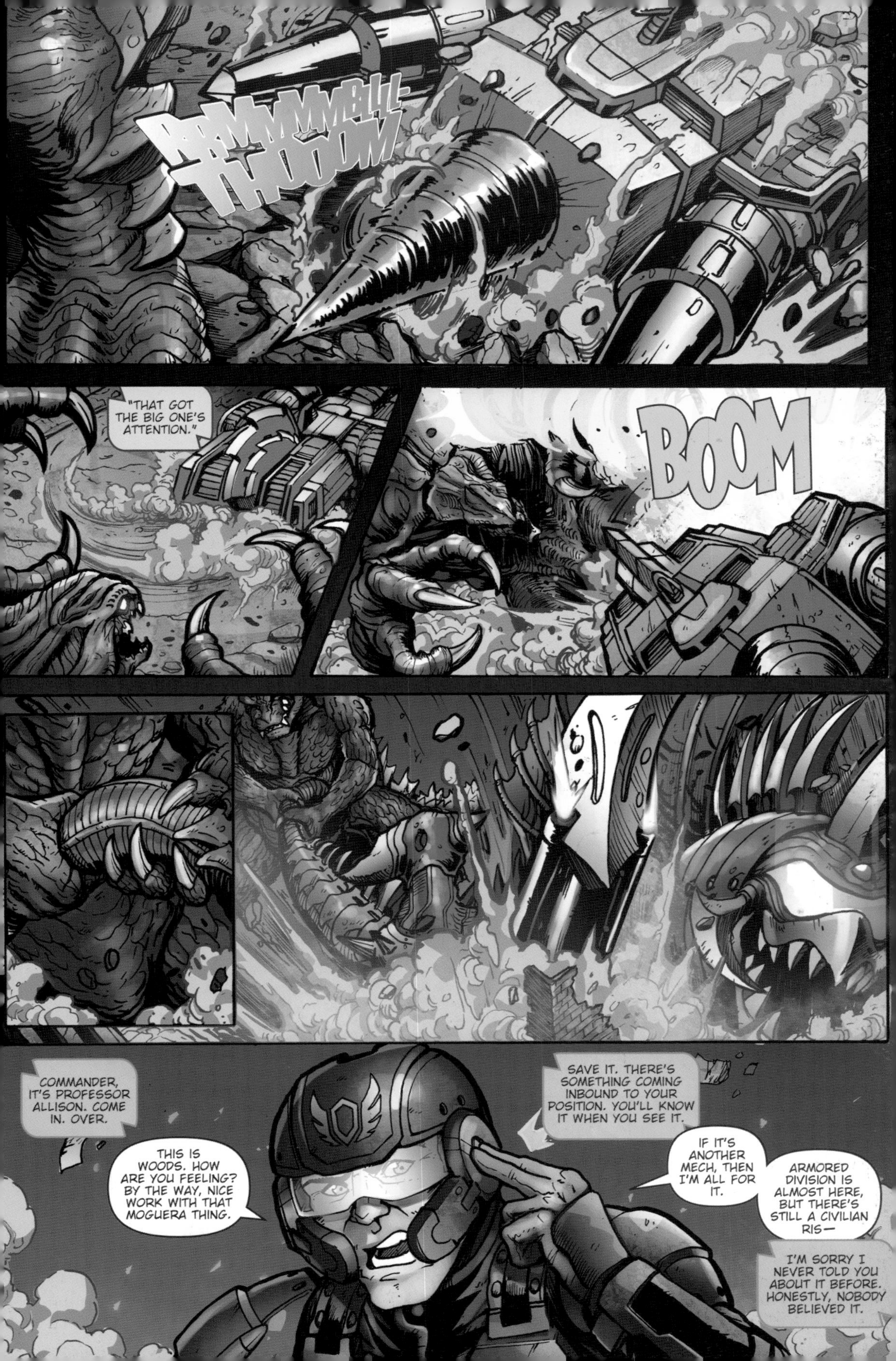

RRMMMMBLLL-THOOOM
"THAT GOT THE BIG ONE'S ATTENTION."
BOOM
COMMANDER, IT'S PROFESSOR ALLISON. COME IN. OVER.
THIS IS WOODS. HOW ARE YOU FEELING? BY THE WAY, NICE WORK WITH THAT MOGUERA THING.
SAVE IT. THERE'S SOMETHING COMING INBOUND TO YOUR POSITION. YOU'LL KNOW IT WHEN YOU SEE IT.
IF IT'S ANOTHER MECH, THEN I'M ALL FOR IT.
ARMORED DIVISION IS ALMOST HERE, BUT THERE'S STILL A CIVILIAN RIS—
I'M SORRY I NEVER TOLD YOU ABOUT IT BEFORE. HONESTLY, NOBODY BELIEVED IT.

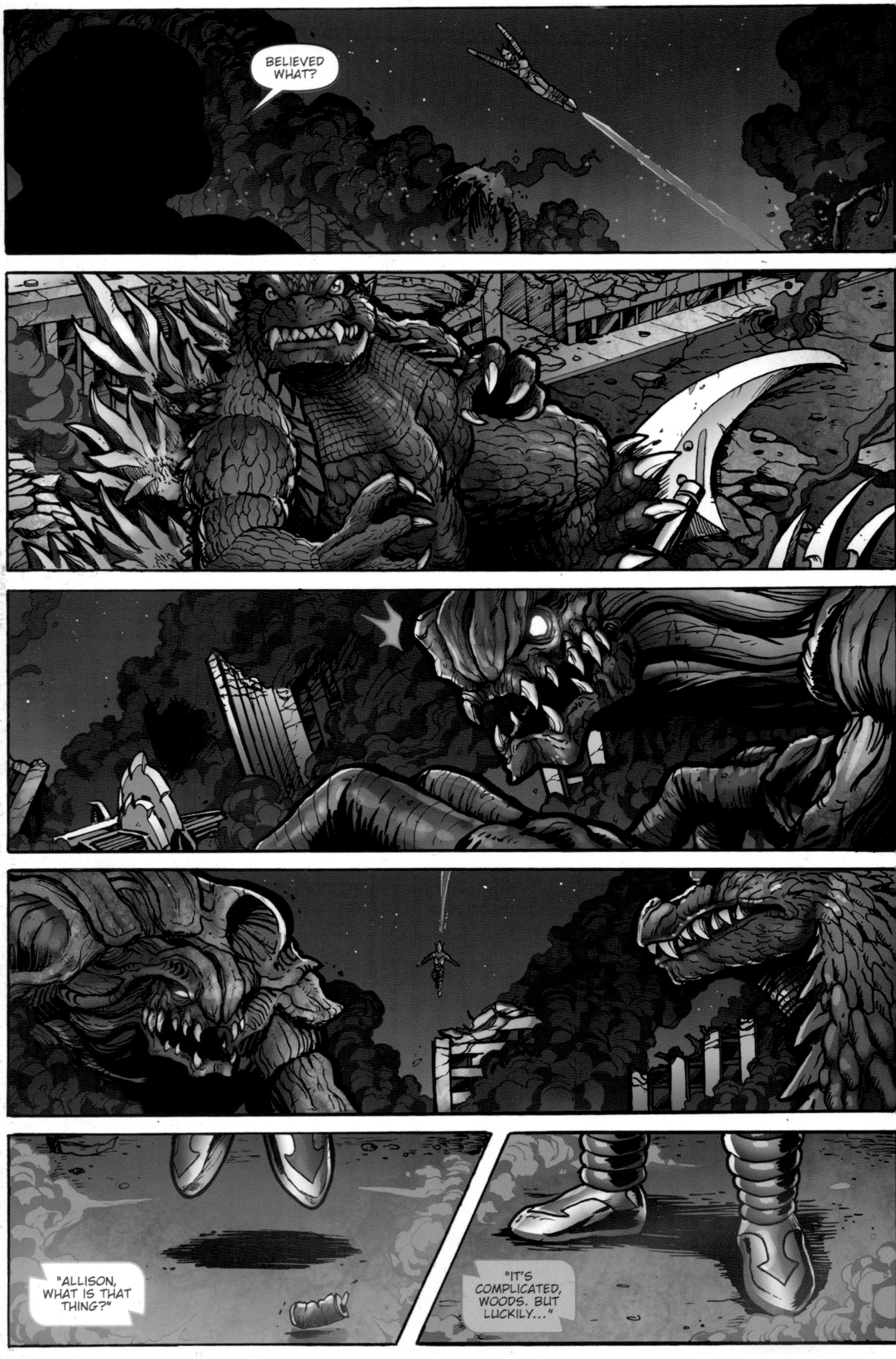

BELIEVED WHAT?
"ALLISON, WHAT IS THAT THING?"
"IT'S COMPLICATED, WOODS. BUT LUCKILY..."

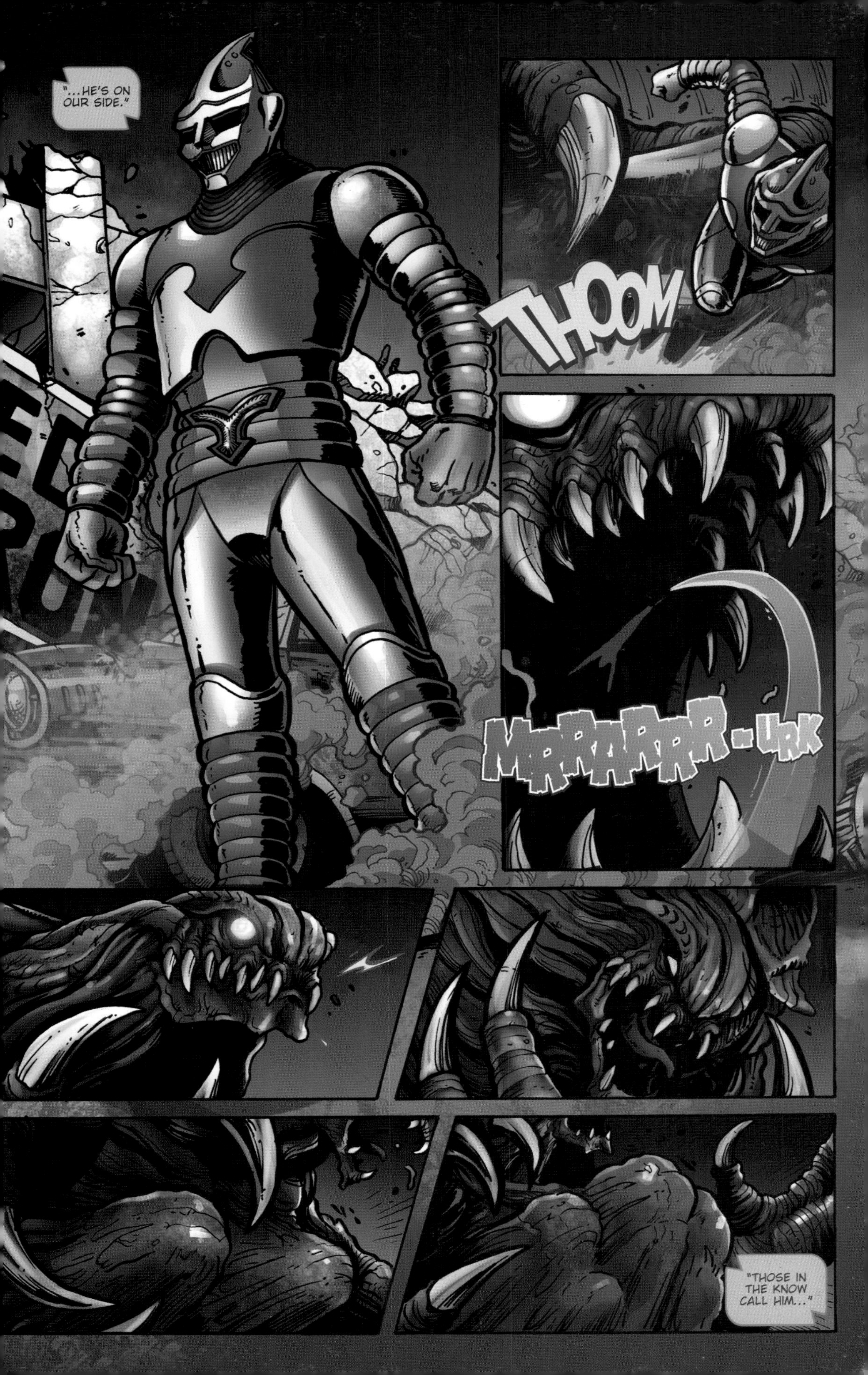
"...HE'S ON OUR SIDE."
THOOM
MRRRARRR - URK
"THOSE IN THE KNOW CALL HIM..."

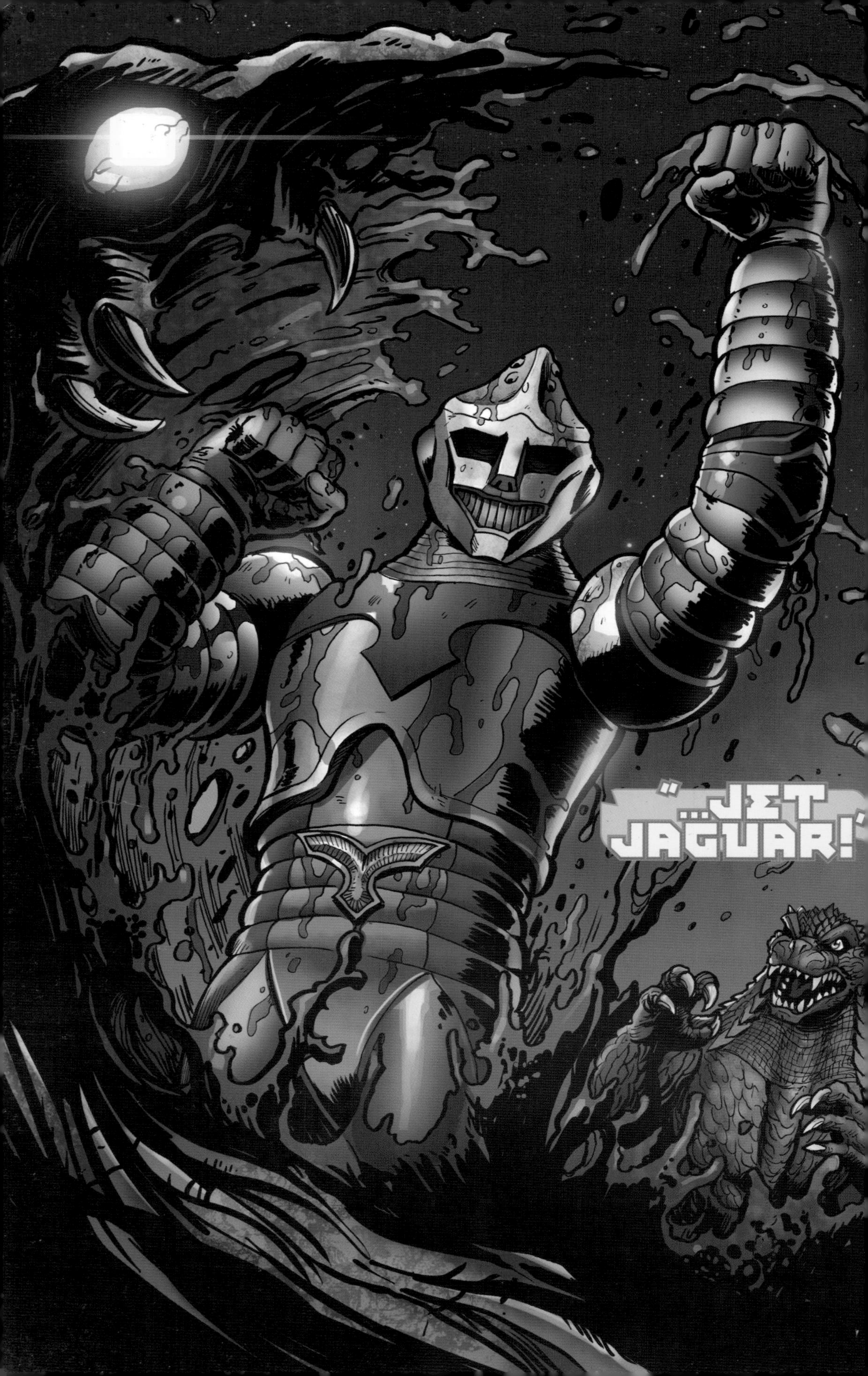
"...JET JAGUAR!"

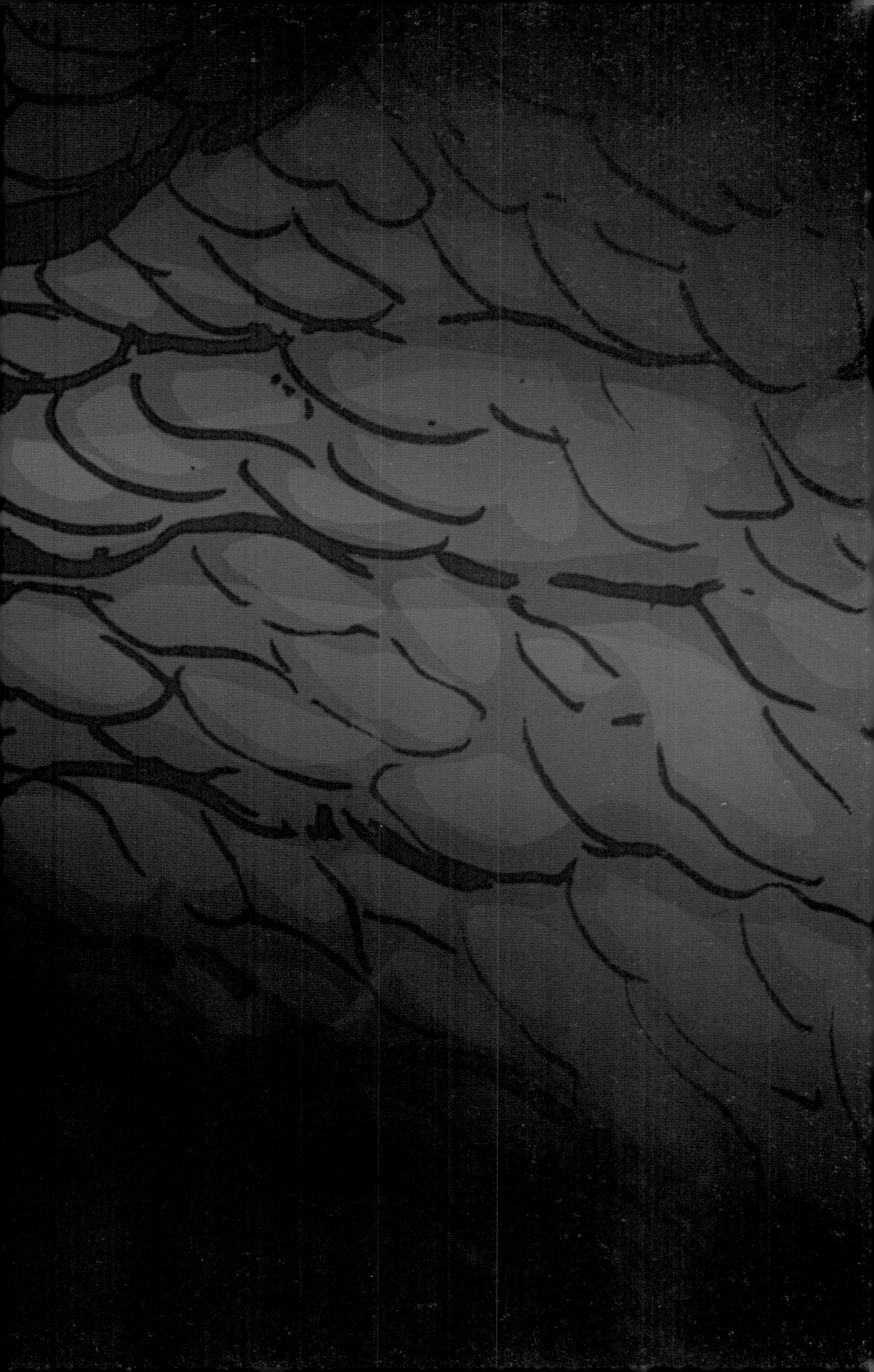

CHAPTER THREE:
VIVA JET JAGUAR

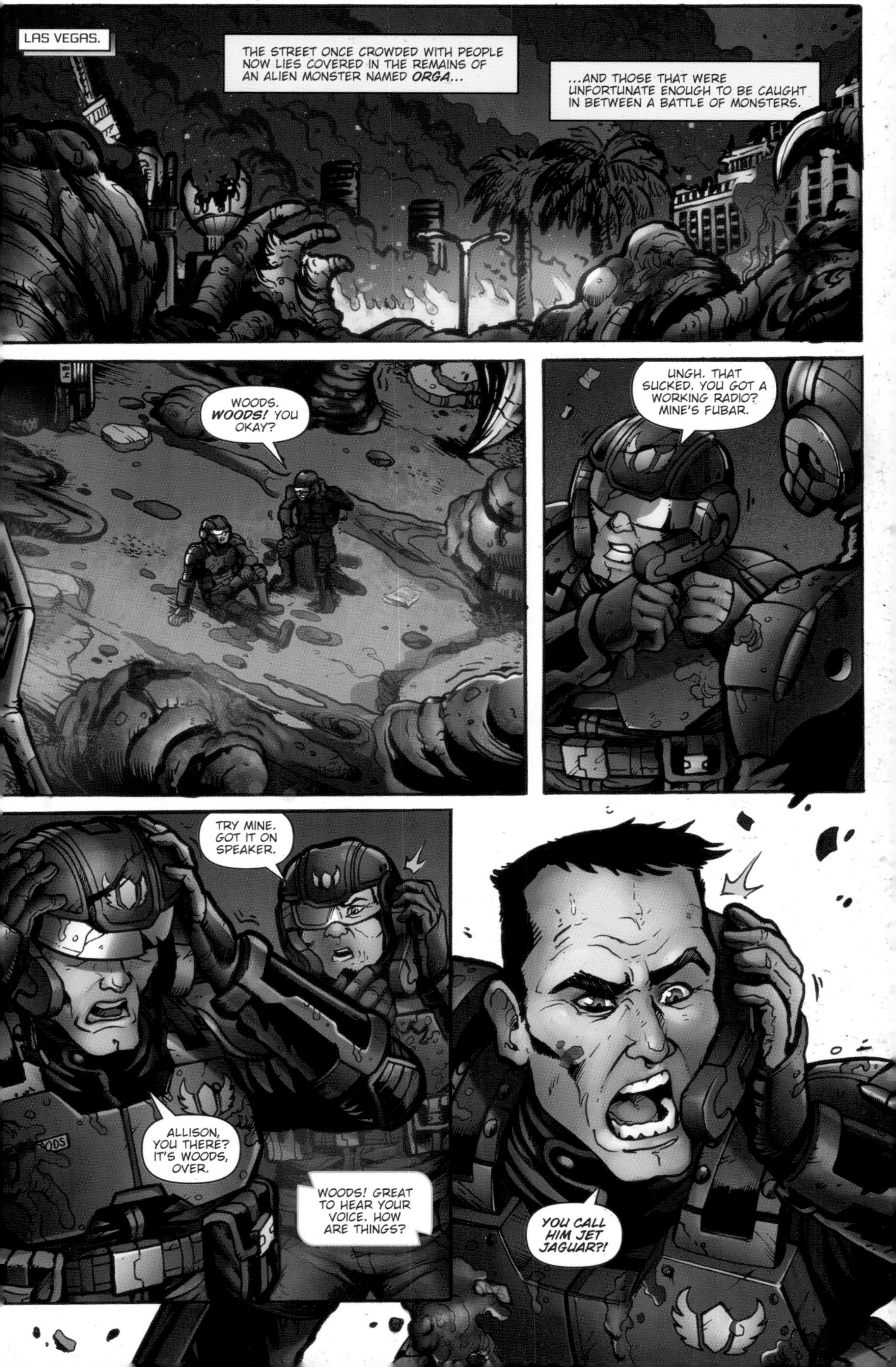
LAS VEGAS.
THE STREET ONCE CROWDED WITH PEOPLE NOW LIES COVERED IN THE REMAINS OF AN ALIEN MONSTER NAMED ORGA...
...AND THOSE THAT WERE UNFORTUNATE ENOUGH TO BE CAUGHT IN BETWEEN A BATTLE OF MONSTERS.
WOODS. WOODS! YOU OKAY?
UNGH. THAT SUCKED. YOU GOT A WORKING RADIO? MINE'S FUBAR.
TRY MINE. GOT IT ON SPEAKER.
ALLISON, YOU THERE? IT'S WOODS, OVER.
WOODS! GREAT TO HEAR YOUR VOICE. HOW ARE THINGS?
YOU CALL HIM JET JAGUAR?!

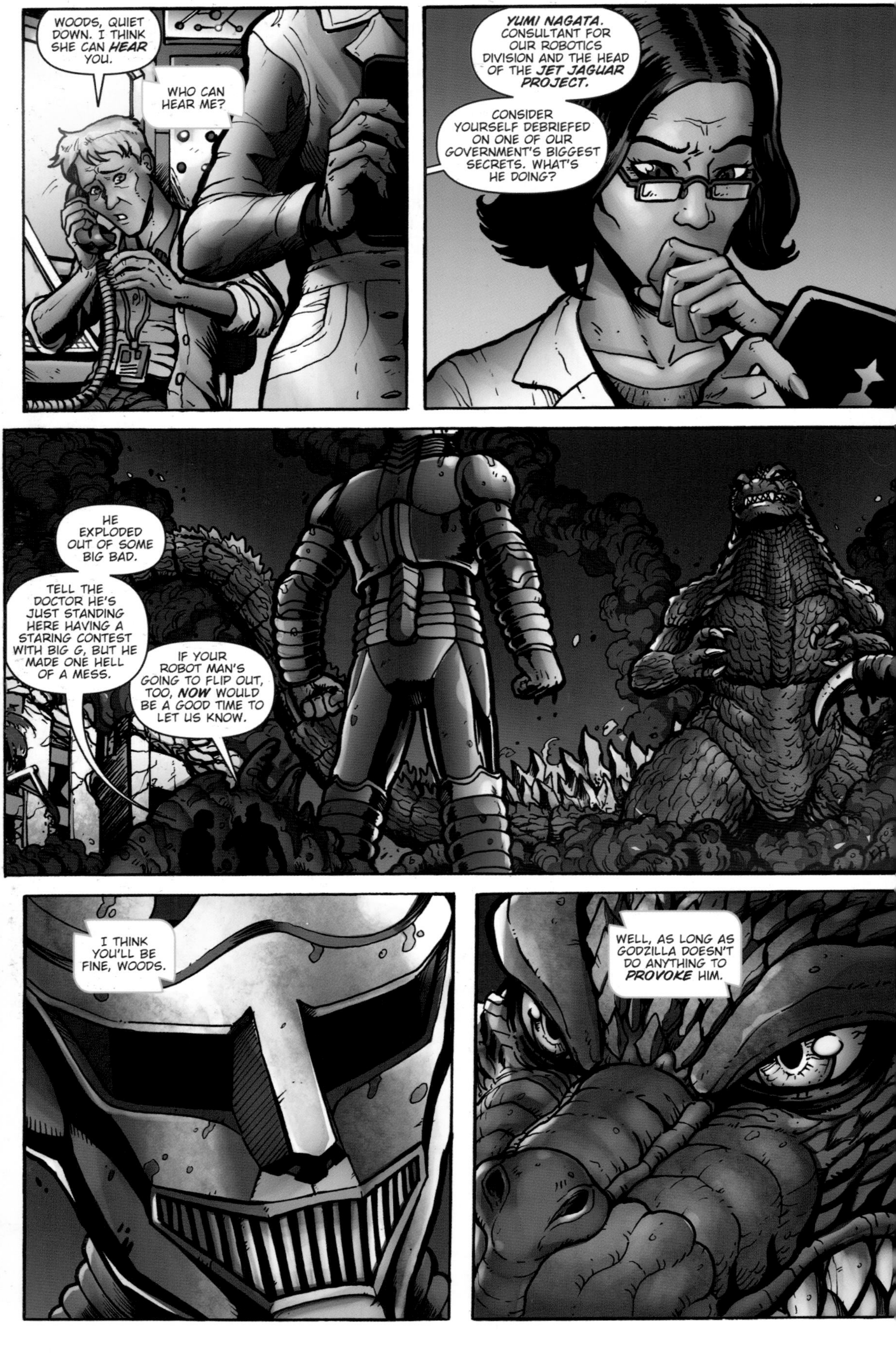
WOODS, QUIET DOWN. I THINK SHE CAN HEAR YOU.
WHO CAN HEAR ME?
YUMI NAGATA. CONSULTANT FOR OUR ROBOTICS DIVISION AND THE HEAD OF THE JET JAGUAR PROJECT.
CONSIDER YOURSELF DEBRIEFED ON ONE OF OUR GOVERNMENT'S BIGGEST SECRETS. WHAT'S HE DOING?
HE EXPLODED OUT OF SOME BIG BAD.
TELL THE DOCTOR HE'S JUST STANDING HERE HAVING A STARING CONTEST WITH BIG G, BUT HE MADE ONE HELL OF A MESS.
IF YOUR ROBOT MAN'S GOING TO FLIP OUT, TOO, NOW WOULD BE A GOOD TIME TO LET US KNOW.
I THINK YOU'LL BE FINE, WOODS.
WELL, AS LONG AS GODZILLA DOESN'T DO ANYTHING TO PROVOKE HIM.

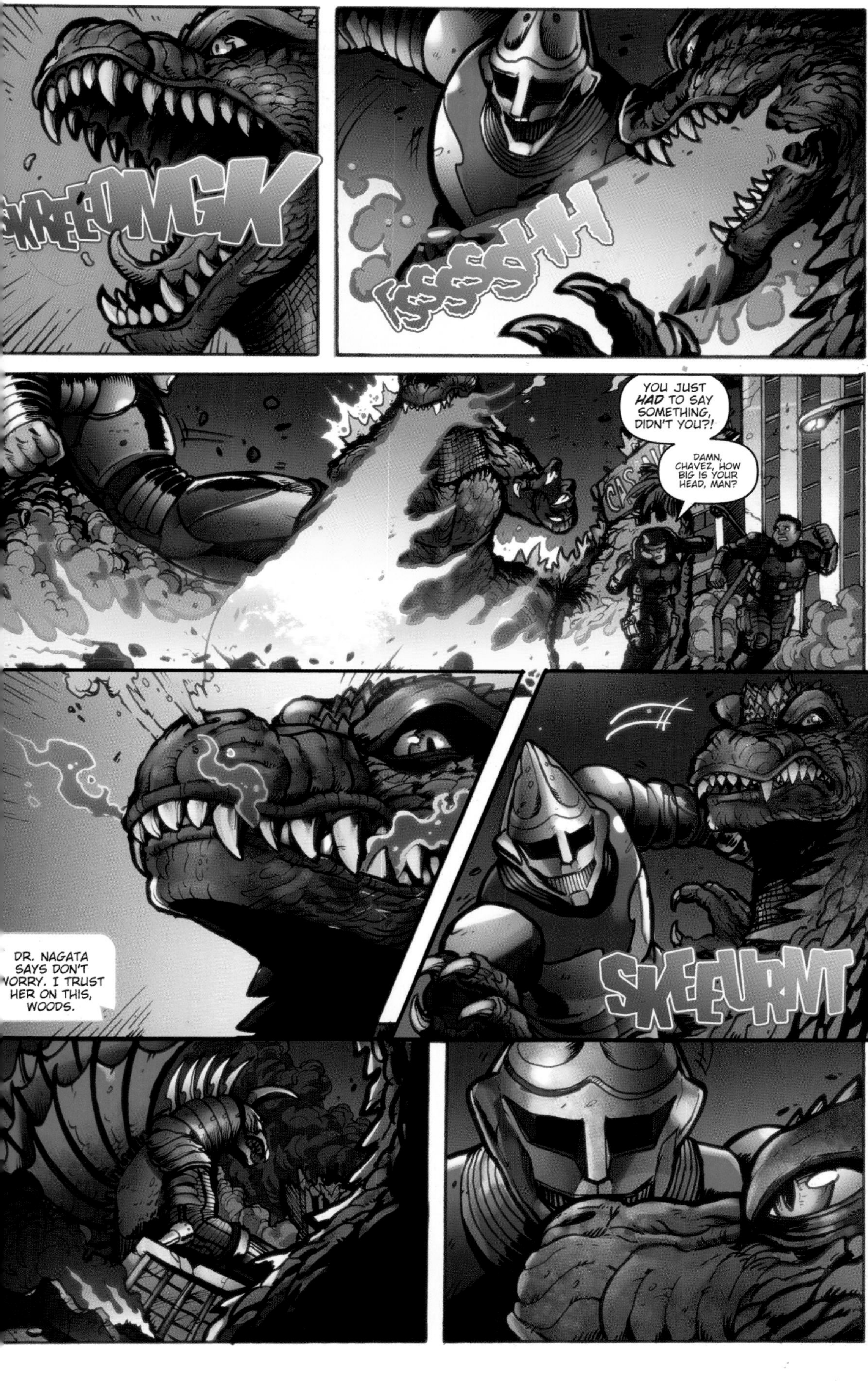

SKREEONGK
FSSSSHH
YOU JUST HAD TO SAY SOMETHING, DIDN'T YOU?!
DAMN, CHAVEZ, HOW BIG IS YOUR HEAD, MAN?
DR. NAGATA SAYS DON'T WORRY. I TRUST HER ON THIS, WOODS.
SKEEURNT

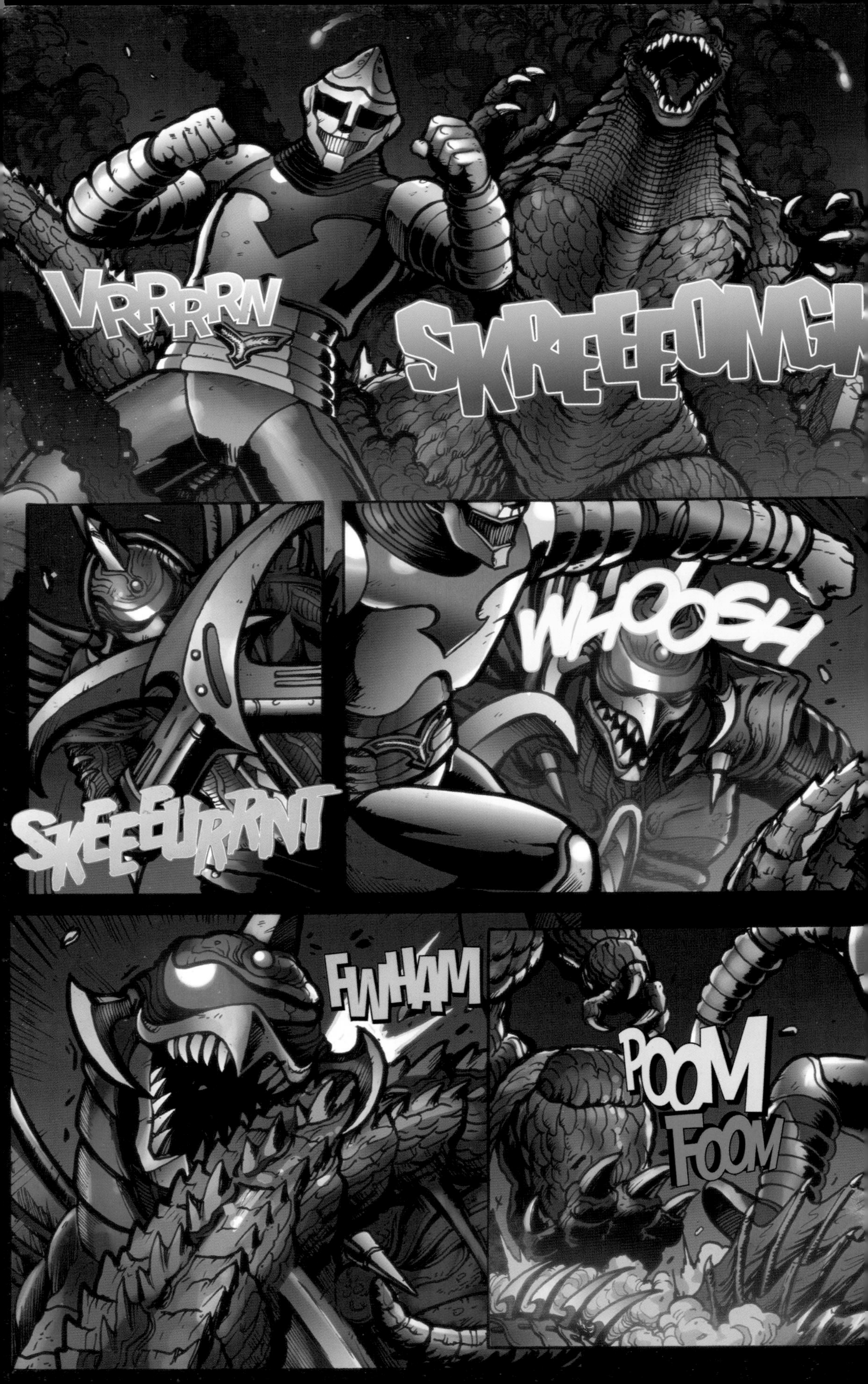
VRRRRRN
SKREEEEONGK
SKEEEURRRNT
WHOOSH
FWHAM
POOM
FOOM

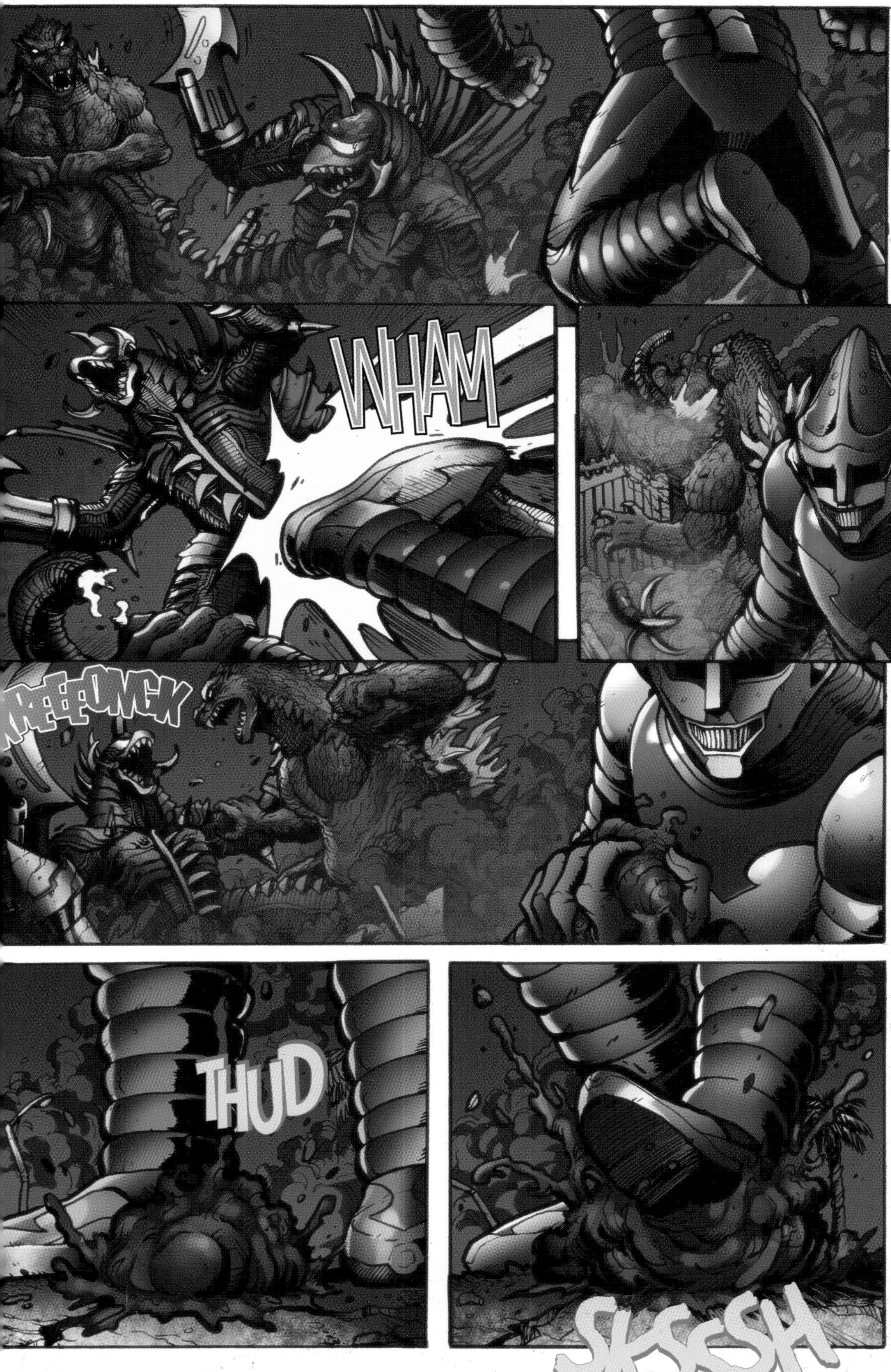
WHAM
REEEOMGK
THUD
SKSSSH

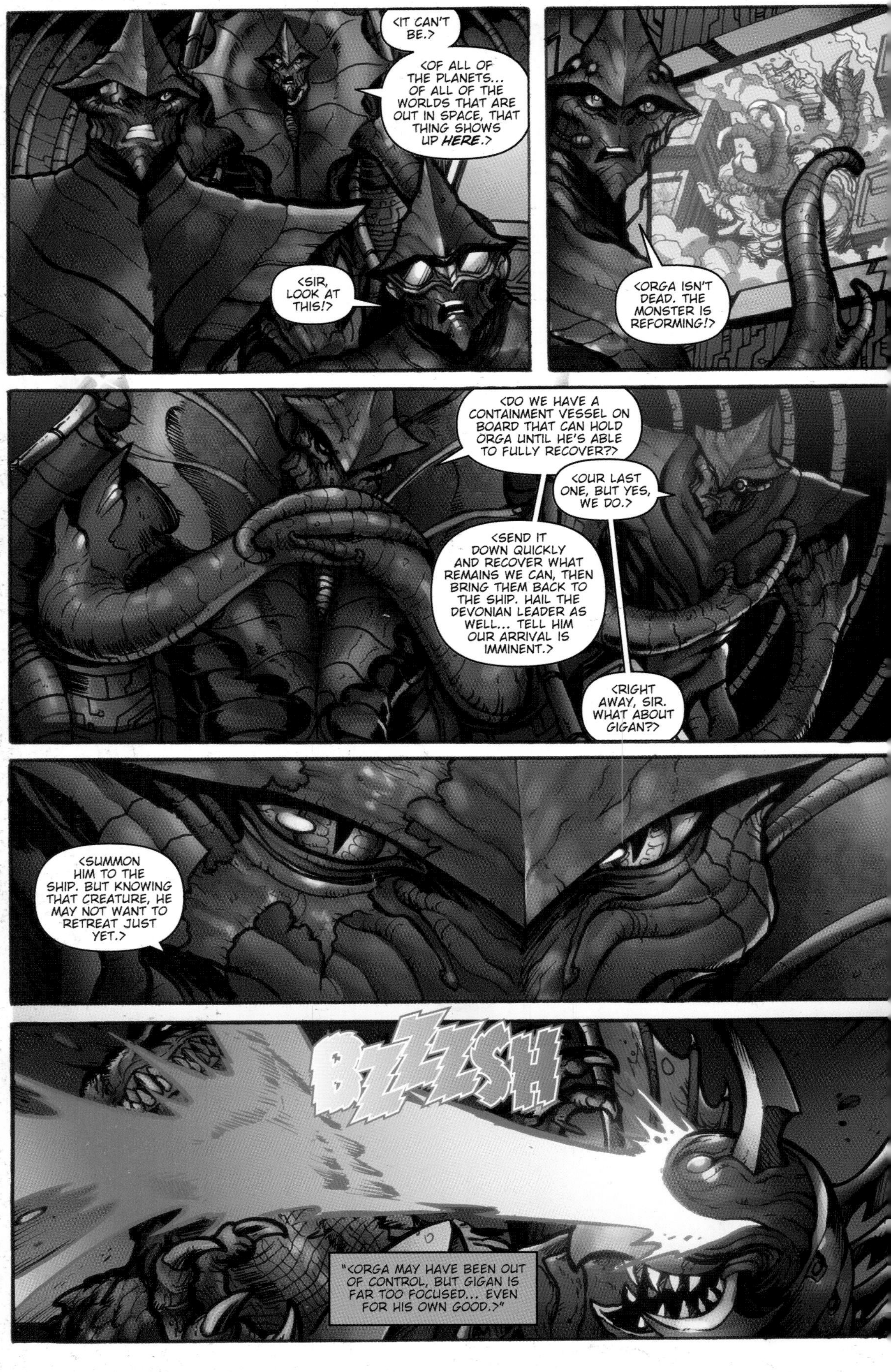
<IT CAN'T BE.>
<OF ALL OF THE PLANETS... OF ALL OF THE WORLDS THAT ARE OUT IN SPACE, THAT THING SHOWS UP *HERE*.>
<SIR, LOOK AT THIS!>
<ORGA ISN'T DEAD. THE MONSTER IS REFORMING!>
<DO WE HAVE A CONTAINMENT VESSEL ON BOARD THAT CAN HOLD ORGA UNTIL HE'S ABLE TO FULLY RECOVER?>
<OUR LAST ONE, BUT YES, WE DO.>
<SEND IT DOWN QUICKLY AND RECOVER WHAT REMAINS WE CAN, THEN BRING THEM BACK TO THE SHIP. HAIL THE DEVONIAN LEADER AS WELL... TELL HIM OUR ARRIVAL IS IMMINENT.>
<RIGHT AWAY, SIR. WHAT ABOUT GIGAN?>
<SUMMON HIM TO THE SHIP. BUT KNOWING THAT CREATURE, HE MAY NOT WANT TO RETREAT JUST YET.>
BZZZSH
"<ORGA MAY HAVE BEEN OUT OF CONTROL, BUT GIGAN IS FAR TOO FOCUSED... EVEN FOR HIS OWN GOOD.>"

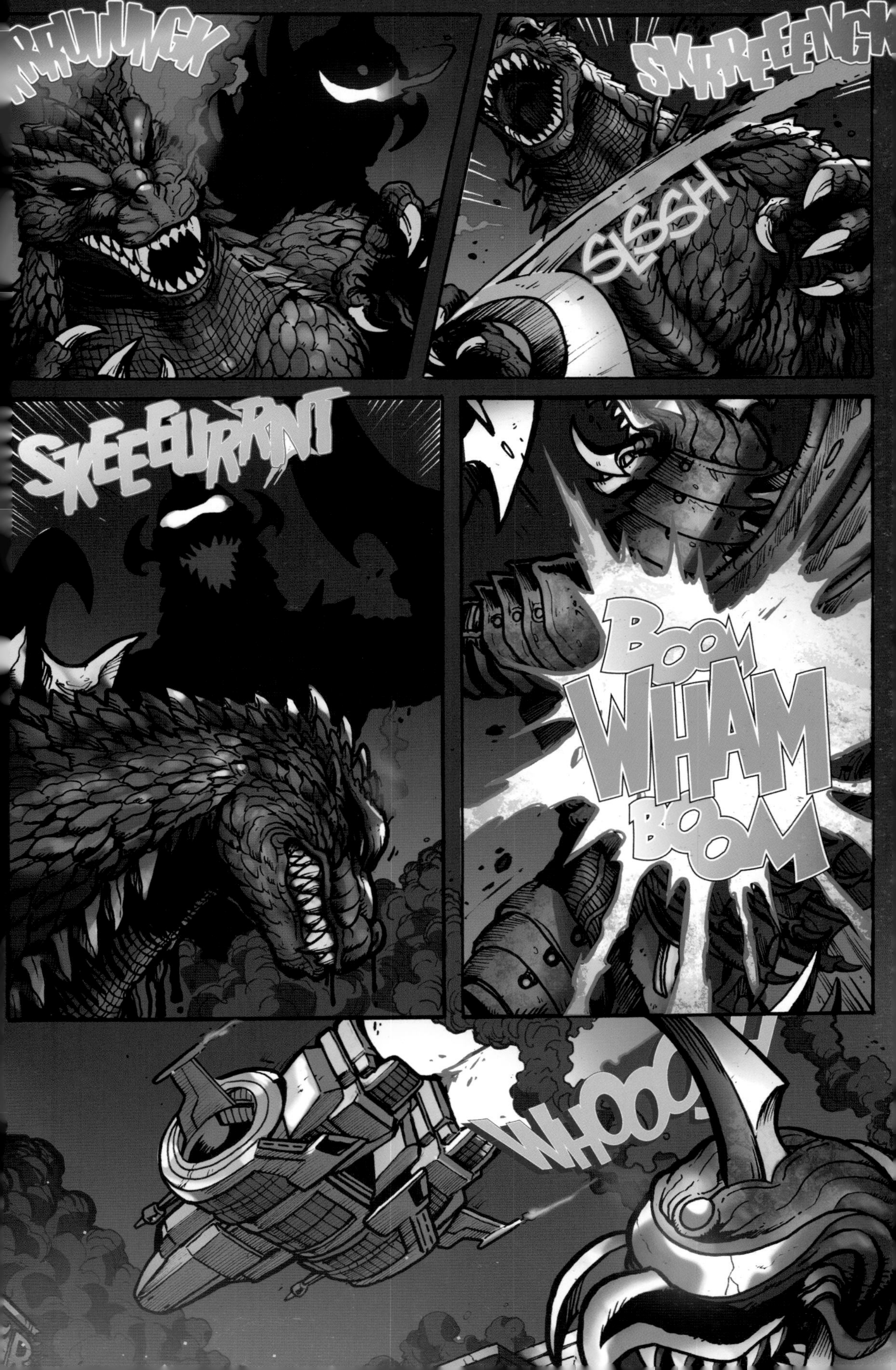
RRRUUUNGK
SKRREEENGK
SLSSH
SKEEEURRRNT
BOOM
WHAM
BOOM
WHOOO

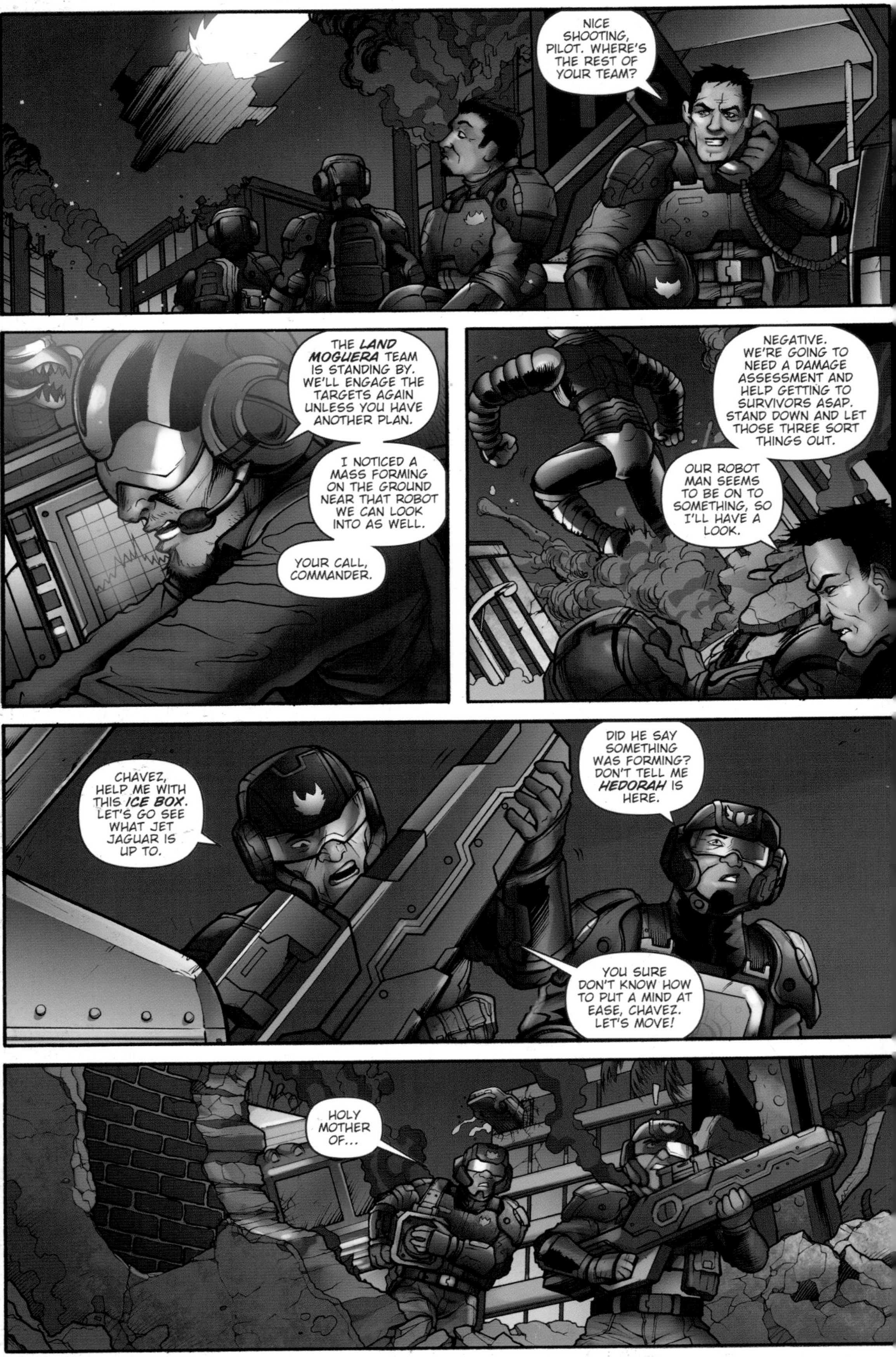
NICE SHOOTING, PILOT. WHERE'S THE REST OF YOUR TEAM?
THE LAND MOGUERA TEAM IS STANDING BY. WE'LL ENGAGE THE TARGETS AGAIN UNLESS YOU HAVE ANOTHER PLAN.
I NOTICED A MASS FORMING ON THE GROUND NEAR THAT ROBOT WE CAN LOOK INTO AS WELL.
YOUR CALL, COMMANDER.
NEGATIVE. WE'RE GOING TO NEED A DAMAGE ASSESSMENT AND HELP GETTING TO SURVIVORS ASAP. STAND DOWN AND LET THOSE THREE SORT THINGS OUT.
OUR ROBOT MAN SEEMS TO BE ON TO SOMETHING, SO I'LL HAVE A LOOK.
CHAVEZ, HELP ME WITH THIS ICE BOX. LET'S GO SEE WHAT JET JAGUAR IS UP TO.
DID HE SAY SOMETHING WAS FORMING? DON'T TELL ME HEDORAH IS HERE.
YOU SURE DON'T KNOW HOW TO PUT A MIND AT EASE, CHAVEZ. LET'S MOVE!
HOLY MOTHER OF...

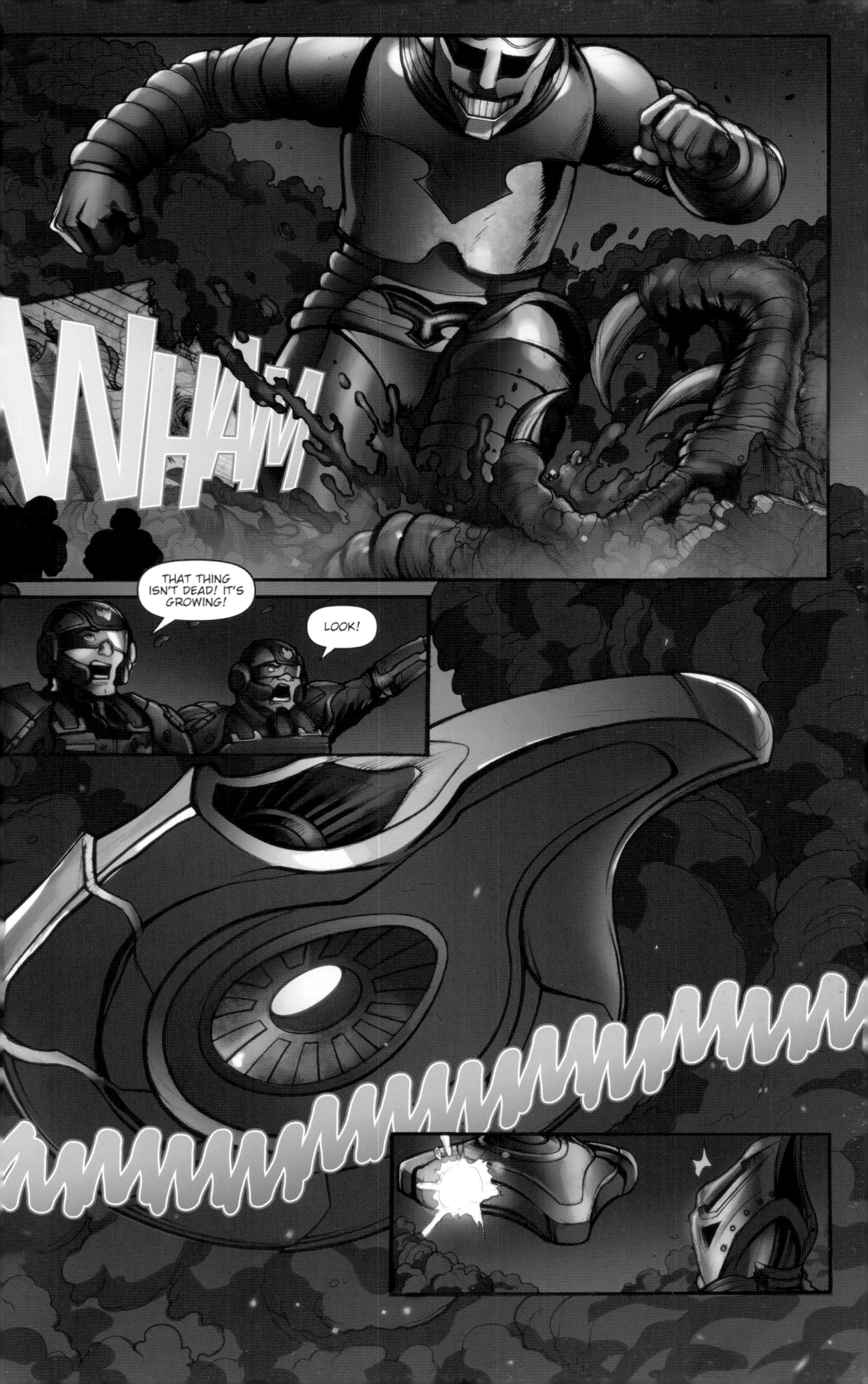
WHAM
THAT THING ISN'T DEAD! IT'S GROWING!
LOOK!
nnnnnnnnnnnnnnnnnnnnnnn

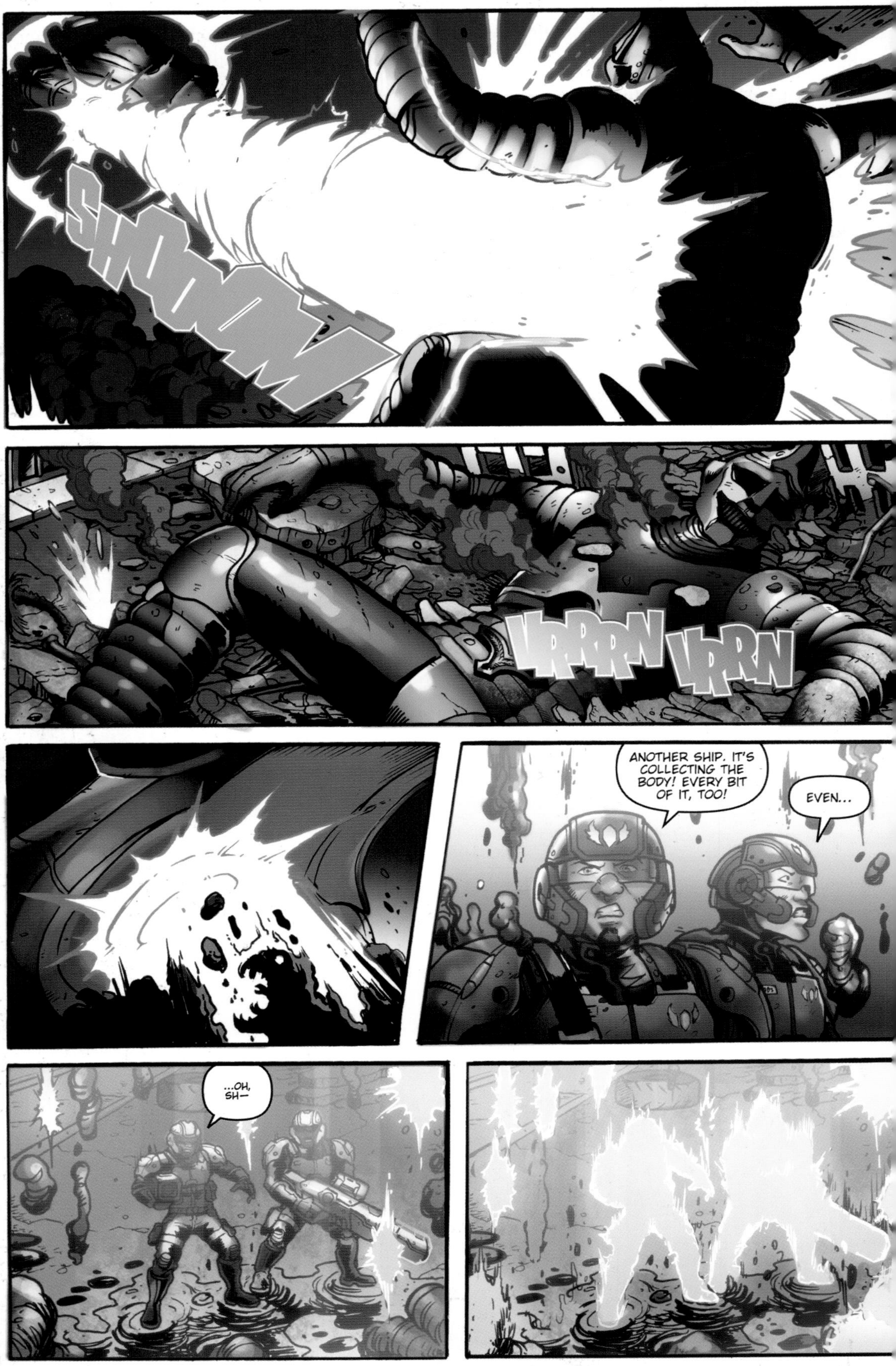
SHOOOM
URRRRN URRRN
ANOTHER SHIP. IT'S COLLECTING THE BODY! EVERY BIT OF IT, TOO!
EVEN...
...OH, SH—

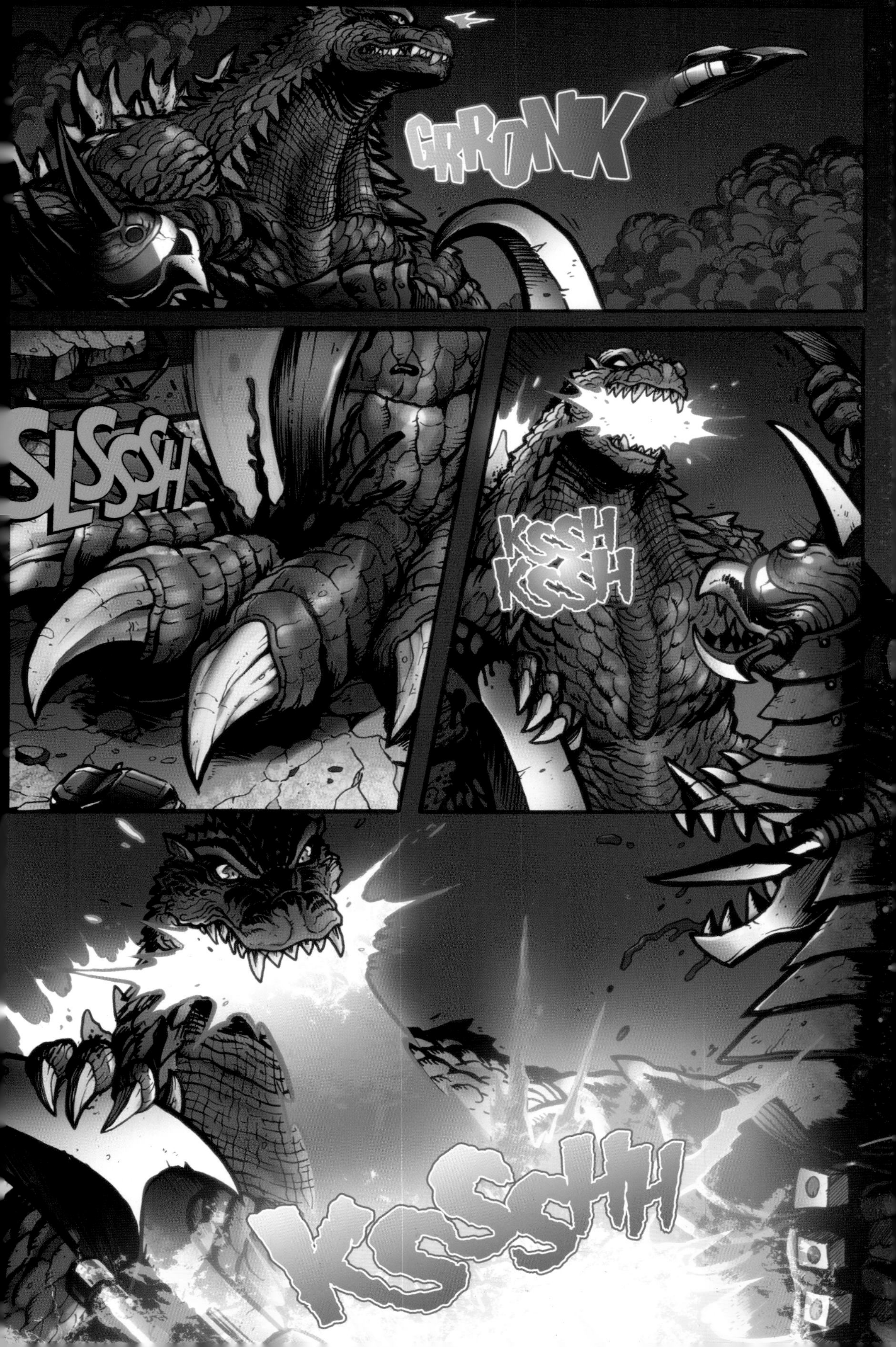
GRRONK
SLSSSH
KSSH KSSH
KSSHH

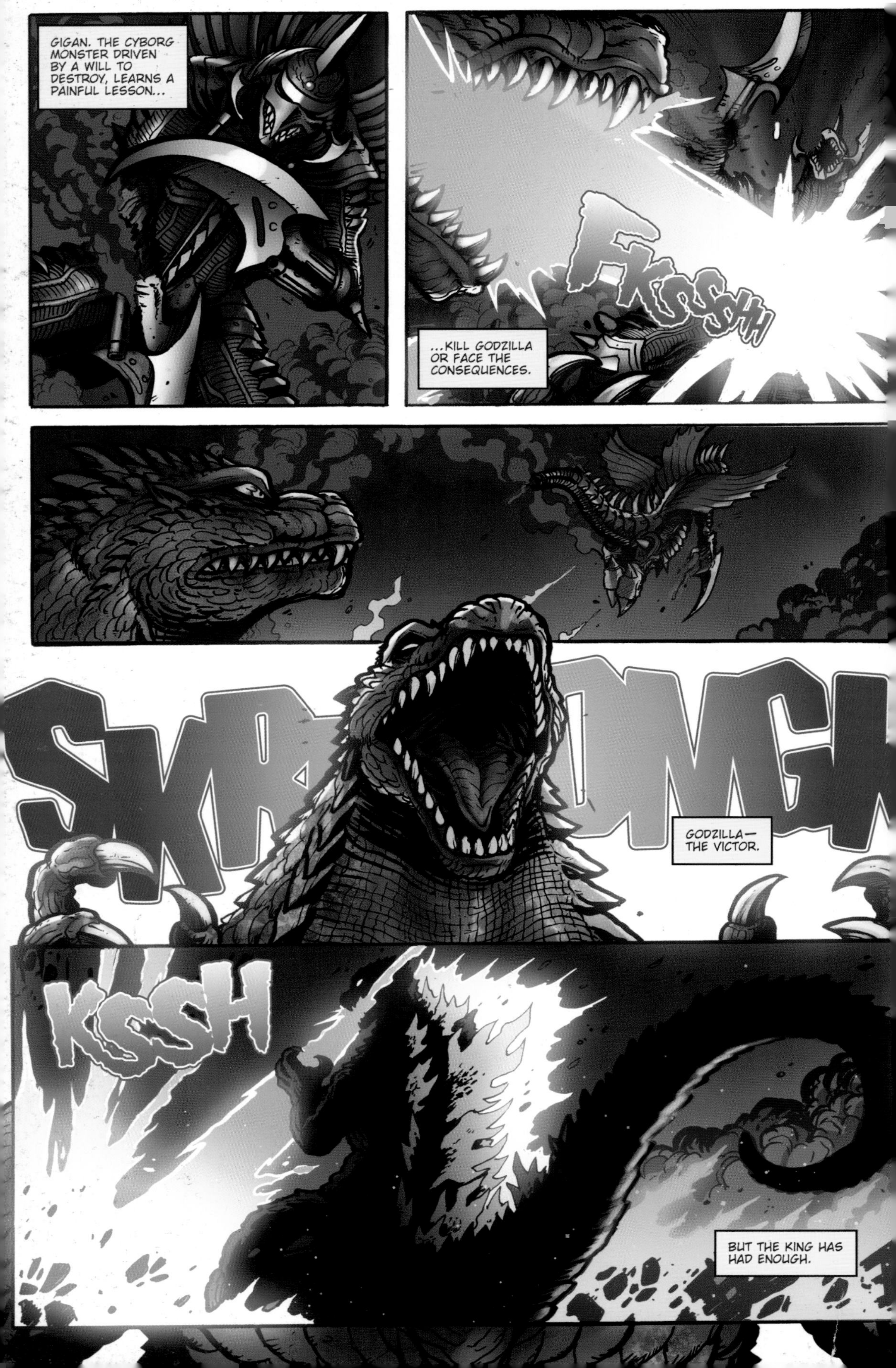
GIGAN. THE CYBORG MONSTER DRIVEN BY A WILL TO DESTROY, LEARNS A PAINFUL LESSON...
FKOSSHH
...KILL GODZILLA OR FACE THE CONSEQUENCES.
GODZILLA— THE VICTOR.
KSSH
BUT THE KING HAS HAD ENOUGH.

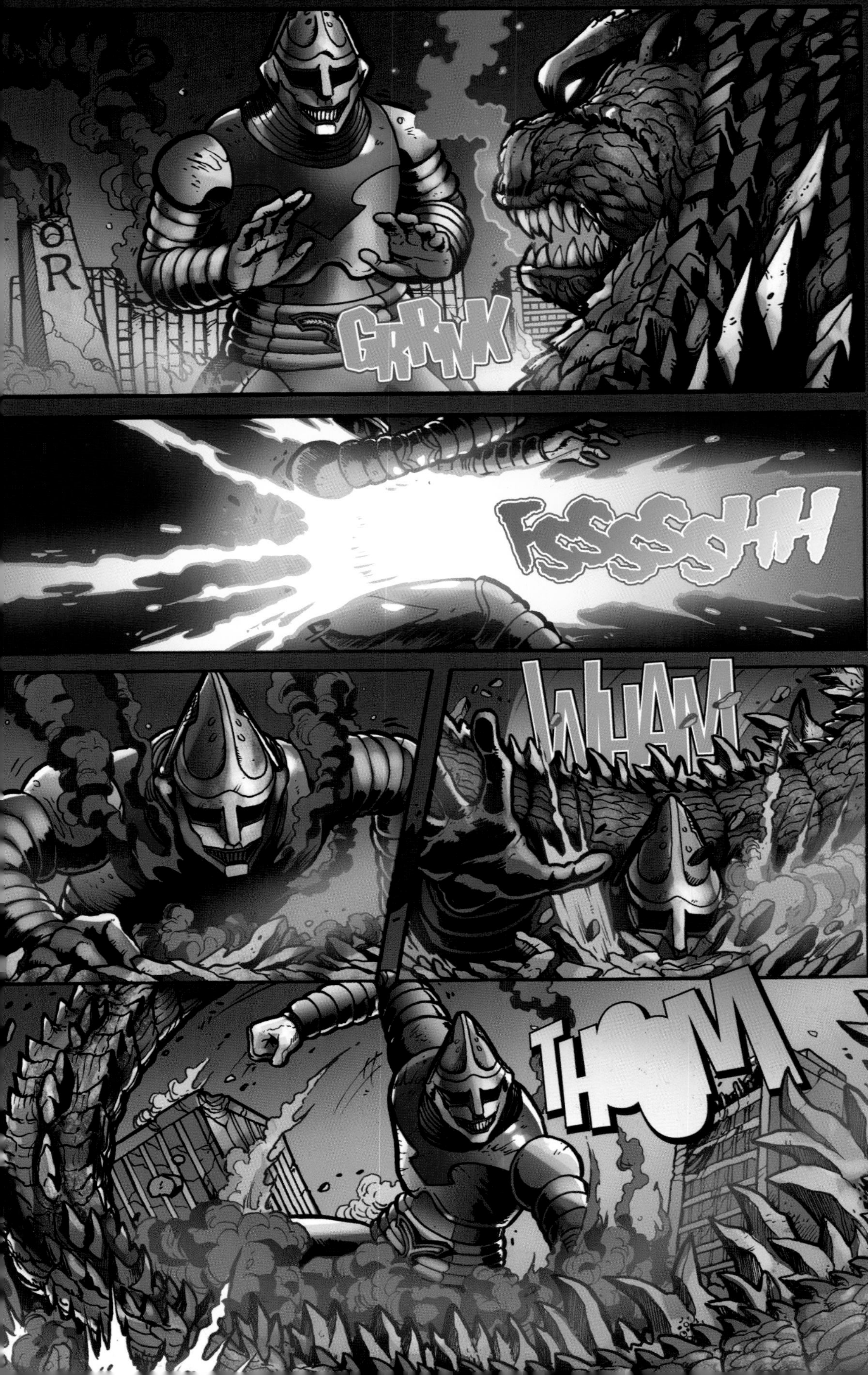
GRRNK
FSSSHH
WHAM
THOOM

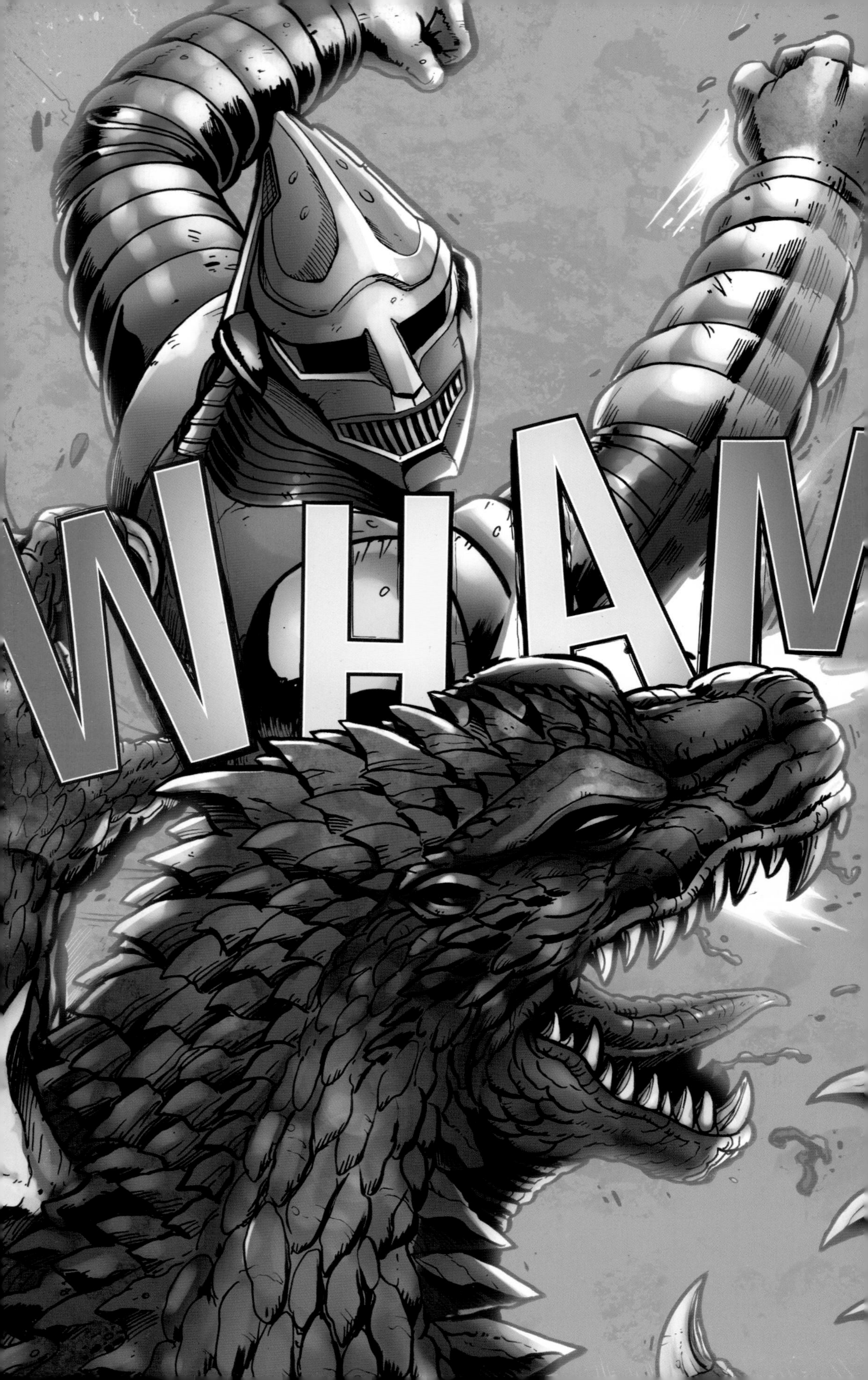
WHAM

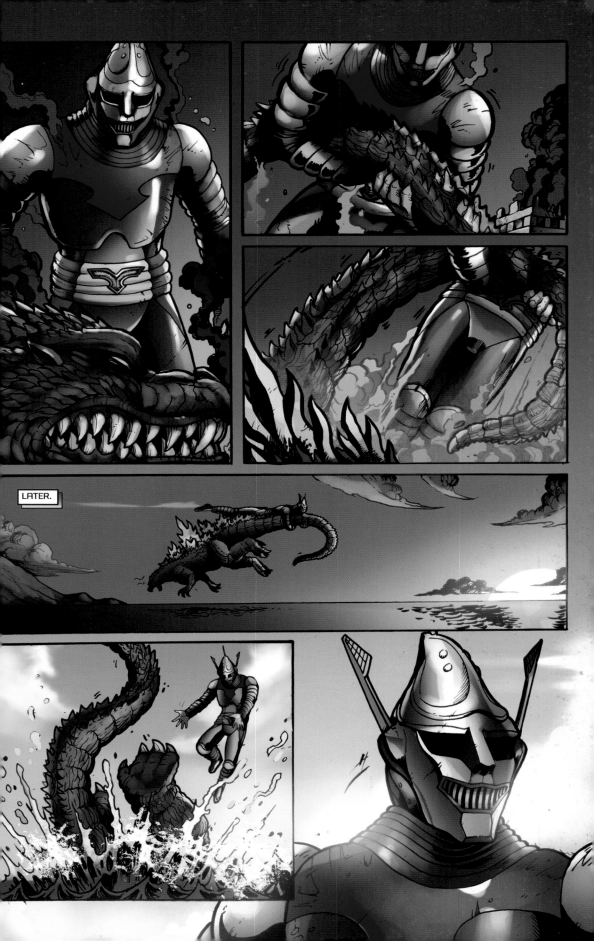

LATER.

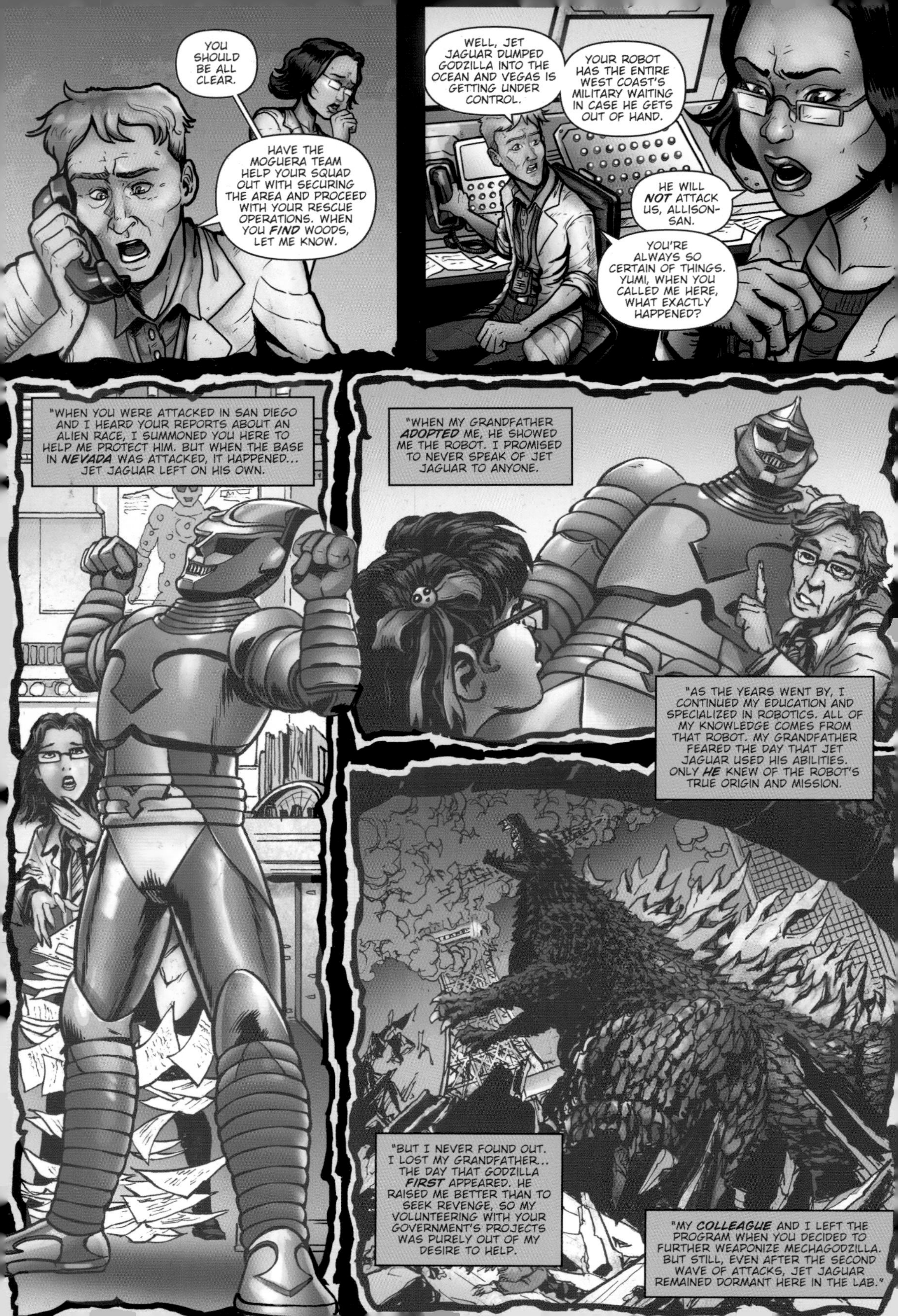
YOU SHOULD BE ALL CLEAR.
HAVE THE MOGUERA TEAM HELP YOUR SQUAD OUT WITH SECURING THE AREA AND PROCEED WITH YOUR RESCUE OPERATIONS. WHEN YOU *FIND* WOODS, LET ME KNOW.
WELL, JET JAGUAR DUMPED GODZILLA INTO THE OCEAN AND VEGAS IS GETTING UNDER CONTROL.
YOUR ROBOT HAS THE ENTIRE WEST COAST'S MILITARY WAITING IN CASE HE GETS OUT OF HAND.
HE WILL *NOT* ATTACK US, ALLISON-SAN.
YOU'RE ALWAYS SO CERTAIN OF THINGS. YUMI, WHEN YOU CALLED ME HERE, WHAT EXACTLY HAPPENED?
"WHEN YOU WERE ATTACKED IN SAN DIEGO AND I HEARD YOUR REPORTS ABOUT AN ALIEN RACE, I SUMMONED YOU HERE TO HELP ME PROTECT HIM. BUT WHEN THE BASE IN *NEVADA* WAS ATTACKED, IT HAPPENED... JET JAGUAR LEFT ON HIS OWN.
"WHEN MY GRANDFATHER *ADOPTED* ME, HE SHOWED ME THE ROBOT. I PROMISED TO NEVER SPEAK OF JET JAGUAR TO ANYONE.
"AS THE YEARS WENT BY, I CONTINUED MY EDUCATION AND SPECIALIZED IN ROBOTICS. ALL OF MY KNOWLEDGE COMES FROM THAT ROBOT. MY GRANDFATHER FEARED THE DAY THAT JET JAGUAR USED HIS ABILITIES. ONLY *HE* KNEW OF THE ROBOT'S TRUE ORIGIN AND MISSION.
"BUT I NEVER FOUND OUT. I LOST MY GRANDFATHER... THE DAY THAT GODZILLA *FIRST* APPEARED. HE RAISED ME BETTER THAN TO SEEK REVENGE, SO MY VOLUNTEERING WITH YOUR GOVERNMENT'S PROJECTS WAS PURELY OUT OF MY DESIRE TO HELP.
"MY *COLLEAGUE* AND I LEFT THE PROGRAM WHEN YOU DECIDED TO FURTHER WEAPONIZE MECHAGODZILLA. BUT STILL, EVEN AFTER THE SECOND WAVE OF ATTACKS, JET JAGUAR REMAINED DORMANT HERE IN THE LAB."

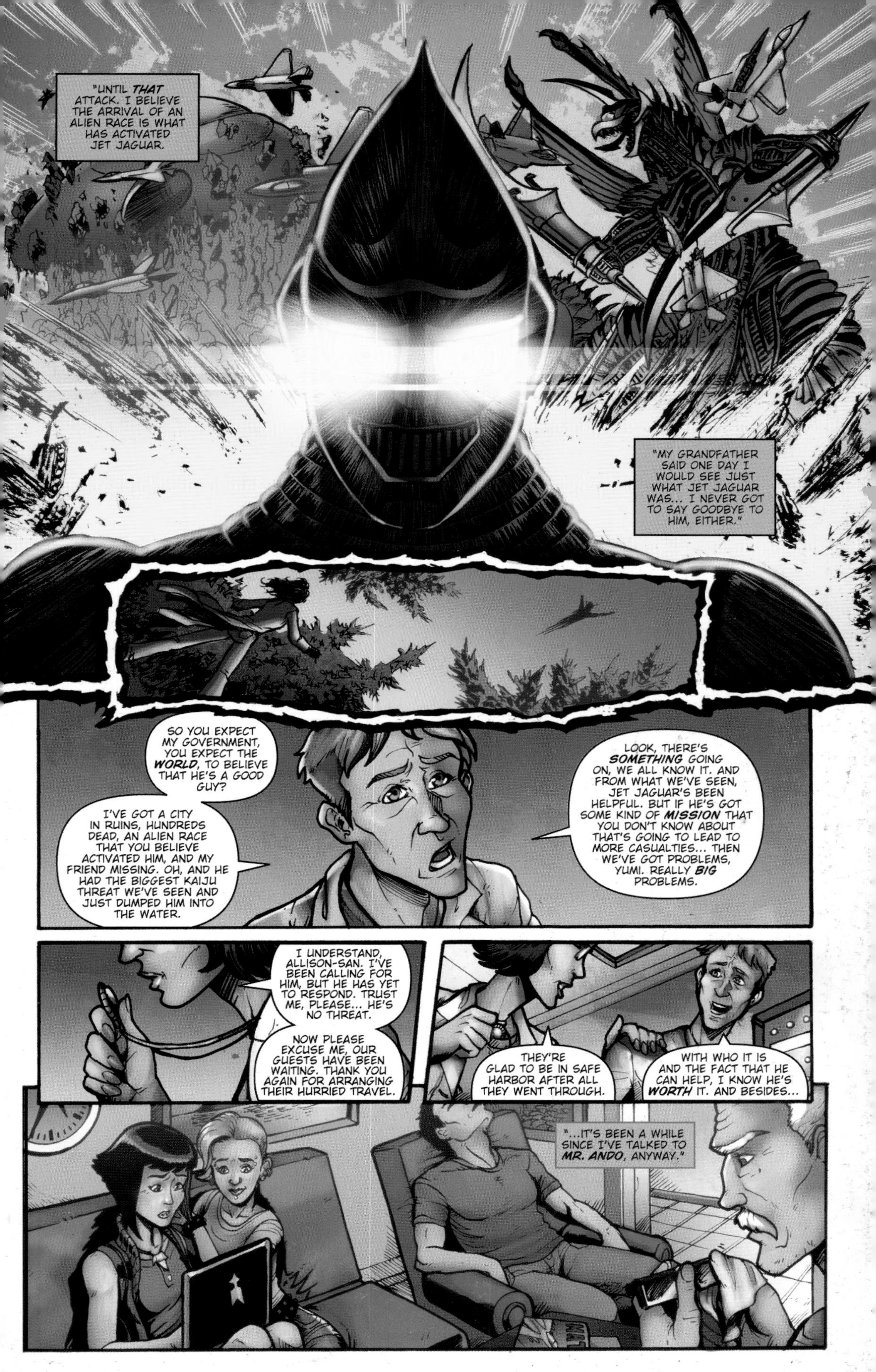
"UNTIL THAT ATTACK. I BELIEVE THE ARRIVAL OF AN ALIEN RACE IS WHAT HAS ACTIVATED JET JAGUAR.
"MY GRANDFATHER SAID ONE DAY I WOULD SEE JUST WHAT JET JAGUAR WAS... I NEVER GOT TO SAY GOODBYE TO HIM, EITHER."
SO YOU EXPECT MY GOVERNMENT, YOU EXPECT THE WORLD, TO BELIEVE THAT HE'S A GOOD GUY?
I'VE GOT A CITY IN RUINS, HUNDREDS DEAD, AN ALIEN RACE THAT YOU BELIEVE ACTIVATED HIM, AND MY FRIEND MISSING. OH, AND HE HAD THE BIGGEST KAIJU THREAT WE'VE SEEN AND JUST DUMPED HIM INTO THE WATER.
LOOK, THERE'S SOMETHING GOING ON, WE ALL KNOW IT. AND FROM WHAT WE'VE SEEN, JET JAGUAR'S BEEN HELPFUL. BUT IF HE'S GOT SOME KIND OF MISSION THAT YOU DON'T KNOW ABOUT THAT'S GOING TO LEAD TO MORE CASUALTIES... THEN WE'VE GOT PROBLEMS, YUMI. REALLY BIG PROBLEMS.
I UNDERSTAND, ALLISON-SAN. I'VE BEEN CALLING FOR HIM, BUT HE HAS YET TO RESPOND. TRUST ME, PLEASE... HE'S NO THREAT.
NOW PLEASE EXCUSE ME, OUR GUESTS HAVE BEEN WAITING. THANK YOU AGAIN FOR ARRANGING THEIR HURRIED TRAVEL.
THEY'RE GLAD TO BE IN SAFE HARBOR AFTER ALL THEY WENT THROUGH.
WITH WHO IT IS AND THE FACT THAT HE CAN HELP, I KNOW HE'S WORTH IT. AND BESIDES...
"...IT'S BEEN A WHILE SINCE I'VE TALKED TO MR. ANDO, ANYWAY."

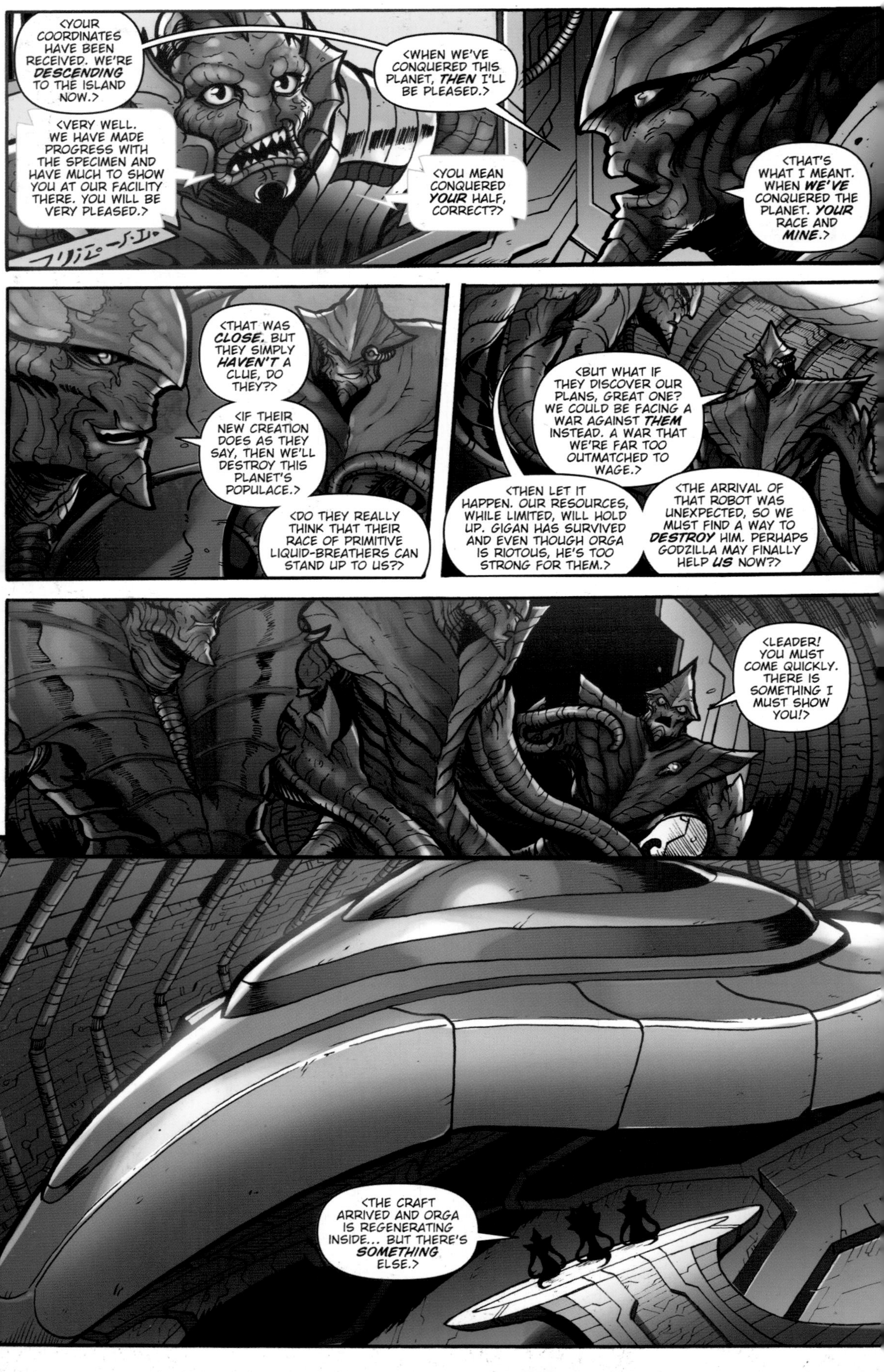
<YOUR COORDINATES HAVE BEEN RECEIVED. WE'RE **DESCENDING** TO THE ISLAND NOW.>
<VERY WELL. WE HAVE MADE PROGRESS WITH THE SPECIMEN AND HAVE MUCH TO SHOW YOU AT OUR FACILITY THERE. YOU WILL BE VERY PLEASED.>
<WHEN WE'VE CONQUERED THIS PLANET, **THEN** I'LL BE PLEASED.>
<YOU MEAN CONQUERED **YOUR** HALF, CORRECT?>
<THAT'S WHAT I MEANT. WHEN **WE'VE** CONQUERED THE PLANET. **YOUR** RACE AND **MINE**.>
<THAT WAS **CLOSE.** BUT THEY SIMPLY **HAVEN'T** A CLUE, DO THEY?>
<IF THEIR NEW CREATION DOES AS THEY SAY, THEN WE'LL DESTROY THIS PLANET'S POPULACE.>
<DO THEY REALLY THINK THAT THEIR RACE OF PRIMITIVE LIQUID-BREATHERS CAN STAND UP TO US?>
<BUT WHAT IF THEY DISCOVER OUR PLANS, GREAT ONE? WE COULD BE FACING A WAR AGAINST **THEM** INSTEAD. A WAR THAT WE'RE FAR TOO OUTMATCHED TO WAGE.>
<THEN LET IT HAPPEN. OUR RESOURCES, WHILE LIMITED, WILL HOLD UP. GIGAN HAS SURVIVED AND EVEN THOUGH ORGA IS RIOTOUS, HE'S TOO STRONG FOR THEM.>
<THE ARRIVAL OF THAT ROBOT WAS UNEXPECTED, SO WE MUST FIND A WAY TO **DESTROY** HIM. PERHAPS GODZILLA MAY FINALLY HELP **US** NOW?>
<LEADER! YOU MUST COME QUICKLY. THERE IS SOMETHING I MUST SHOW YOU!>
<THE CRAFT ARRIVED AND ORGA IS REGENERATING INSIDE... BUT THERE'S **SOMETHING** ELSE.>

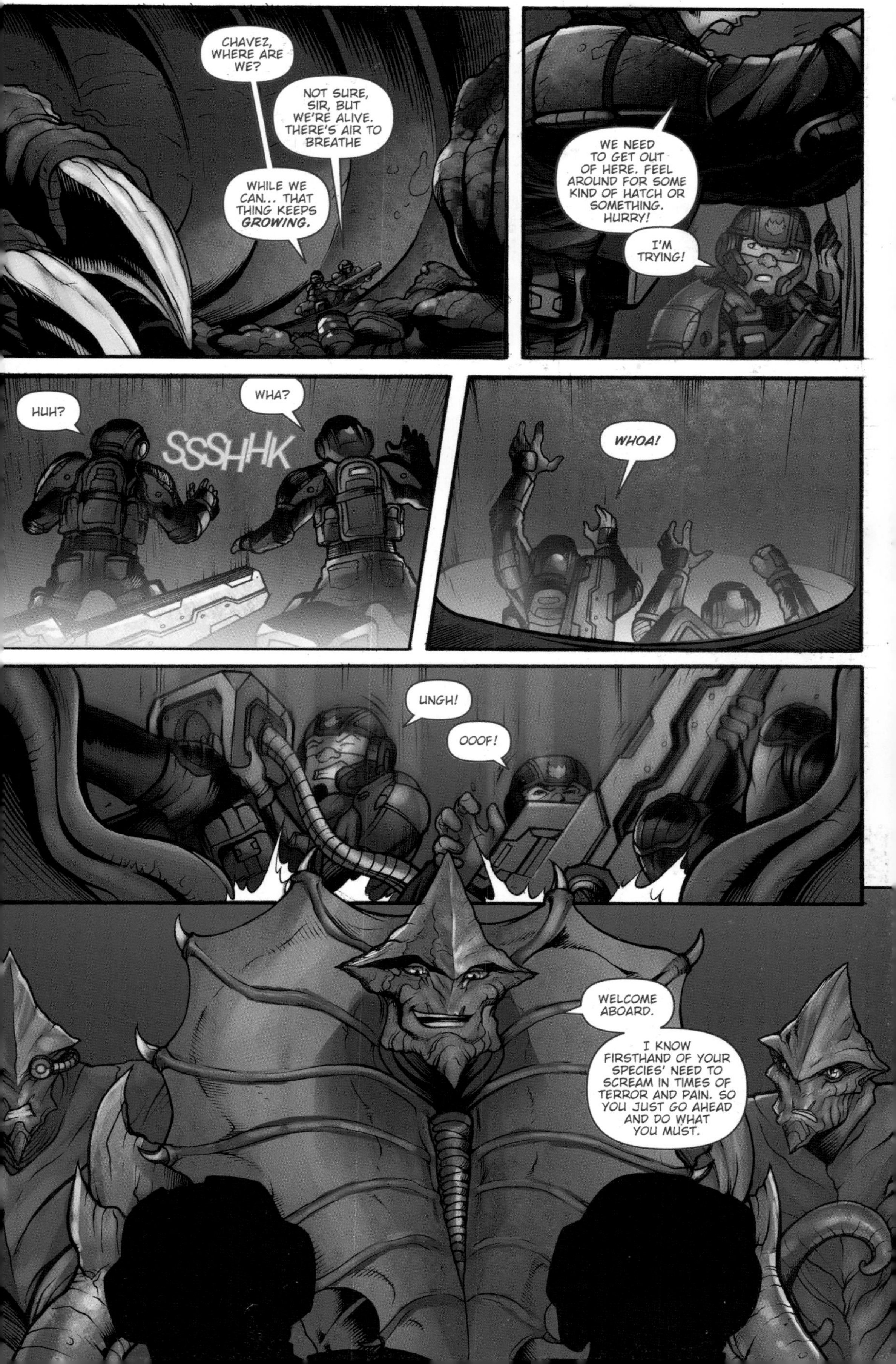
CHAVEZ, WHERE ARE WE?
NOT SURE, SIR, BUT WE'RE ALIVE. THERE'S AIR TO BREATHE
WHILE WE CAN... THAT THING KEEPS *GROWING.*
WE NEED TO GET OUT OF HERE. FEEL AROUND FOR SOME KIND OF HATCH OR SOMETHING. HURRY!
I'M TRYING!
HUH?
WHA?
SSSHHK
WHOA!
UNGH!
OOOF!
WELCOME ABOARD.
I KNOW FIRSTHAND OF YOUR SPECIES' NEED TO SCREAM IN TIMES OF TERROR AND PAIN. SO YOU JUST GO AHEAD AND DO WHAT YOU MUST.

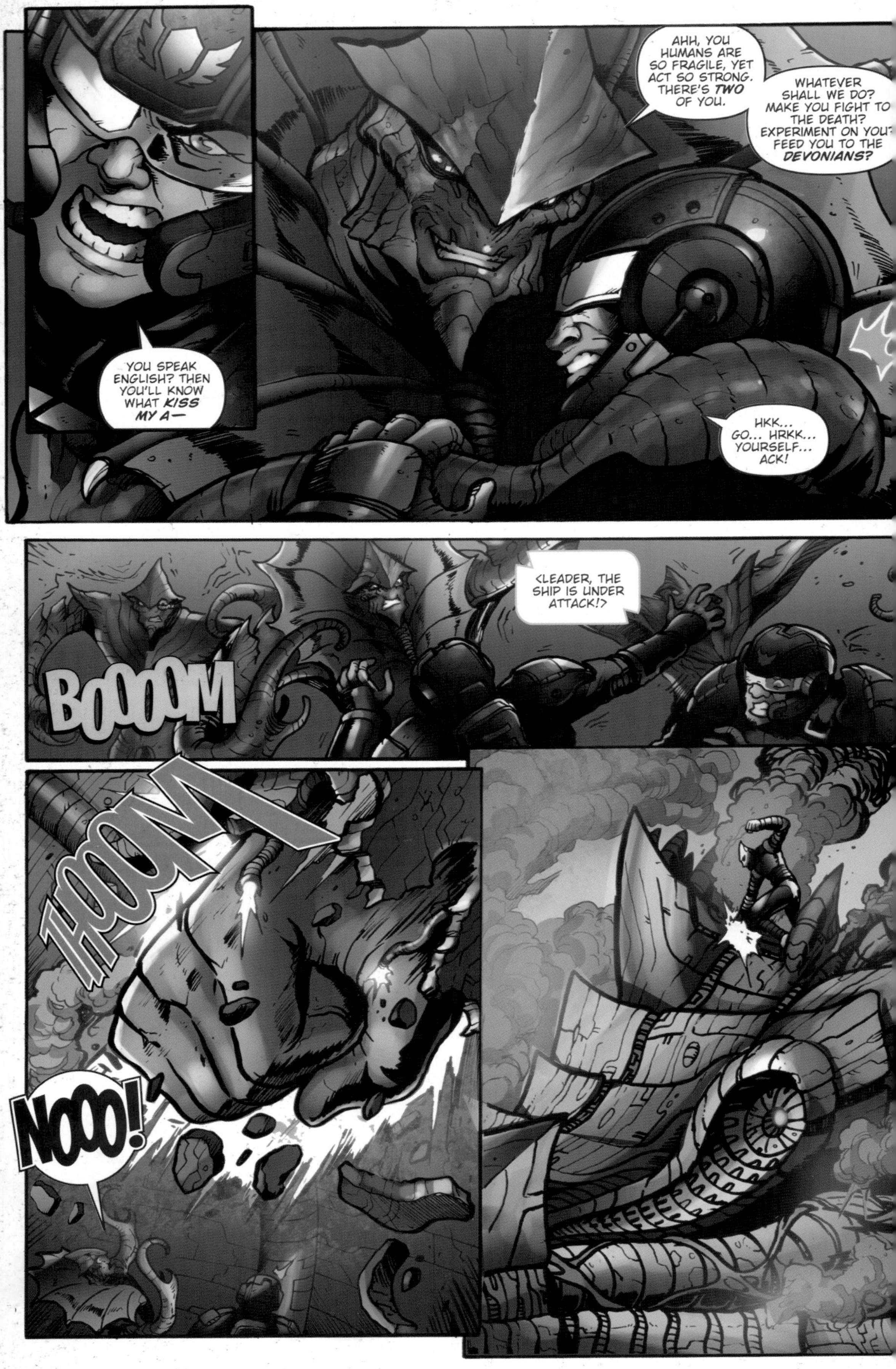
AHH, YOU HUMANS ARE SO FRAGILE, YET ACT SO STRONG. THERE'S TWO OF YOU.
WHATEVER SHALL WE DO? MAKE YOU FIGHT TO THE DEATH? EXPERIMENT ON YOU? FEED YOU TO THE DEVONIANS?
YOU SPEAK ENGLISH? THEN YOU'LL KNOW WHAT KISS MY A—
HKK... GO... HRKK... YOURSELF... ACK!
<LEADER, THE SHIP IS UNDER ATTACK!>
BOOOOM
THOOOM
NOOO!

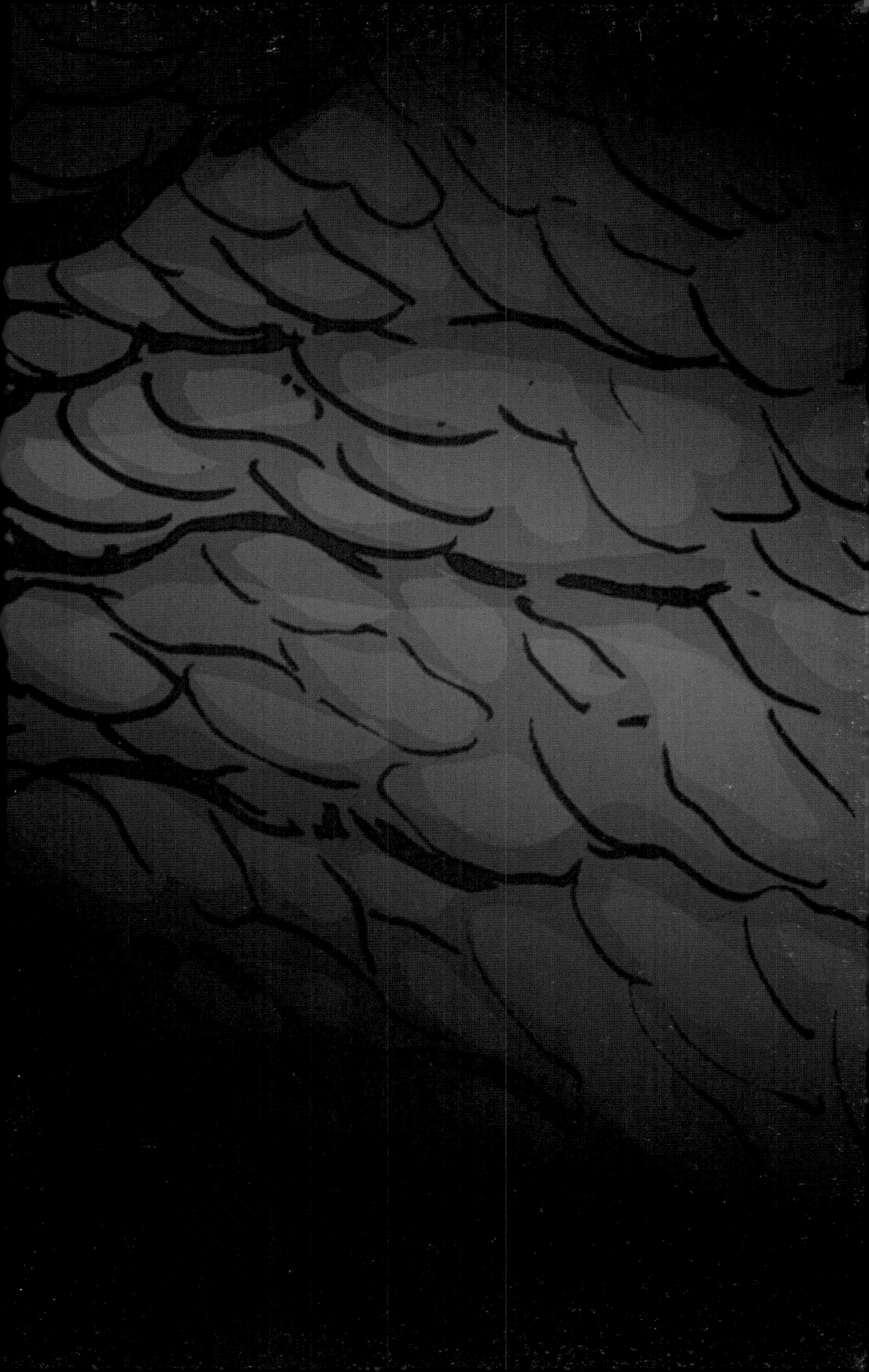

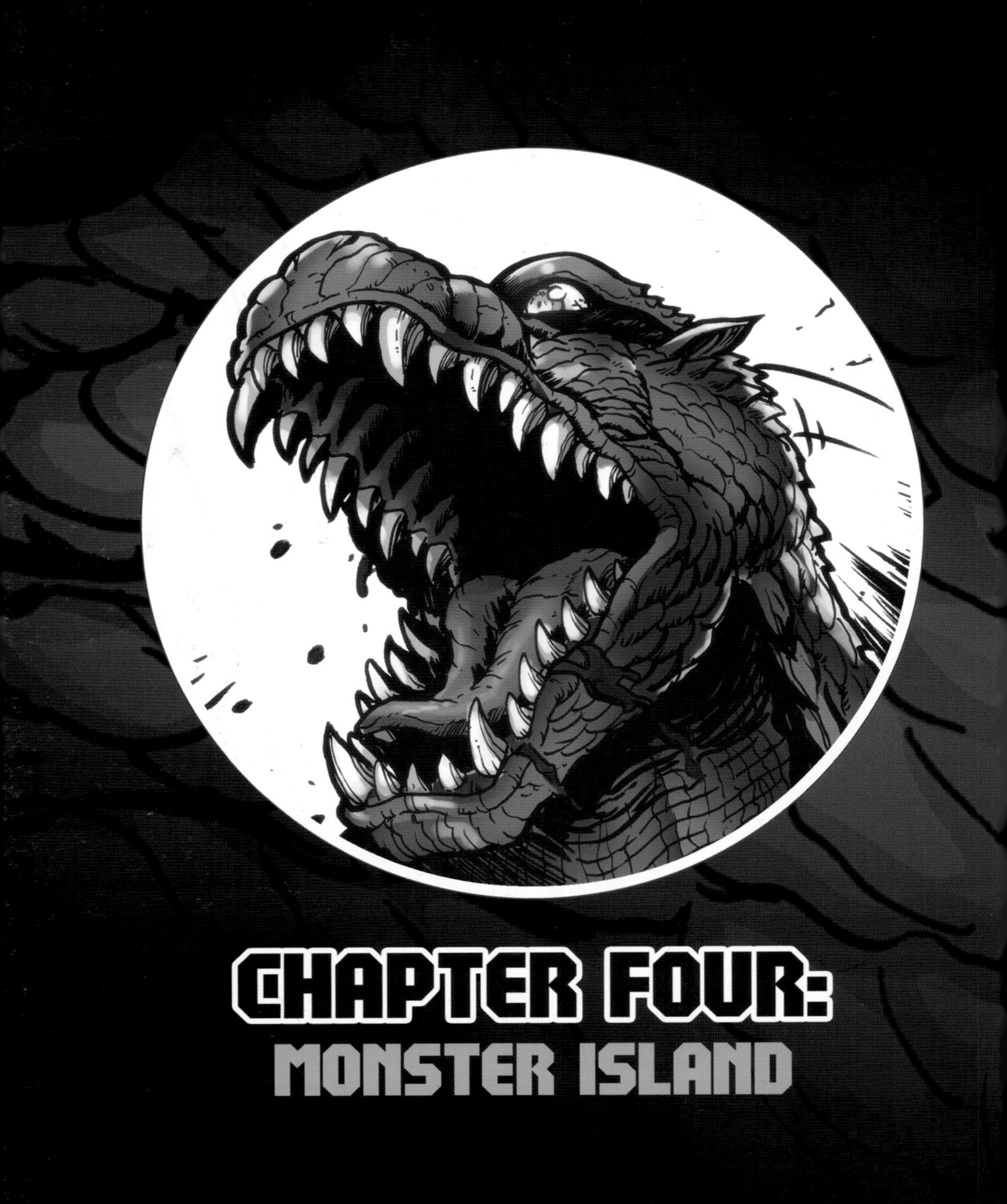

CHAPTER FOUR:
MONSTER ISLAND

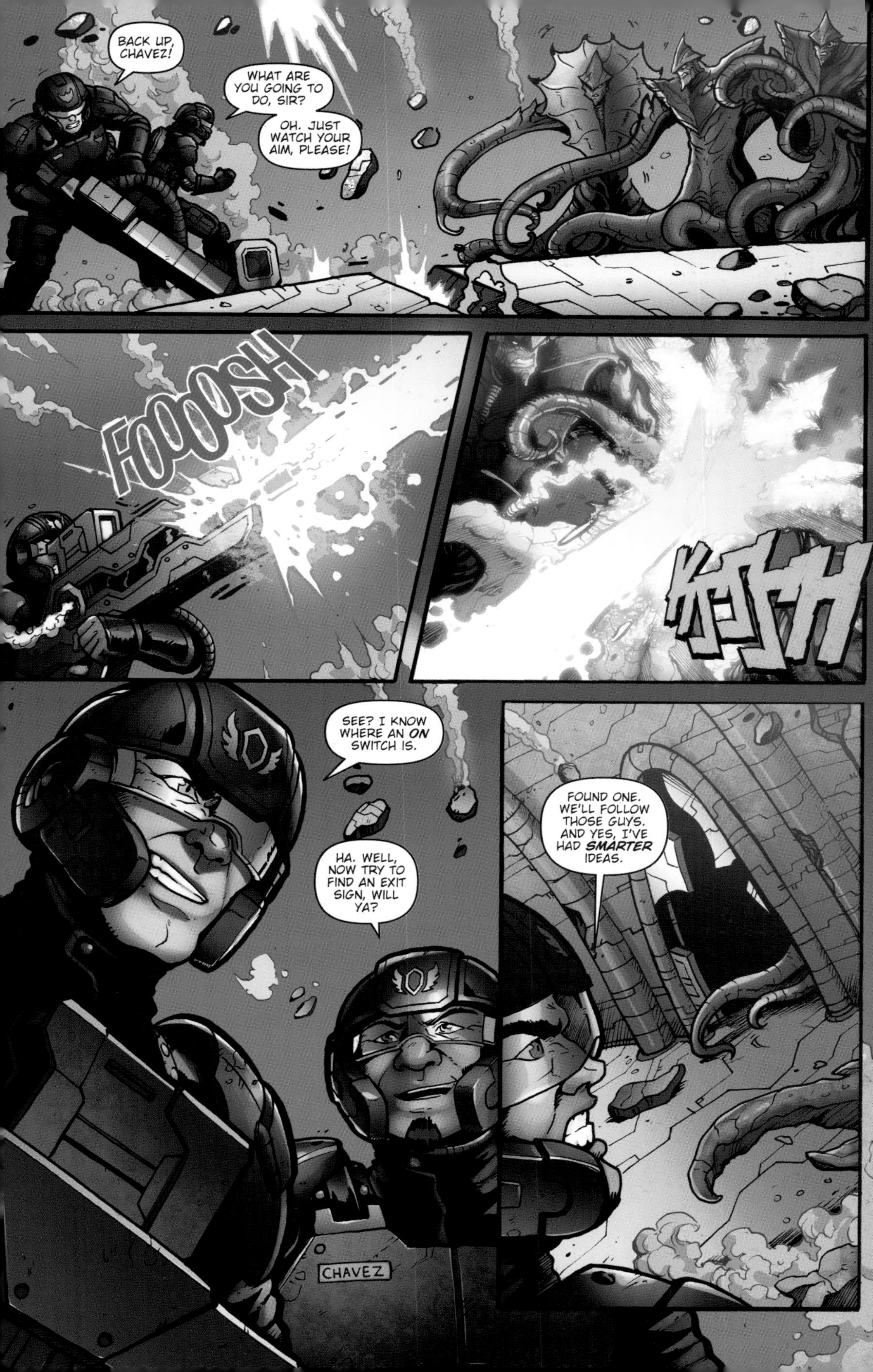
BACK UP, CHAVEZ!
WHAT ARE YOU GOING TO DO, SIR?
OH. JUST WATCH YOUR AIM, PLEASE!
FOOOSH
KOOSH
SEE? I KNOW WHERE AN ON SWITCH IS.
HA. WELL, NOW TRY TO FIND AN EXIT SIGN, WILL YA?
CHAVEZ
FOUND ONE. WE'LL FOLLOW THOSE GUYS. AND YES, I'VE HAD SMARTER IDEAS.

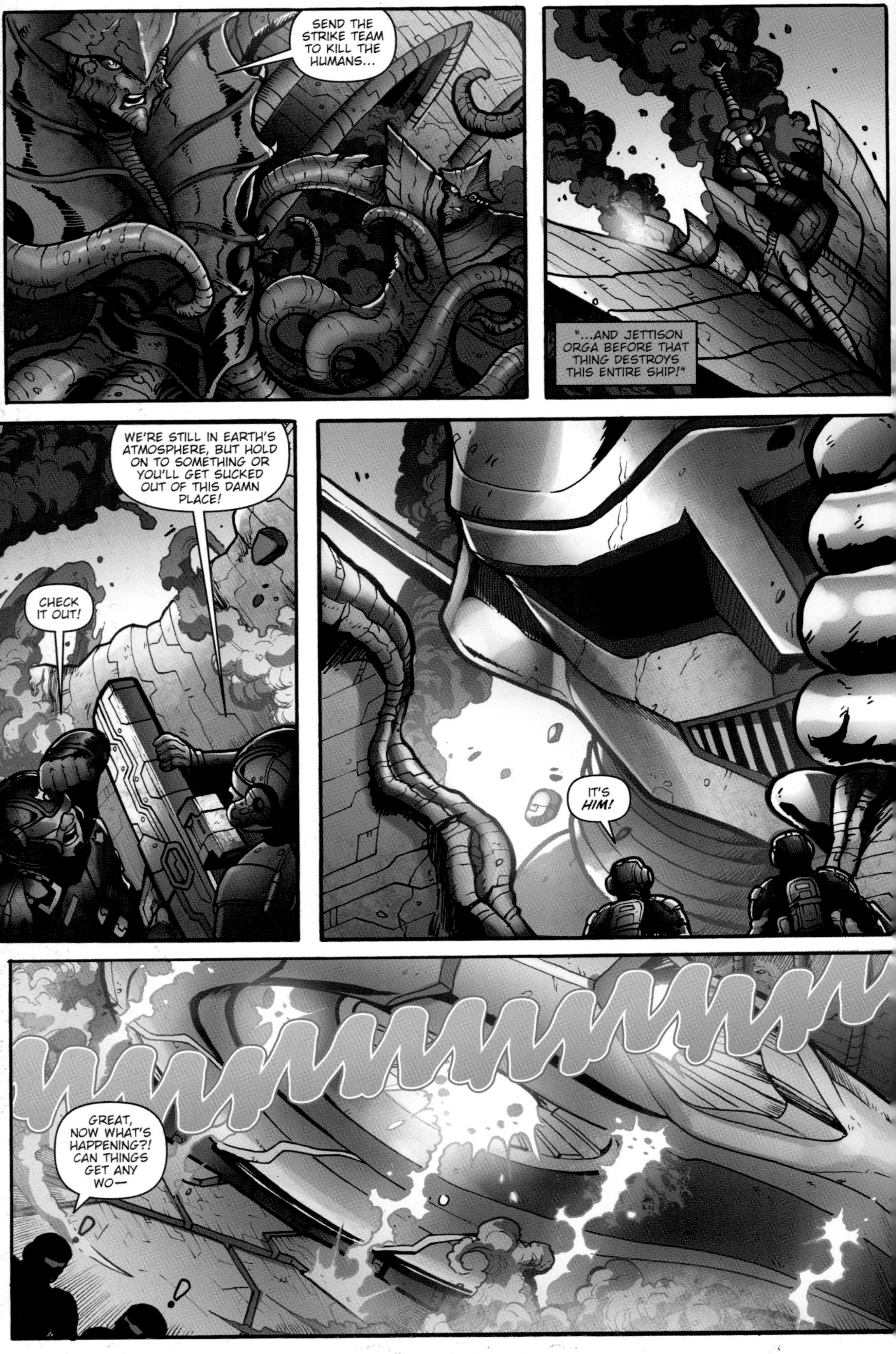
SEND THE STRIKE TEAM TO KILL THE HUMANS...
"...AND JETTISON ORGA BEFORE THAT THING DESTROYS THIS ENTIRE SHIP!"
WE'RE STILL IN EARTH'S ATMOSPHERE, BUT HOLD ON TO SOMETHING OR YOU'LL GET SUCKED OUT OF THIS DAMN PLACE!
CHECK IT OUT!
IT'S *HIM!*
GREAT, NOW WHAT'S HAPPENING?! CAN THINGS GET ANY WO—
!

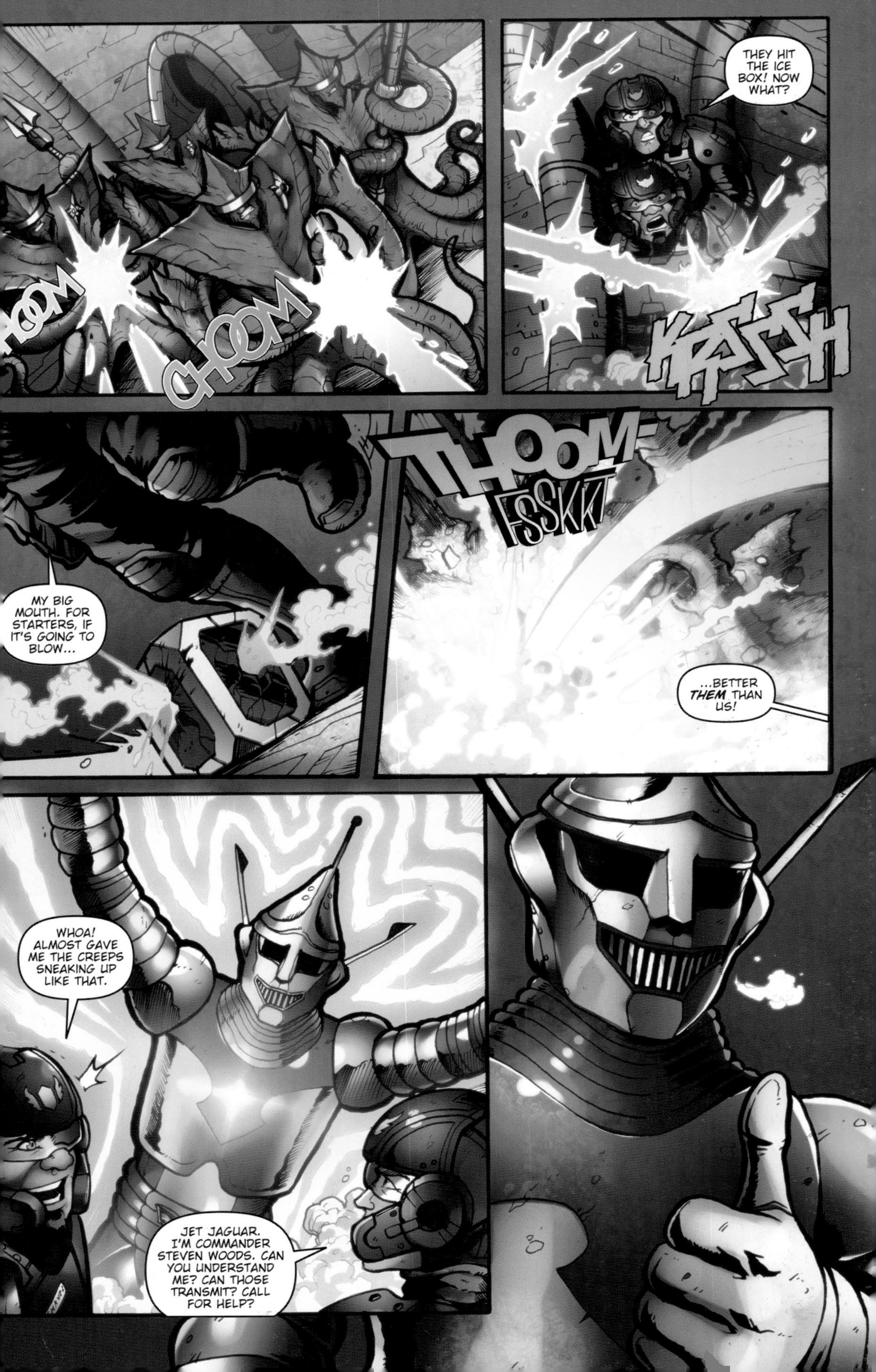

THOOM
CHOOM
THEY HIT THE ICE BOX! NOW WHAT?
KRSSSH
MY BIG MOUTH. FOR STARTERS, IF IT'S GOING TO BLOW...
THOOM-
FSSKKT
...BETTER *THEM* THAN US!
WHOA! ALMOST GAVE ME THE CREEPS SNEAKING UP LIKE THAT.
JET JAGUAR. I'M COMMANDER STEVEN WOODS. CAN YOU UNDERSTAND ME? CAN THOSE TRANSMIT? CALL FOR HELP?

CAN'T YOU HEAR THAT?! WE NEED TO GET OUT OF HERE BEFORE—

WHOA! GUESS THAT'S ONE WAY TO BREAK THE ICE. NO? COME ON, THAT WAS FUNNY.

JET JAGUAR, I NEED TO REACH OUR COMMAND.

CAN YOU— WHOA, WHAT ARE YOU DOING?!

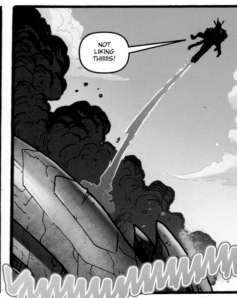

NOT LIKING THIIIIS!

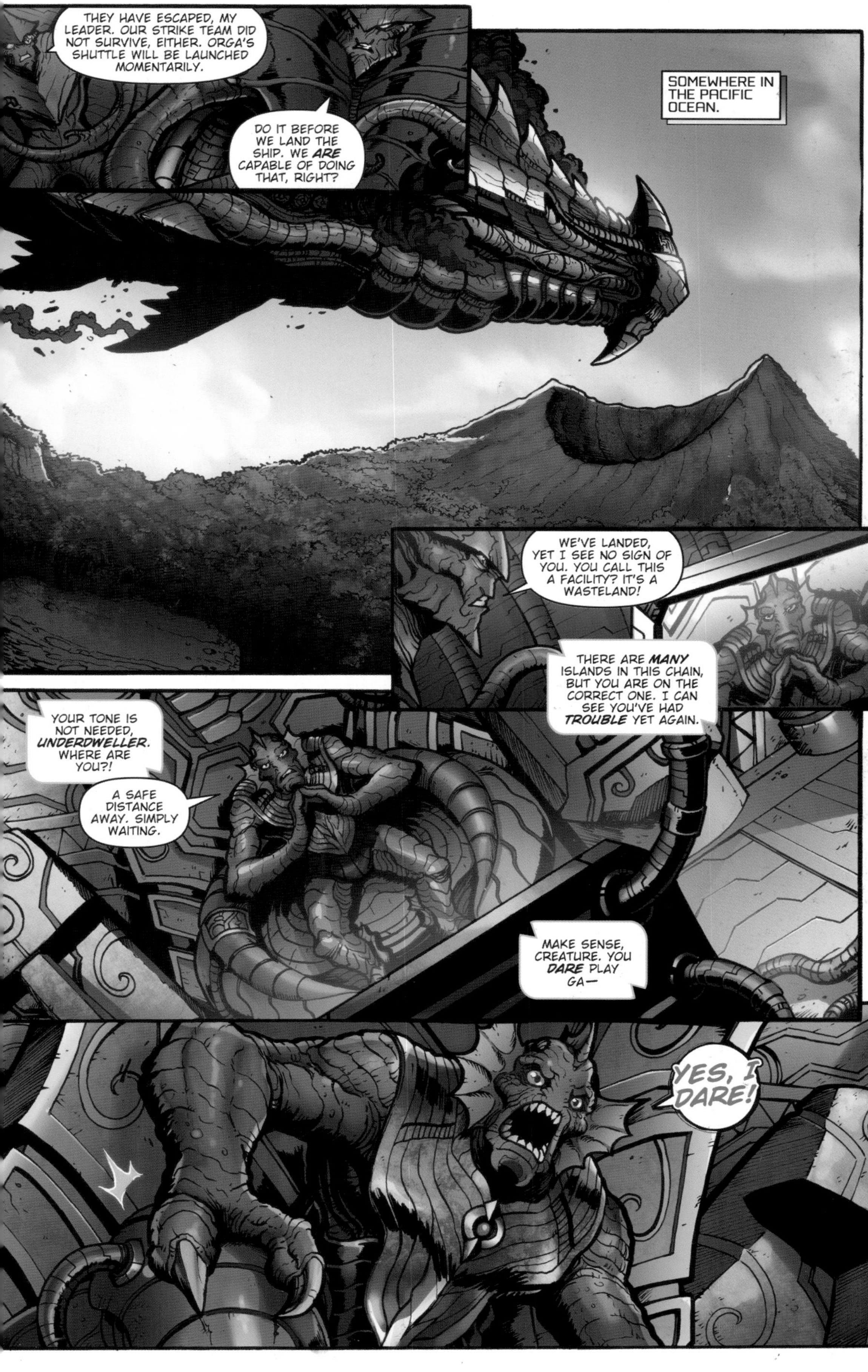
THEY HAVE ESCAPED, MY LEADER. OUR STRIKE TEAM DID NOT SURVIVE, EITHER. ORGA'S SHUTTLE WILL BE LAUNCHED MOMENTARILY.
DO IT BEFORE WE LAND THE SHIP. WE ARE CAPABLE OF DOING THAT, RIGHT?
SOMEWHERE IN THE PACIFIC OCEAN.
WE'VE LANDED, YET I SEE NO SIGN OF YOU. YOU CALL THIS A FACILITY? IT'S A WASTELAND!
THERE ARE MANY ISLANDS IN THIS CHAIN, BUT YOU ARE ON THE CORRECT ONE. I CAN SEE YOU'VE HAD TROUBLE YET AGAIN.
YOUR TONE IS NOT NEEDED, UNDERDWELLER. WHERE ARE YOU?!
A SAFE DISTANCE AWAY. SIMPLY WAITING.
MAKE SENSE, CREATURE. YOU DARE PLAY GA—
YES, I DARE!

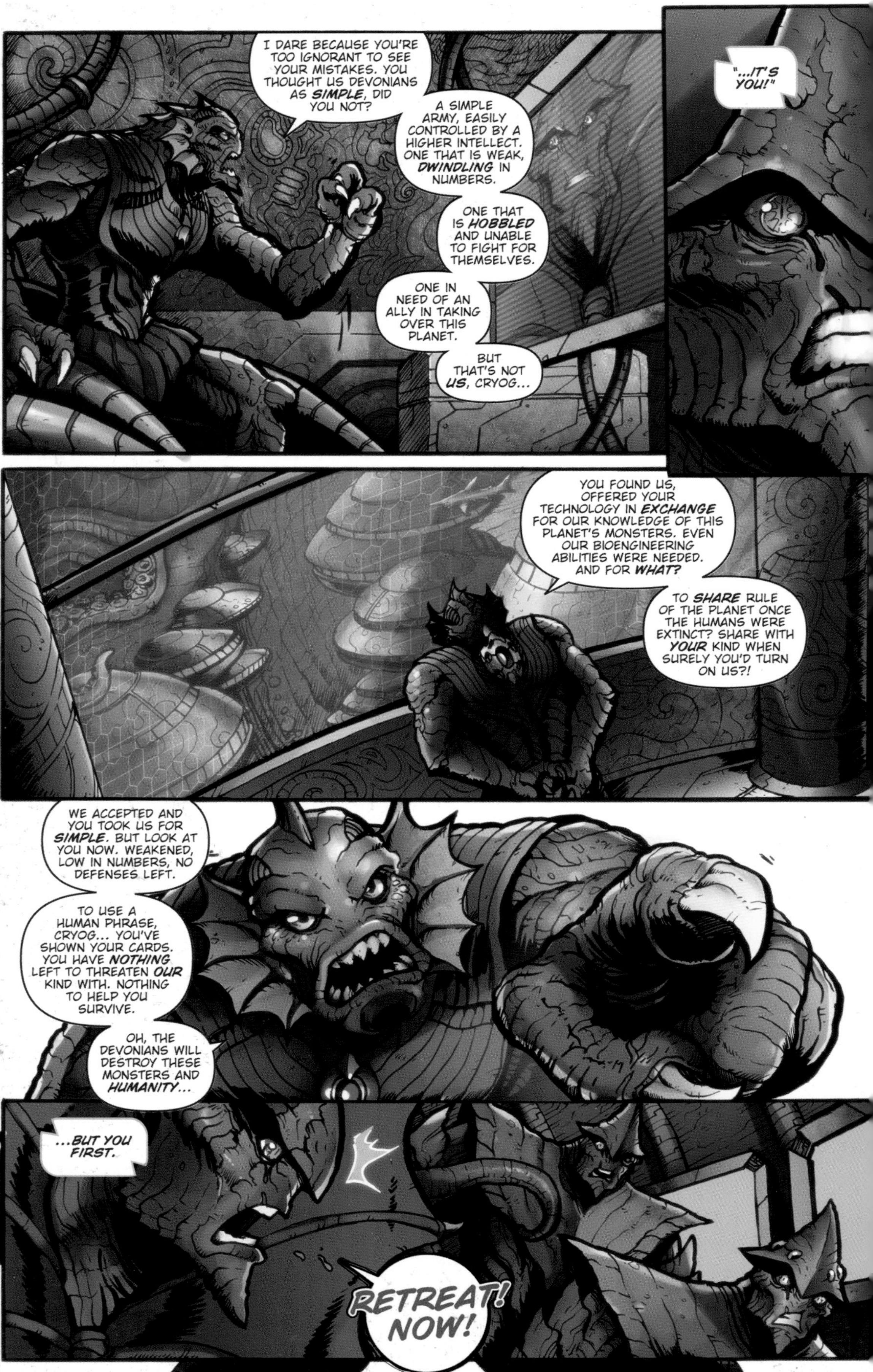
I DARE BECAUSE YOU'RE TOO IGNORANT TO SEE YOUR MISTAKES. YOU THOUGHT US DEVONIANS AS SIMPLE, DID YOU NOT?
A SIMPLE ARMY, EASILY CONTROLLED BY A HIGHER INTELLECT. ONE THAT IS WEAK, DWINDLING IN NUMBERS.
ONE THAT IS HOBBLED AND UNABLE TO FIGHT FOR THEMSELVES.
ONE IN NEED OF AN ALLY IN TAKING OVER THIS PLANET.
BUT THAT'S NOT US, CRYOG...
"...IT'S YOU!"
YOU FOUND US, OFFERED YOUR TECHNOLOGY IN EXCHANGE FOR OUR KNOWLEDGE OF THIS PLANET'S MONSTERS. EVEN OUR BIOENGINEERING ABILITIES WERE NEEDED. AND FOR WHAT?
TO SHARE RULE OF THE PLANET ONCE THE HUMANS WERE EXTINCT? SHARE WITH YOUR KIND WHEN SURELY YOU'D TURN ON US?!
WE ACCEPTED AND YOU TOOK US FOR SIMPLE. BUT LOOK AT YOU NOW. WEAKENED, LOW IN NUMBERS, NO DEFENSES LEFT.
TO USE A HUMAN PHRASE, CRYOG... YOU'VE SHOWN YOUR CARDS. YOU HAVE NOTHING LEFT TO THREATEN OUR KIND WITH. NOTHING TO HELP YOU SURVIVE.
OH, THE DEVONIANS WILL DESTROY THESE MONSTERS AND HUMANITY...
...BUT YOU FIRST.
RETREAT! NOW!

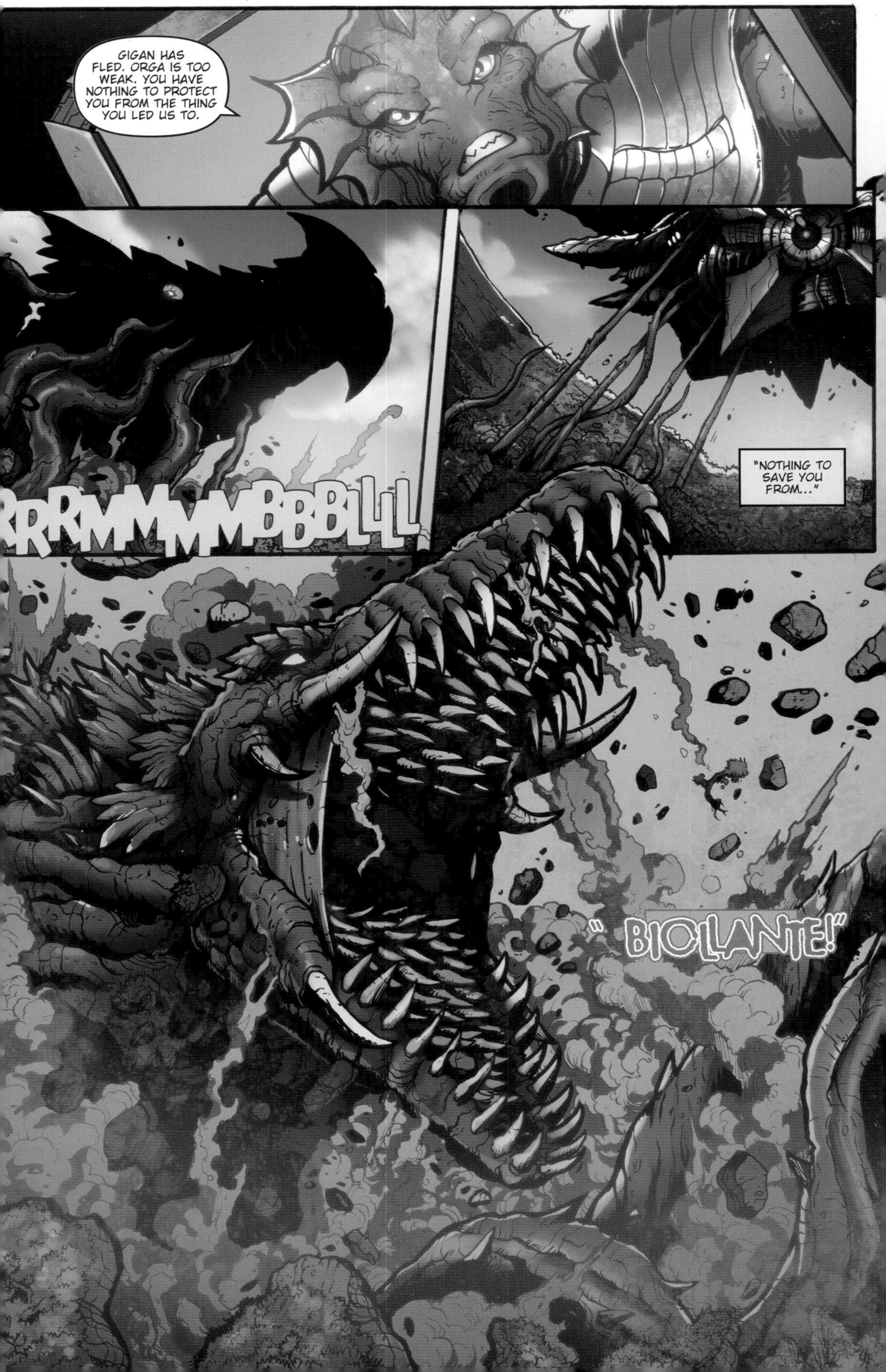
GIGAN HAS FLED. ORGA IS TOO WEAK. YOU HAVE NOTHING TO PROTECT YOU FROM THE THING YOU LED US TO.
RRRMMMMMBBBLLLL
"NOTHING TO SAVE YOU FROM..."
"...BIOLLANTE!"

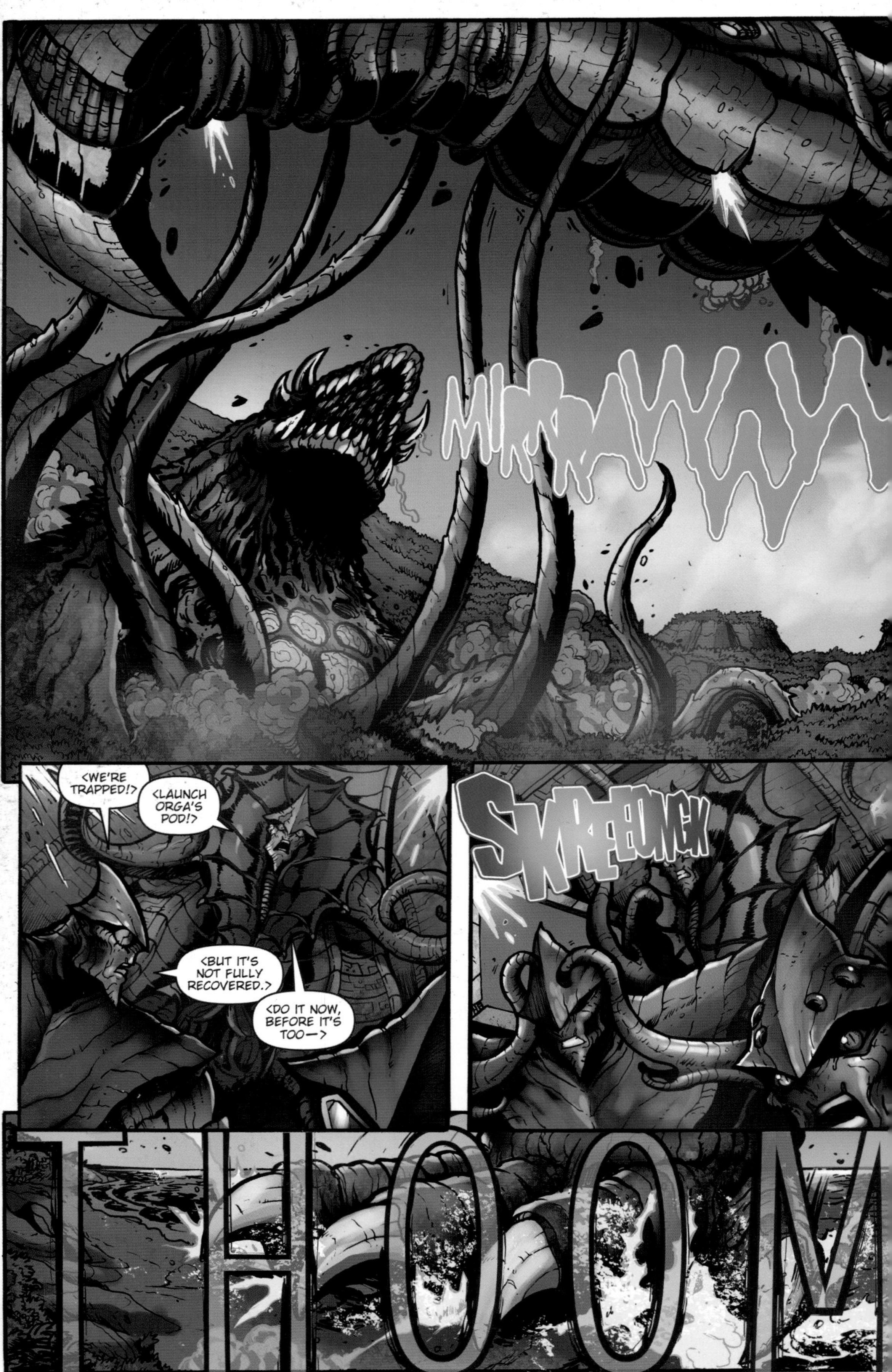
MRRAWWW
<WE'RE TRAPPED!>
<LAUNCH ORGA'S POD!>
<BUT IT'S NOT FULLY RECOVERED.>
<DO IT NOW, BEFORE IT'S TOO—>
SKREEOMGK
THOOM

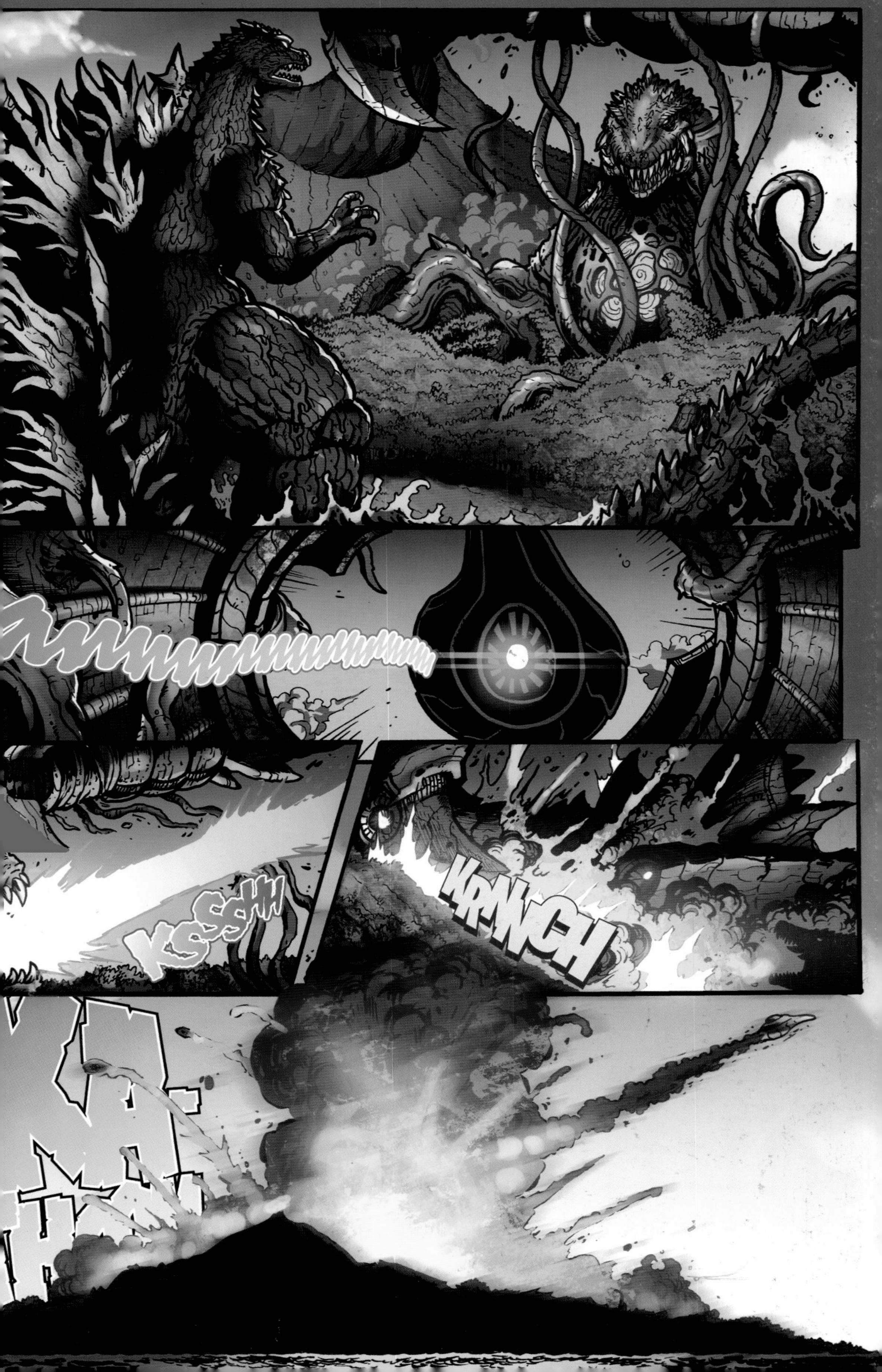
KSSSHH
KRANCH

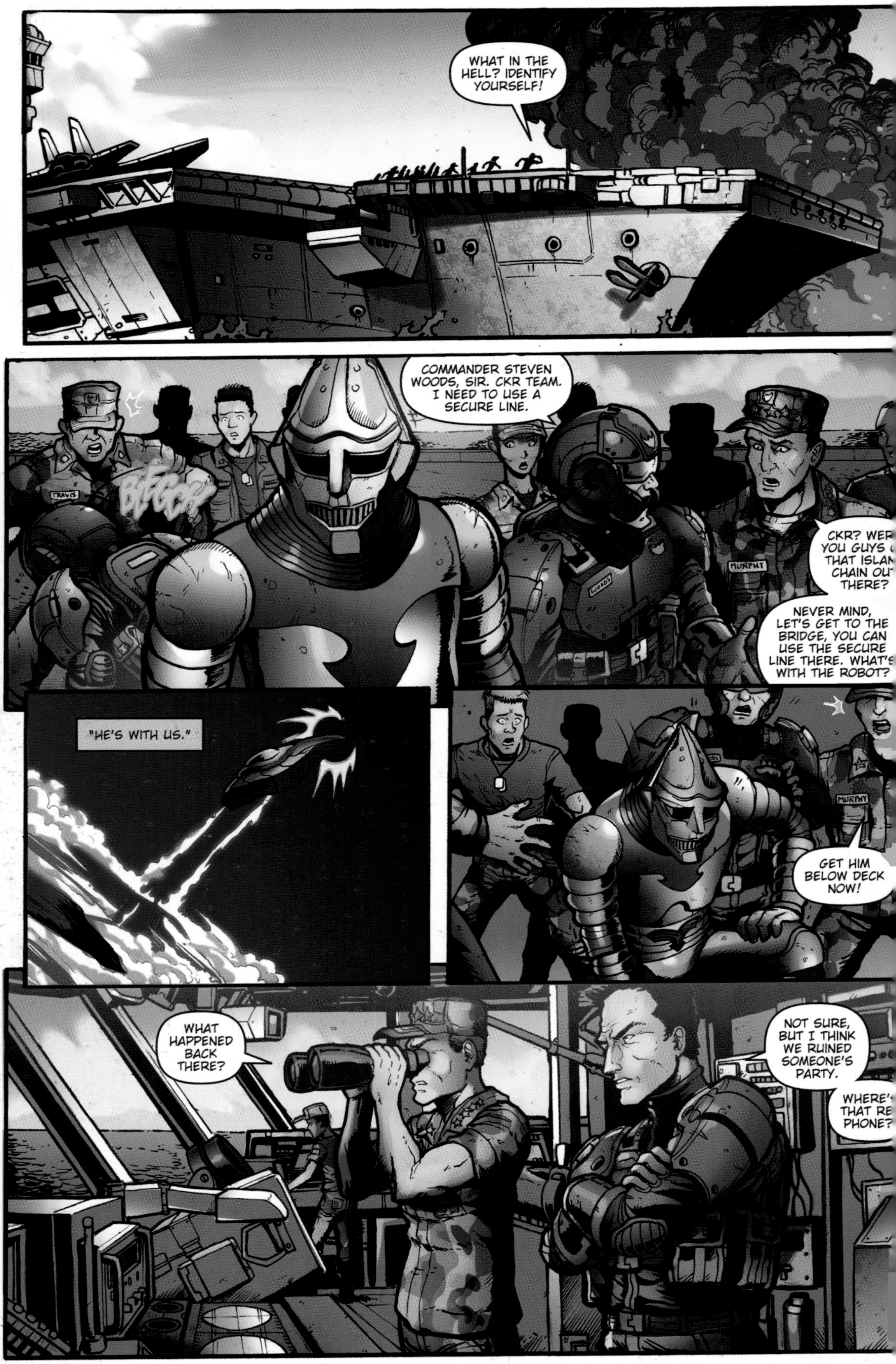
WHAT IN THE HELL? IDENTIFY YOURSELF!
COMMANDER STEVEN WOODS, SIR. CKR TEAM. I NEED TO USE A SECURE LINE.
TRAVIS
WOODS
MURPHY
CKR? WER YOU GUYS THAT ISLAN CHAIN OUT THERE?
NEVER MIND, LET'S GET TO THE BRIDGE, YOU CAN USE THE SECURE LINE THERE. WHAT'S WITH THE ROBOT?
"HE'S WITH US."
MURPHY
GET HIM BELOW DECK NOW!
WHAT HAPPENED BACK THERE?
NOT SURE, BUT I THINK WE RUINED SOMEONE'S PARTY.
WHERE' THAT RE PHONE?

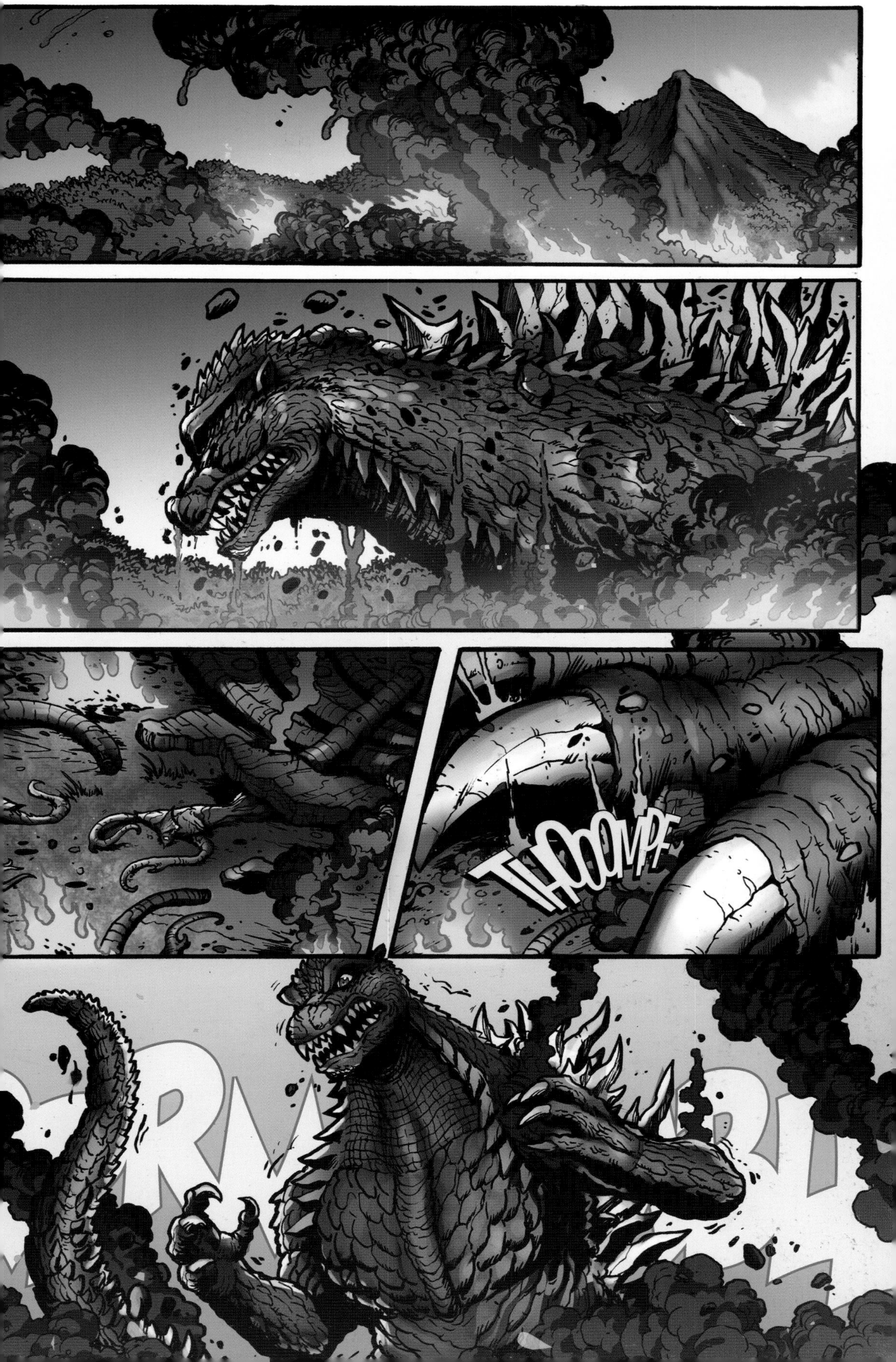
THOOOMPF

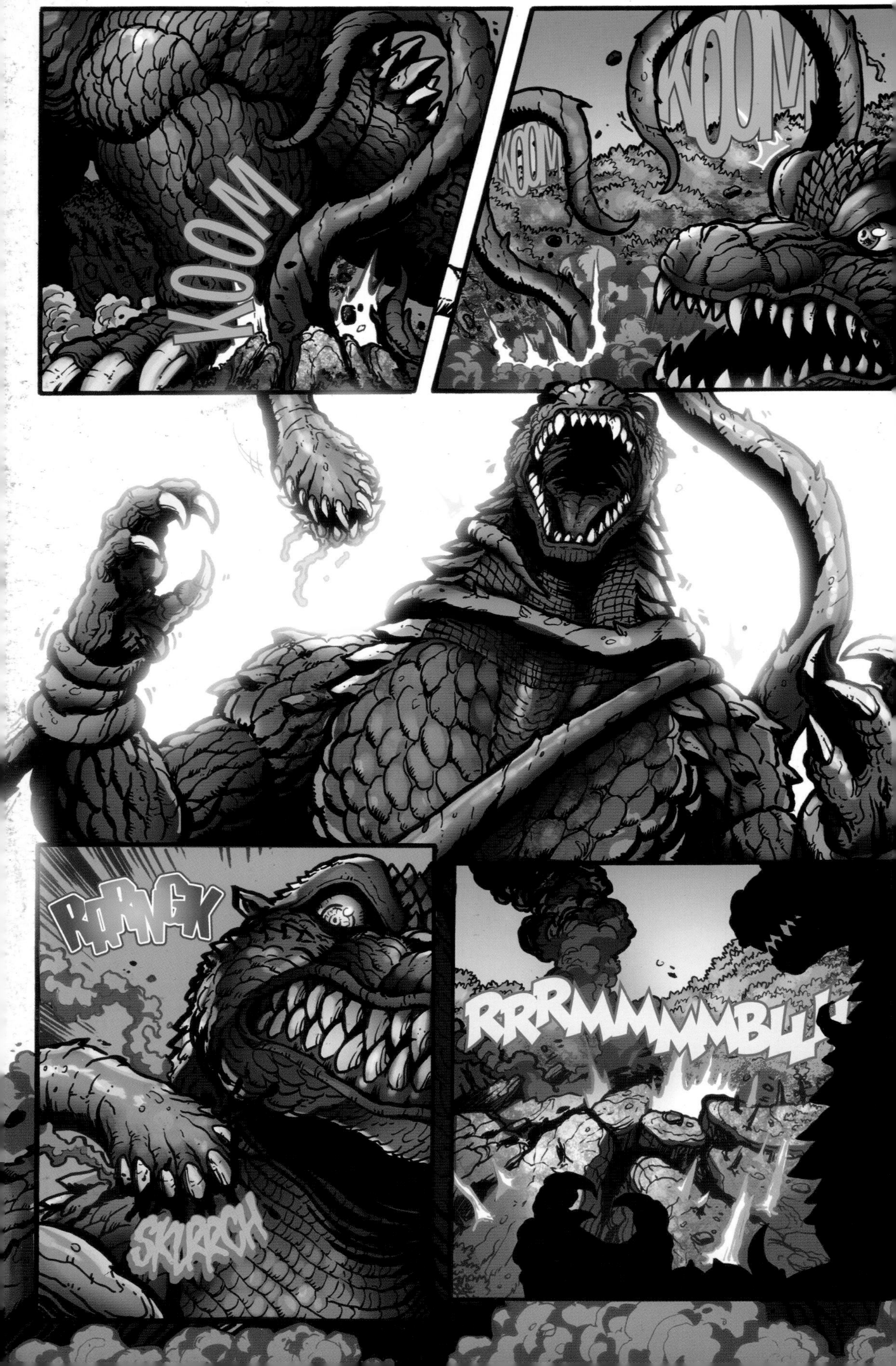
KOOM
KOOM
KOOM
RRRNGK
SKURRCH
RRRMMMMMBLL

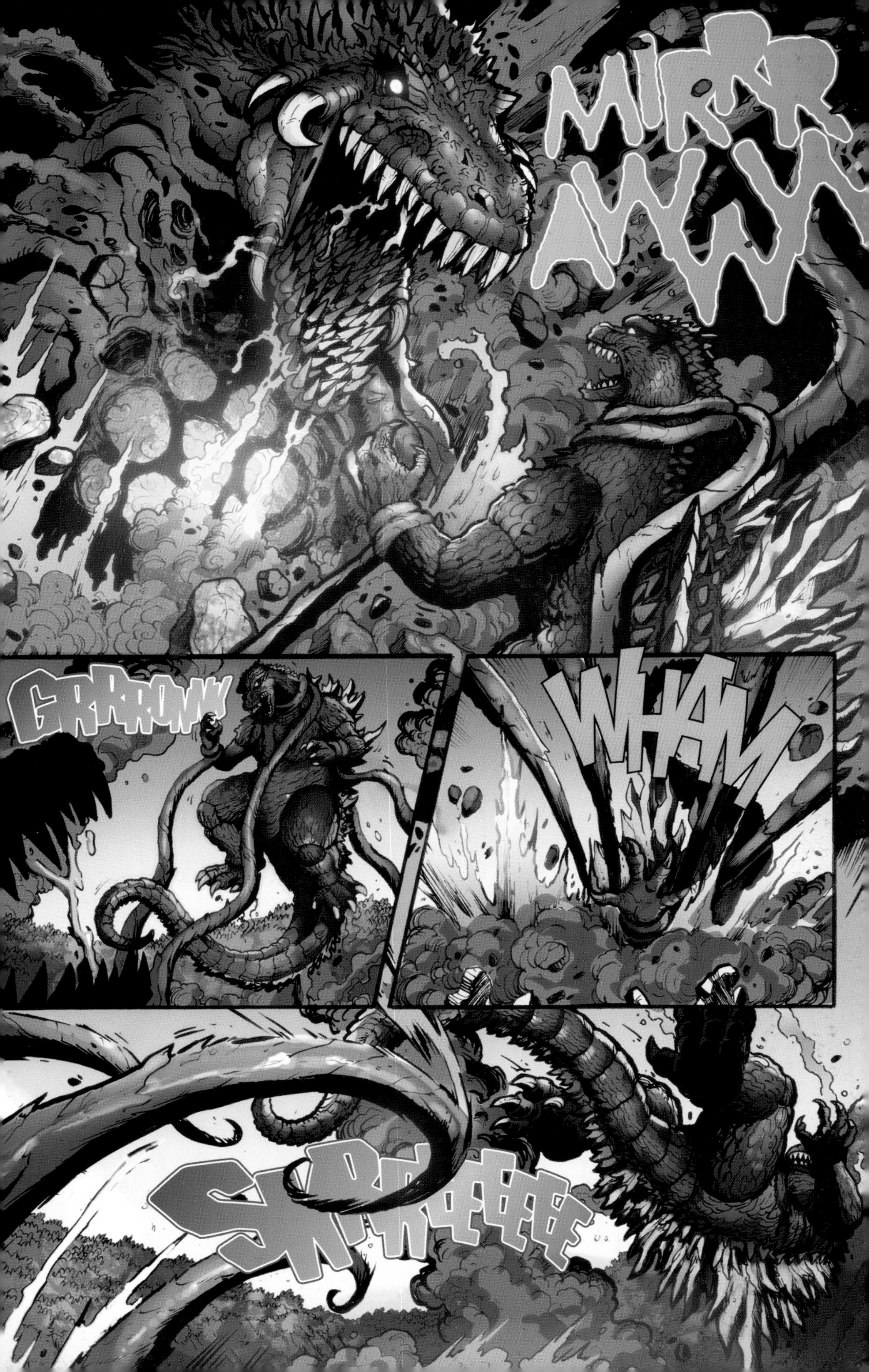
MIRR
AWWW
GRRRONNK
WHAM
SKRREEEE

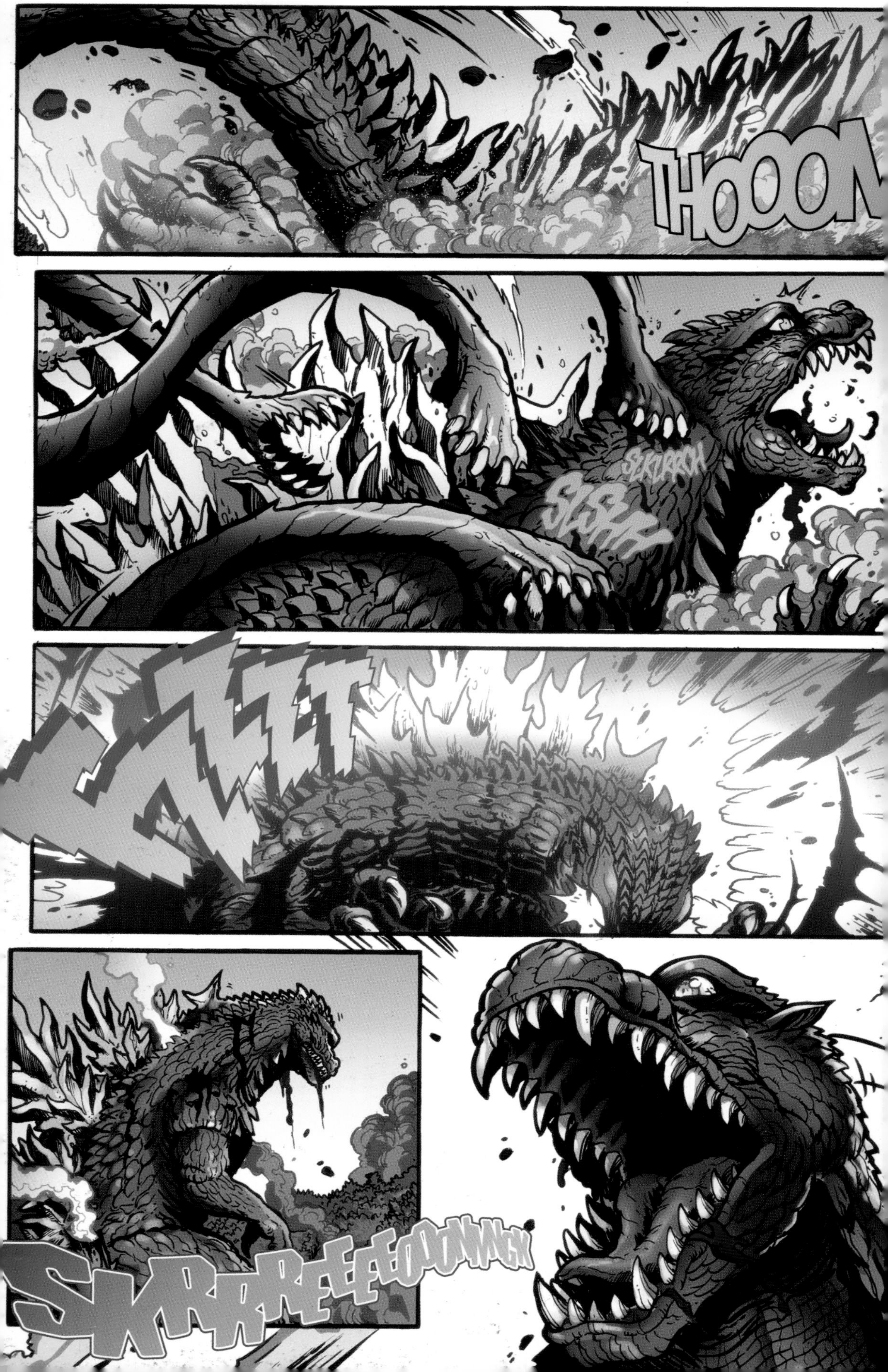
THOOOM
SKZRRCH
SKRRRREEEEOOONNGK

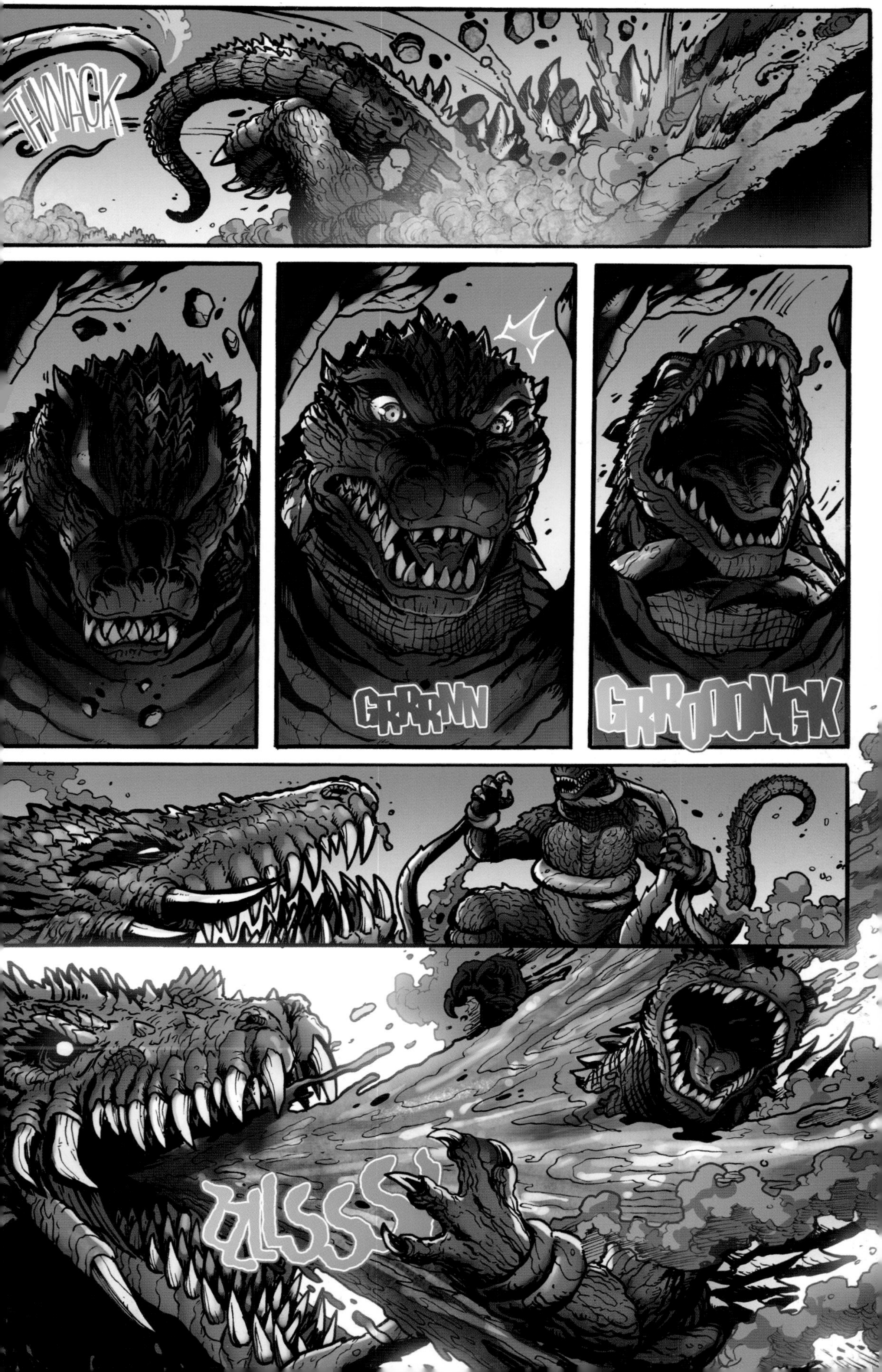
THWACK
GRRRNN
GRROOONGK
ZZLSSS

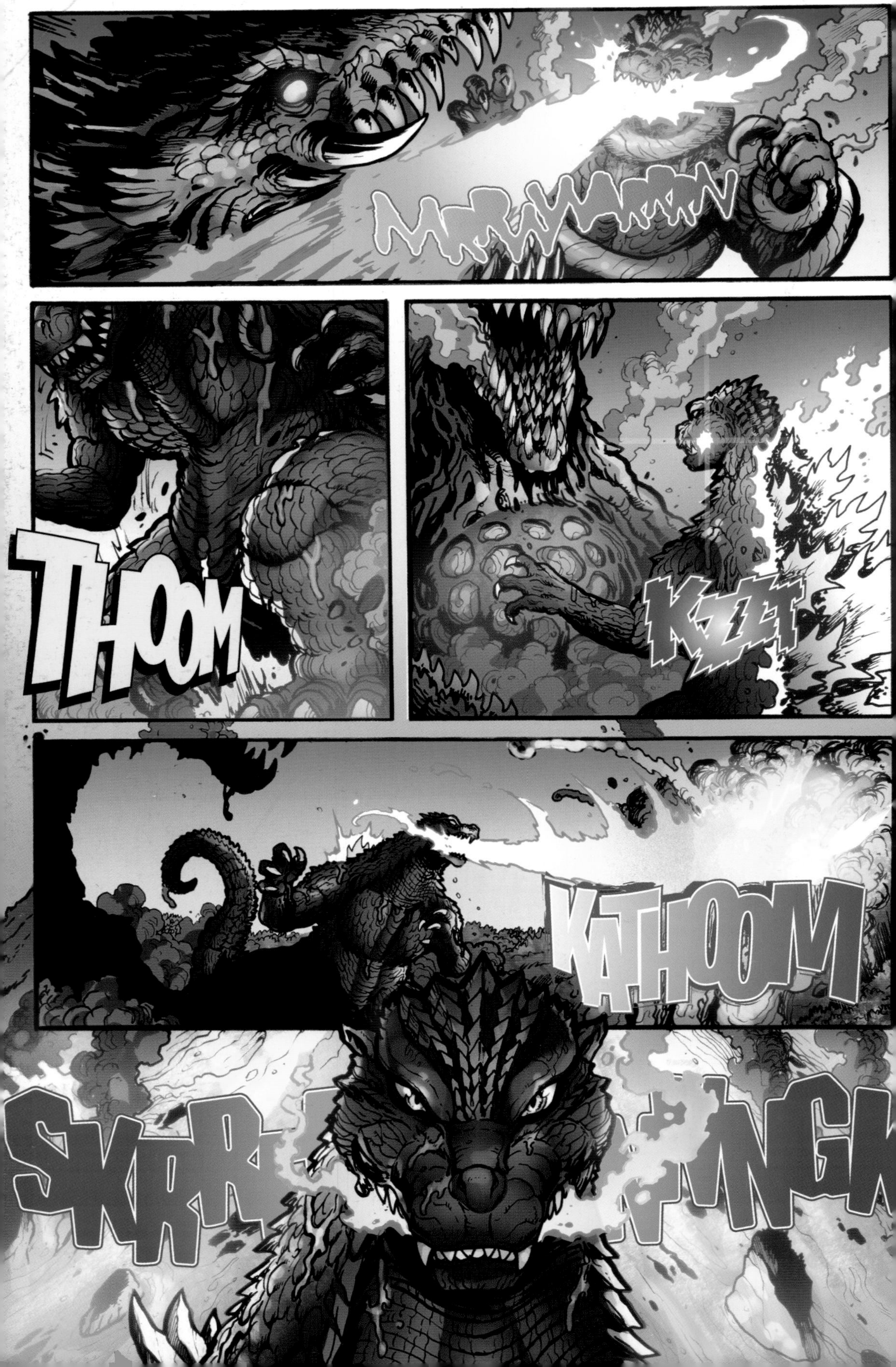
MRRWARRN
THOOM
KZZT
KATHOOM
SKRR-

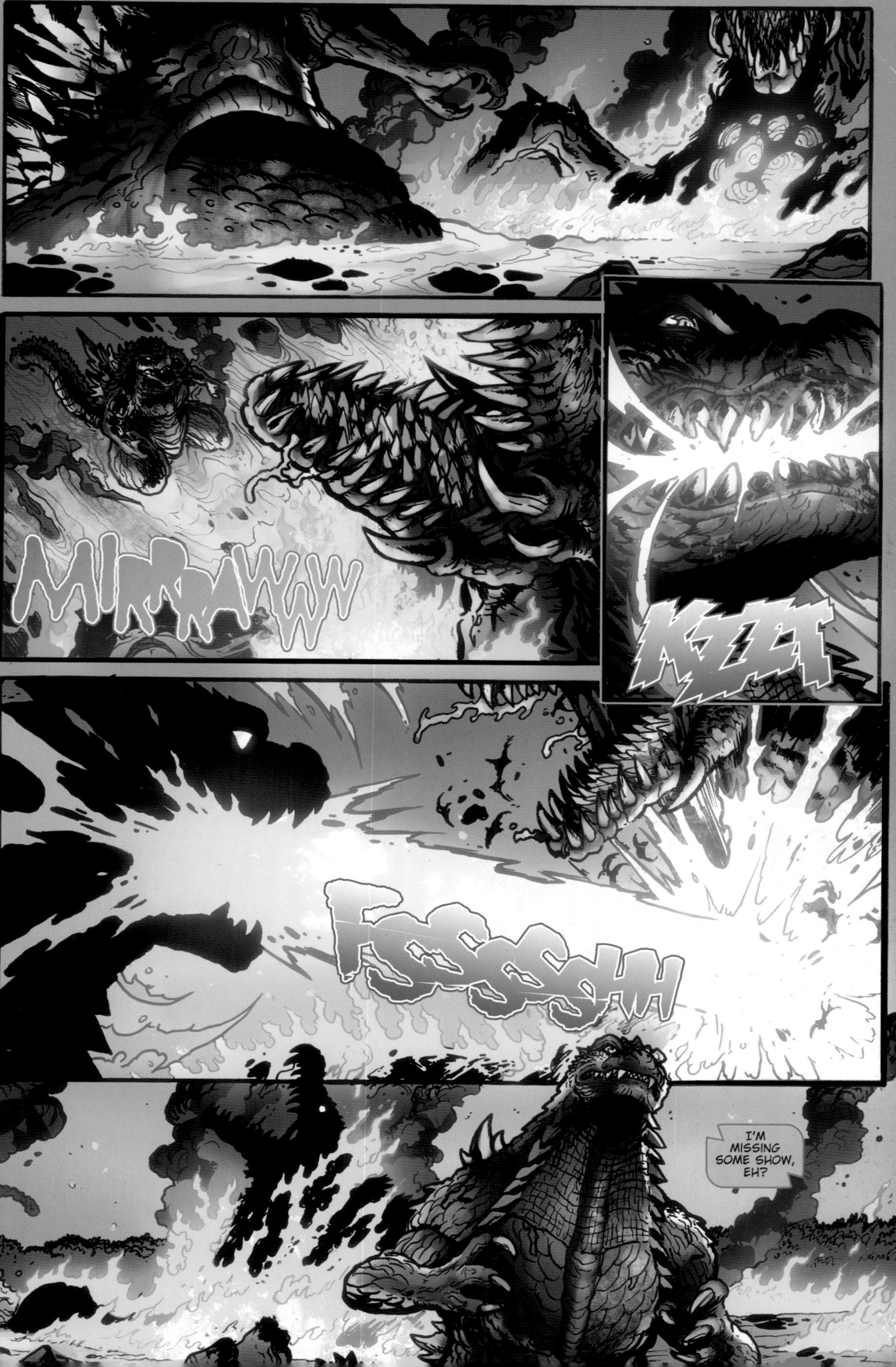
MIRRAWWW
KZZT
FSSSSHH
I'M MISSING SOME SHOW, EH?

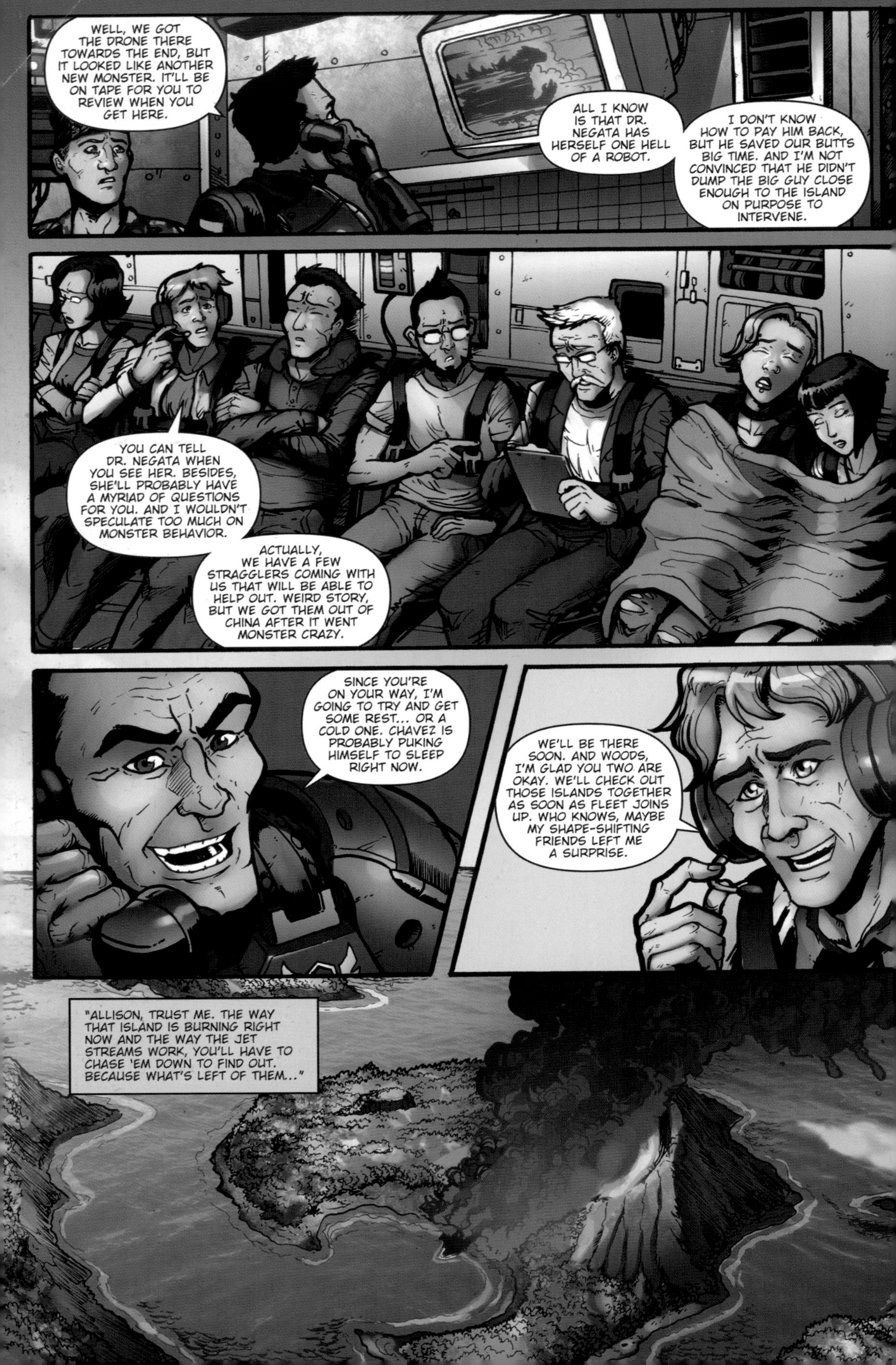
WELL, WE GOT THE DRONE THERE TOWARDS THE END, BUT IT LOOKED LIKE ANOTHER NEW MONSTER. IT'LL BE ON TAPE FOR YOU TO REVIEW WHEN YOU GET HERE.
ALL I KNOW IS THAT DR. NEGATA HAS HERSELF ONE HELL OF A ROBOT.
I DON'T KNOW HOW TO PAY HIM BACK, BUT HE SAVED OUR BUTTS BIG TIME. AND I'M NOT CONVINCED THAT HE DIDN'T DUMP THE BIG GUY CLOSE ENOUGH TO THE ISLAND ON PURPOSE TO INTERVENE.
YOU CAN TELL DR. NEGATA WHEN YOU SEE HER. BESIDES, SHE'LL PROBABLY HAVE A MYRIAD OF QUESTIONS FOR YOU. AND I WOULDN'T SPECULATE TOO MUCH ON MONSTER BEHAVIOR.
ACTUALLY, WE HAVE A FEW STRAGGLERS COMING WITH US THAT WILL BE ABLE TO HELP OUT. WEIRD STORY, BUT WE GOT THEM OUT OF CHINA AFTER IT WENT MONSTER CRAZY.
SINCE YOU'RE ON YOUR WAY, I'M GOING TO TRY AND GET SOME REST... OR A COLD ONE. CHAVEZ IS PROBABLY PUKING HIMSELF TO SLEEP RIGHT NOW.
WE'LL BE THERE SOON. AND WOODS, I'M GLAD YOU TWO ARE OKAY. WE'LL CHECK OUT THOSE ISLANDS TOGETHER AS SOON AS FLEET JOINS UP. WHO KNOWS, MAYBE MY SHAPE-SHIFTING FRIENDS LEFT ME A SURPRISE.
"ALLISON, TRUST ME. THE WAY THAT ISLAND IS BURNING RIGHT NOW AND THE WAY THE JET STREAMS WORK, YOU'LL HAVE TO CHASE 'EM DOWN TO FIND OUT. BECAUSE WHAT'S LEFT OF THEM..."

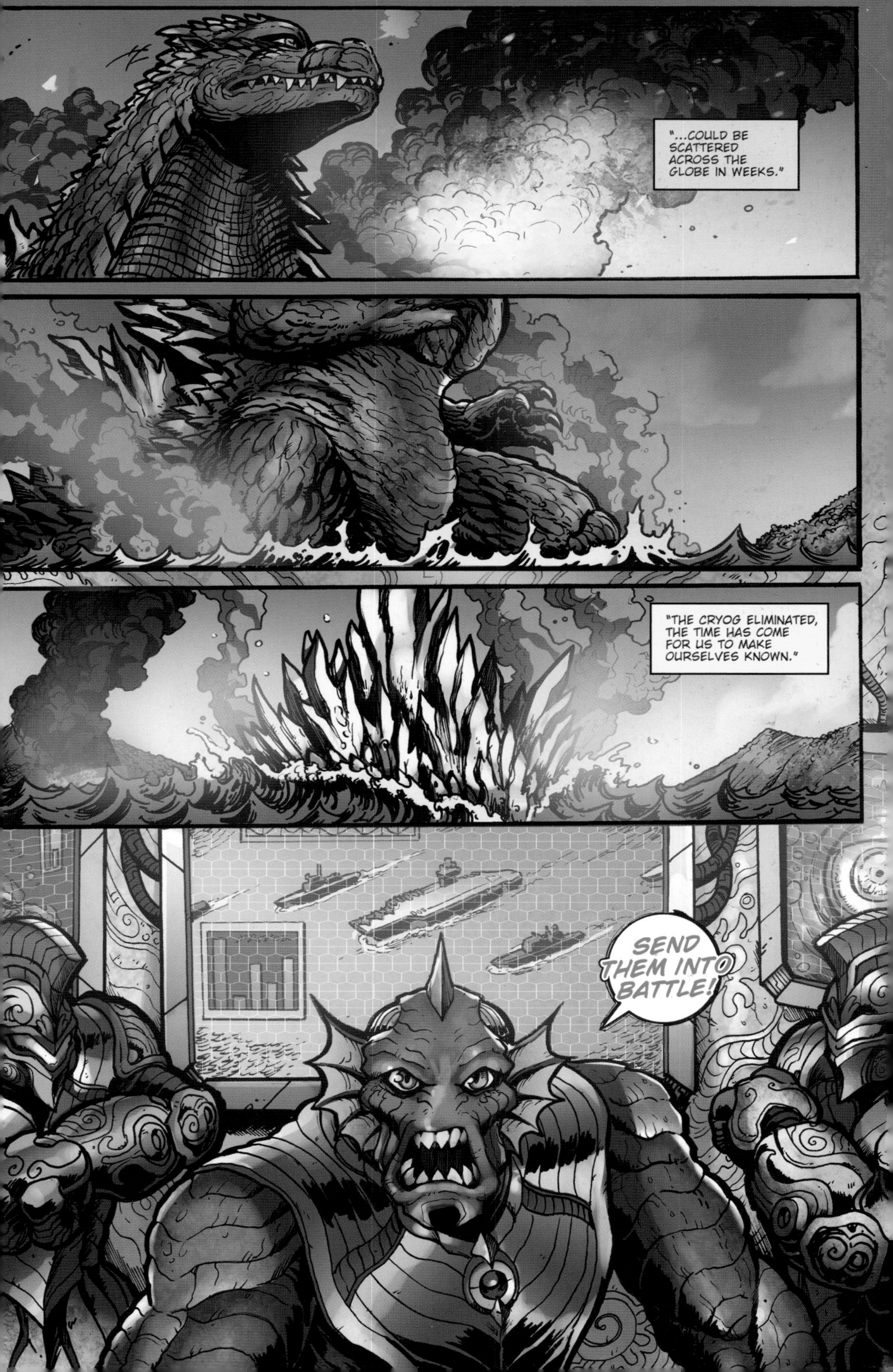
"...COULD BE SCATTERED ACROSS THE GLOBE IN WEEKS."
"THE CRYOG ELIMINATED, THE TIME HAS COME FOR US TO MAKE OURSELVES KNOWN."
SEND THEM INTO BATTLE!

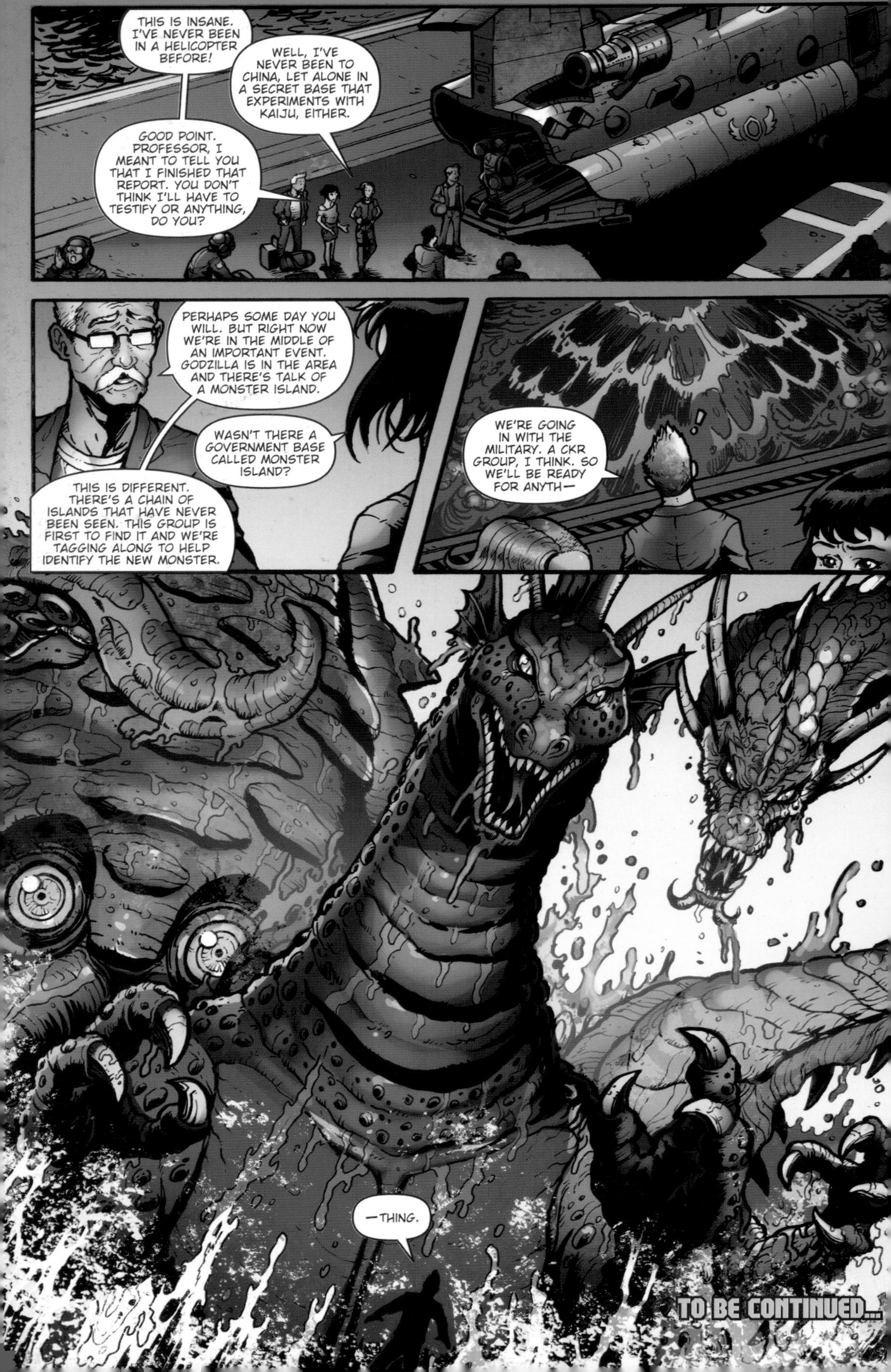
THIS IS INSANE. I'VE NEVER BEEN IN A HELICOPTER BEFORE!
WELL, I'VE NEVER BEEN TO CHINA, LET ALONE IN A SECRET BASE THAT EXPERIMENTS WITH KAIJU, EITHER.
GOOD POINT. PROFESSOR, I MEANT TO TELL YOU THAT I FINISHED THAT REPORT. YOU DON'T THINK I'LL HAVE TO TESTIFY OR ANYTHING, DO YOU?
PERHAPS SOME DAY YOU WILL. BUT RIGHT NOW WE'RE IN THE MIDDLE OF AN IMPORTANT EVENT. GODZILLA IS IN THE AREA AND THERE'S TALK OF A MONSTER ISLAND.
WASN'T THERE A GOVERNMENT BASE CALLED MONSTER ISLAND?
THIS IS DIFFERENT. THERE'S A CHAIN OF ISLANDS THAT HAVE NEVER BEEN SEEN. THIS GROUP IS FIRST TO FIND IT AND WE'RE TAGGING ALONG TO HELP IDENTIFY THE NEW MONSTER.
WE'RE GOING IN WITH THE MILITARY. A CKR GROUP, I THINK. SO WE'LL BE READY FOR ANYTH—
!
—THING.
TO BE CONTINUED...

ART GALLERY

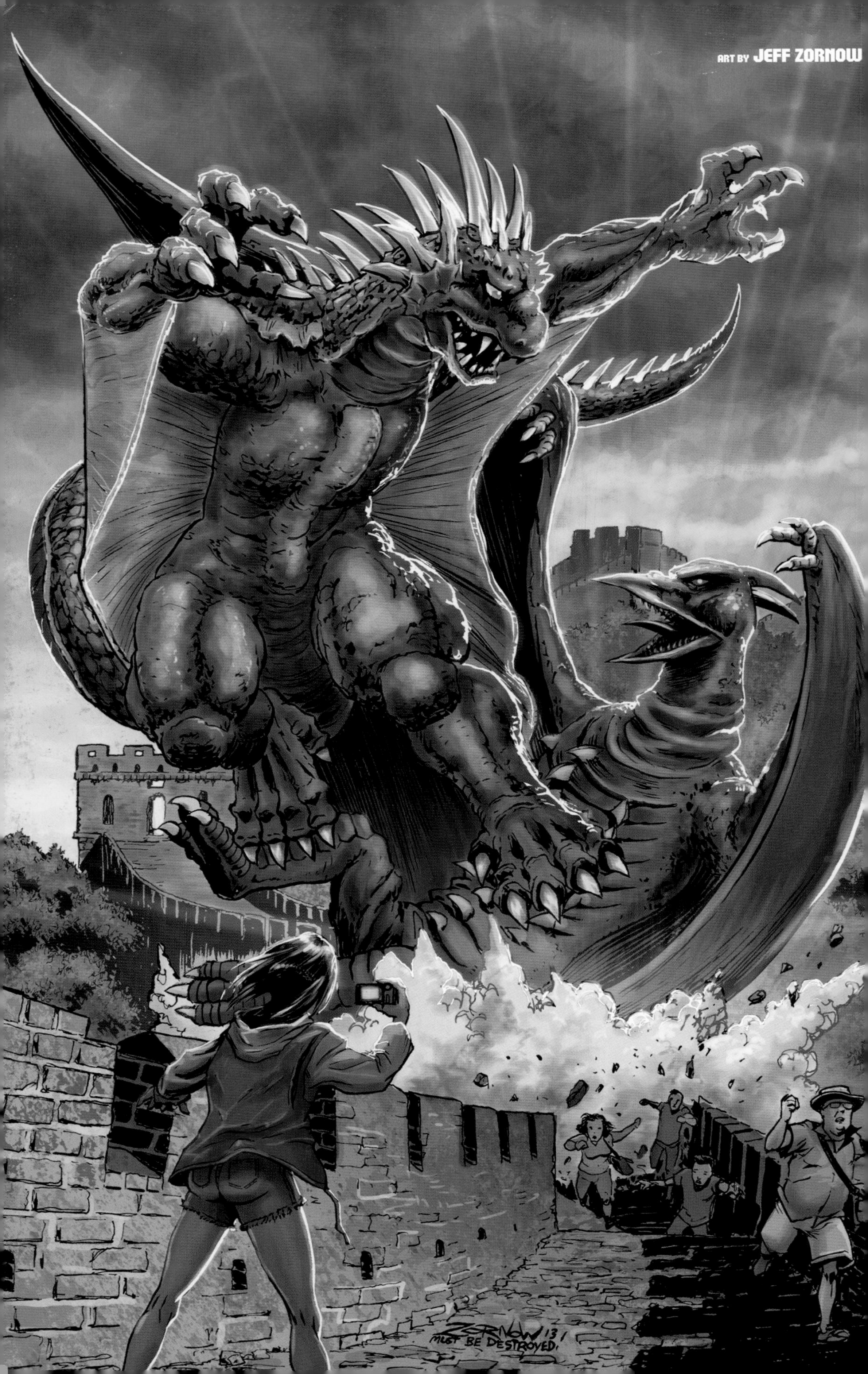
ART BY JEFF ZORNOW
ZORNOW '13
MUST BE DESTROYED!

ART BY **MATT FRANK**

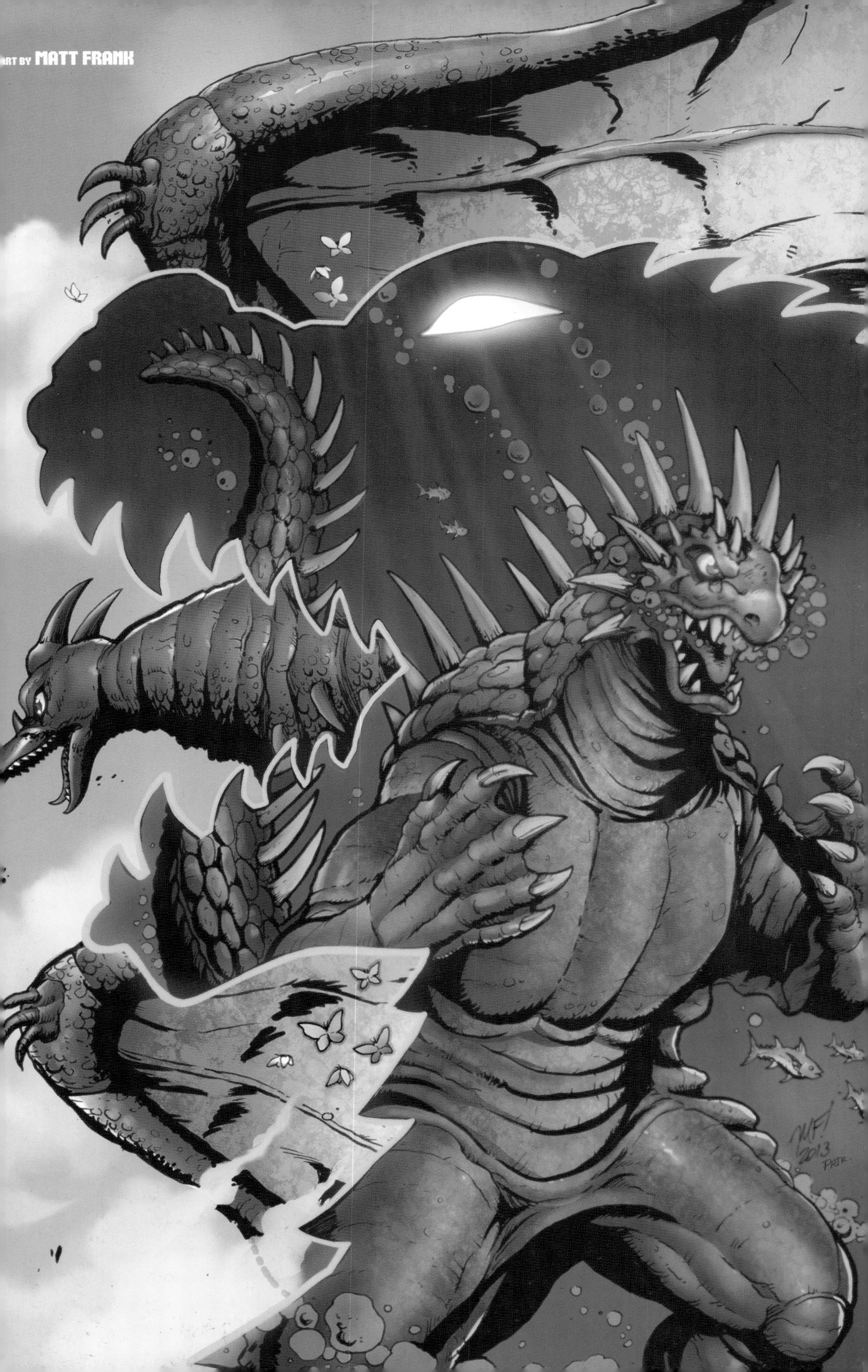
MF 2013

ART BY MATT FRANK

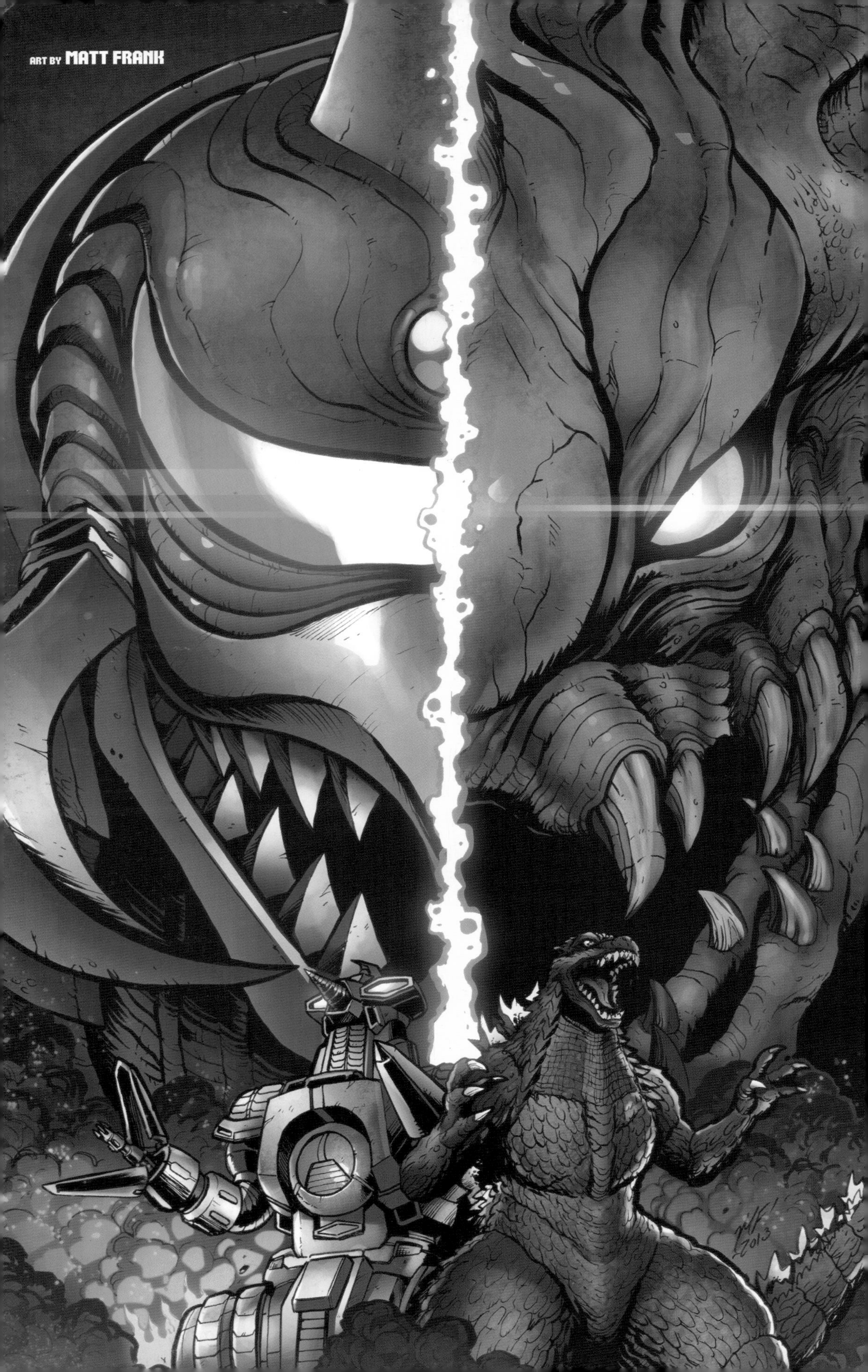
2013

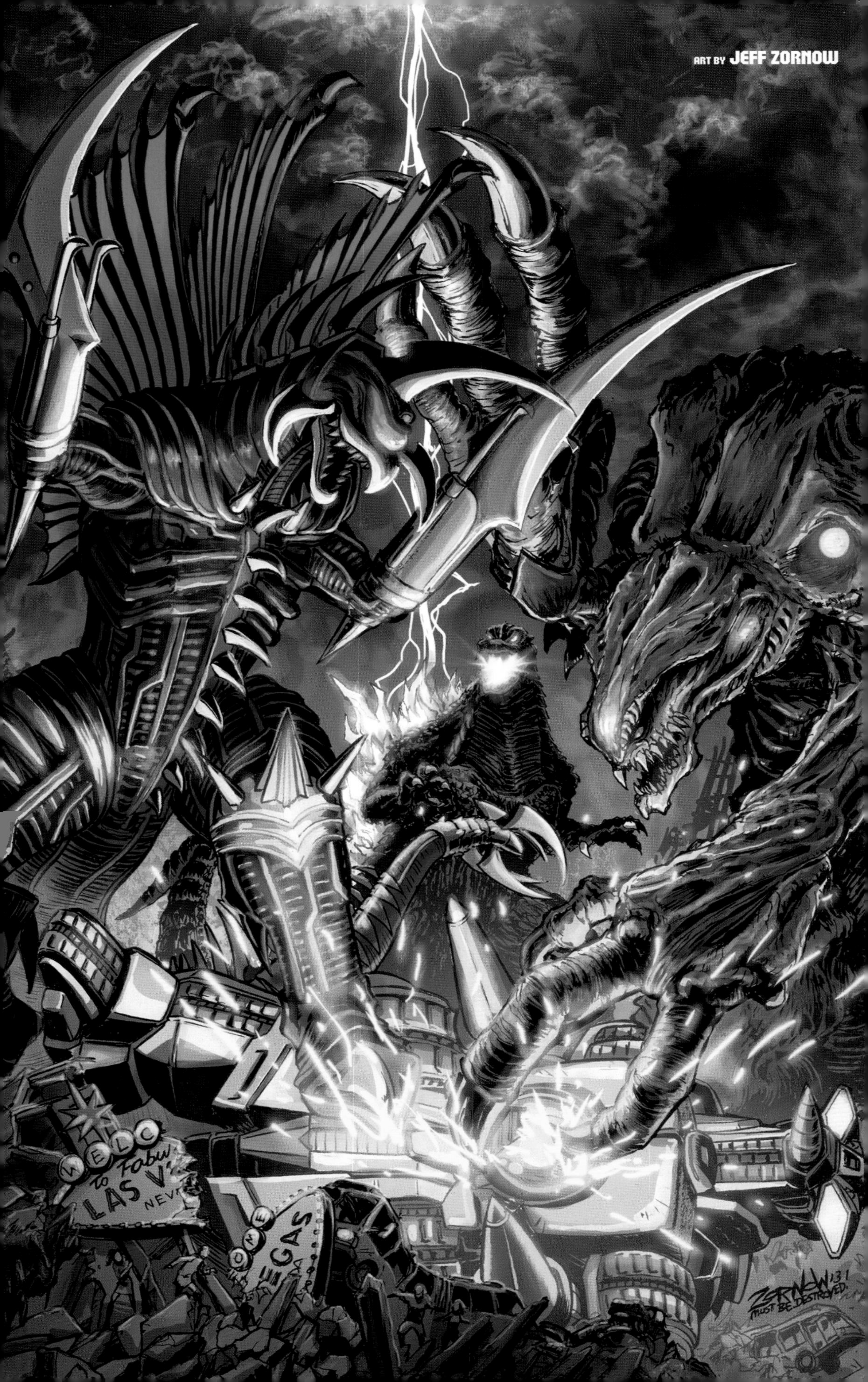
W E L C
to Fabu
LAS V
NEV
O M E
EGAS
ZORNOW '13
MUST BE DESTROYED.
ART BY JEFF ZORNOW

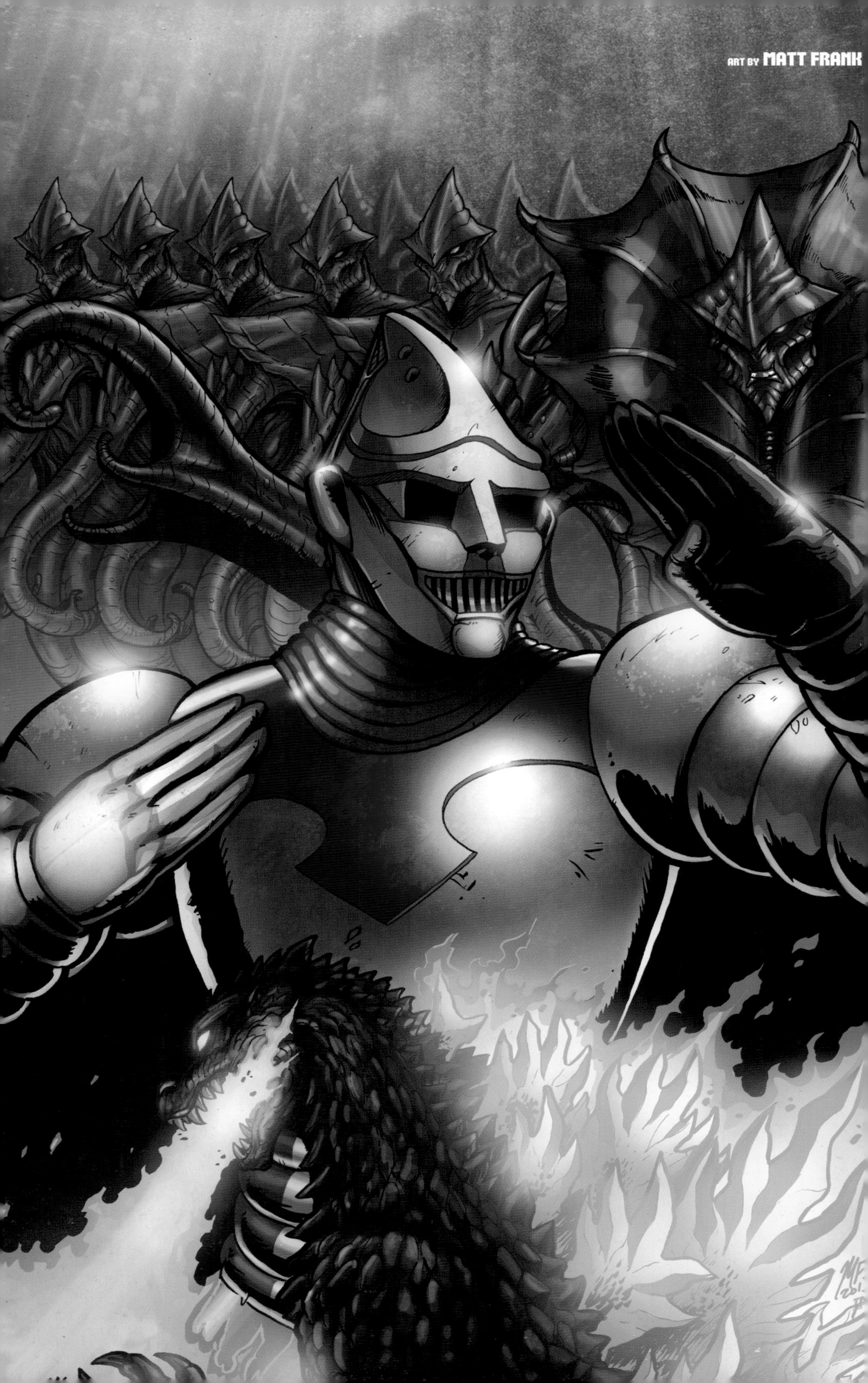
ART BY MATT FRANK

ART BY JEFF ZORNOW

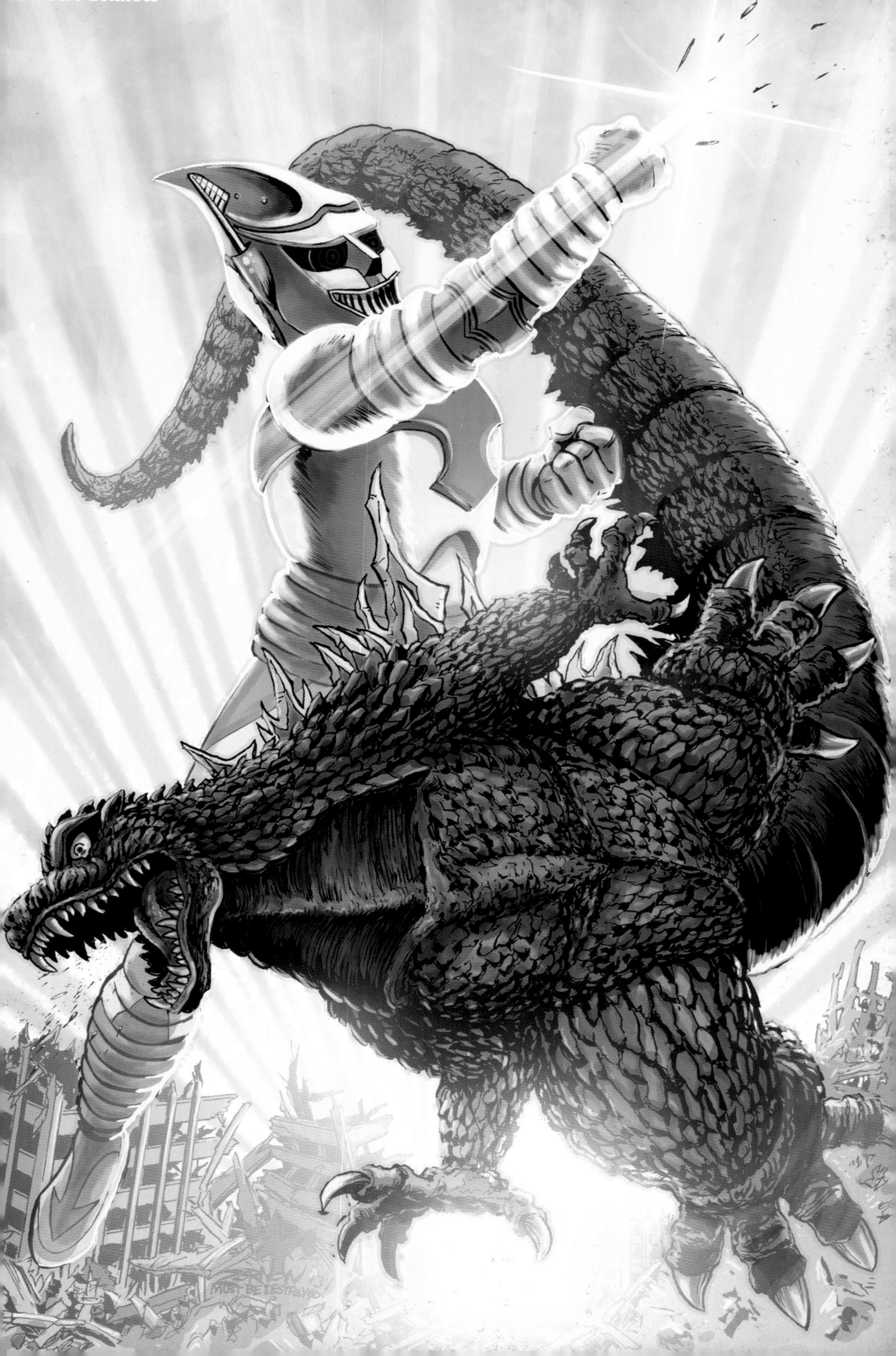

ART BY MATT FRANK

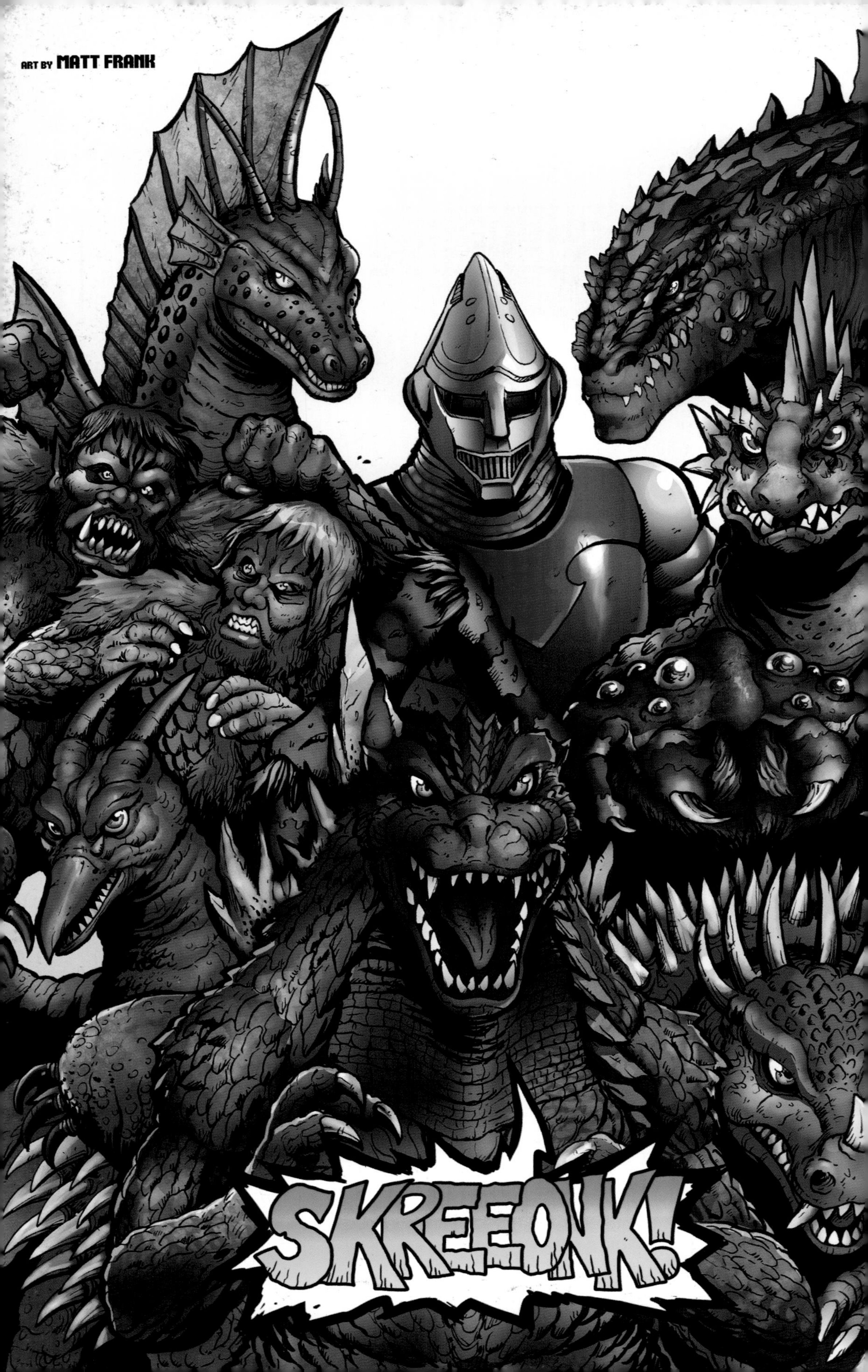
SKREEONK!

ART BY **JEFF ZORNOW**

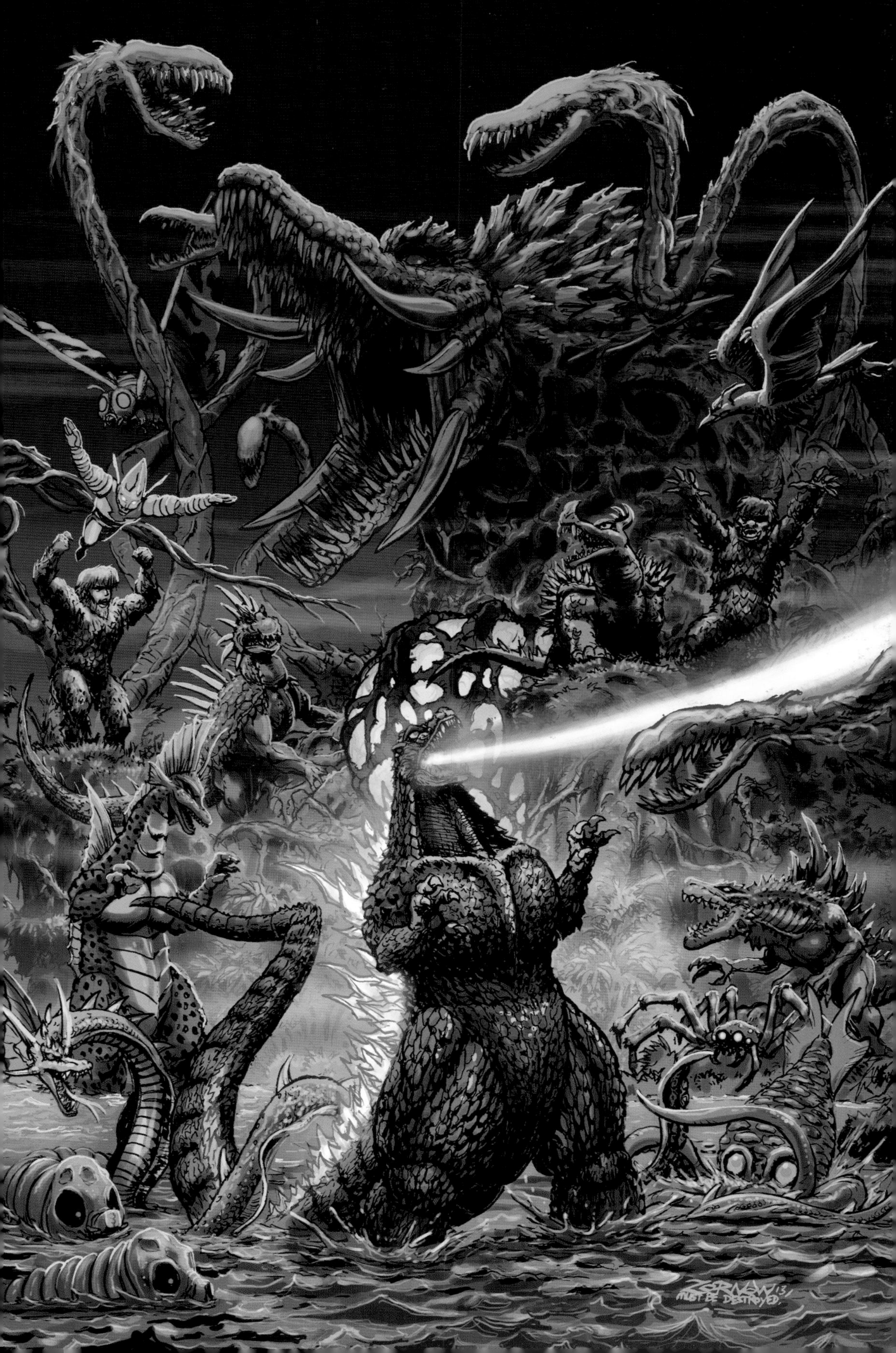
ZORNOW '13
MUST BE DESTROYED!

RODAN SKETCH
BY JEFF ZORNOW

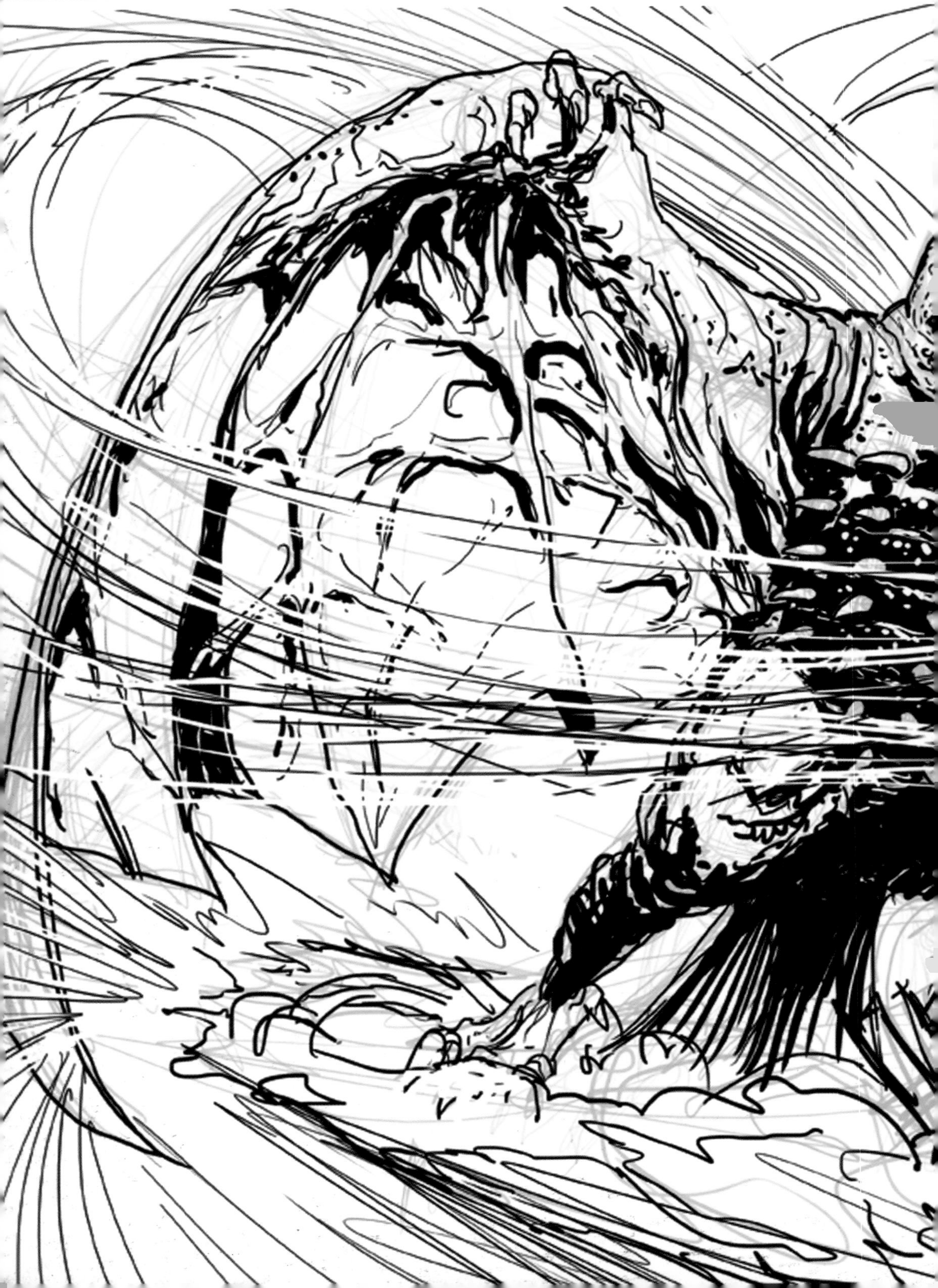

It was decided early on that *Godzilla: Rulers of Earth* would feature the fan-favorite monster Rodan at some point. However, since Rodan's likeness in previous IDW series was based on appearances in more recent films, the team wanted to return him to how he looked in his original films of the '50s and '60s.

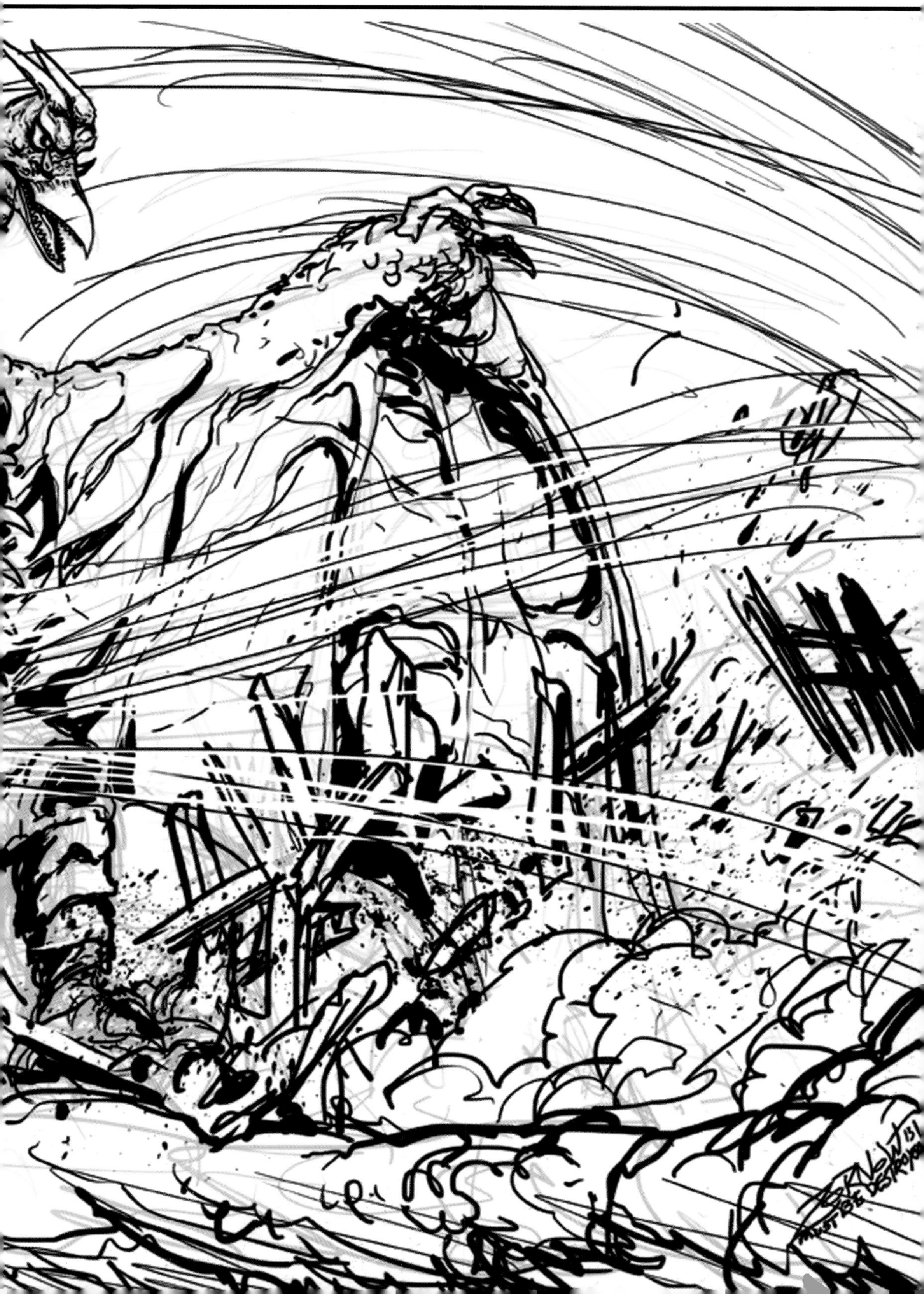

COVER CONCEPTS
BY MATT FRANK

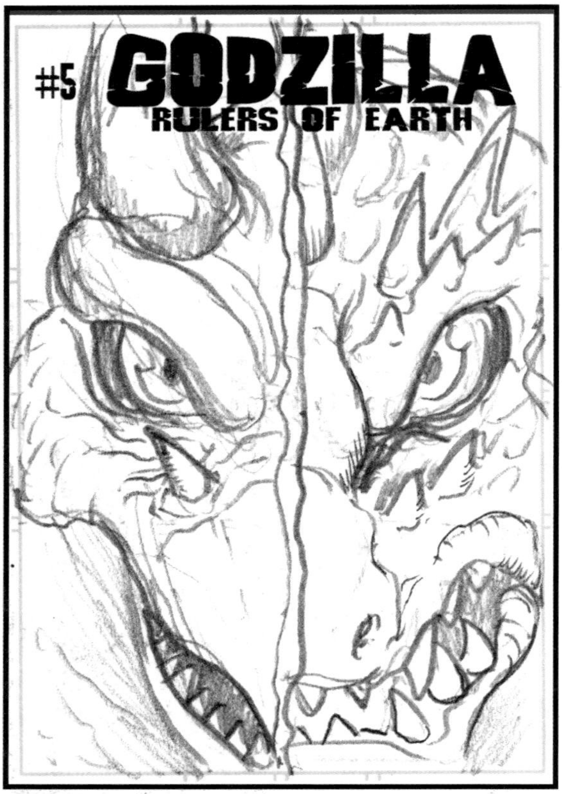
#5
GODZILLA
RULERS OF EARTH

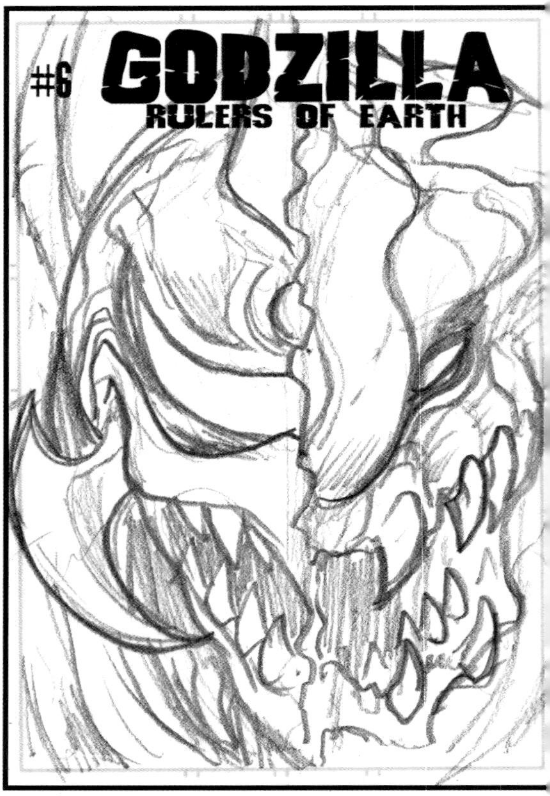
#6
GODZILLA
RULERS OF EARTH

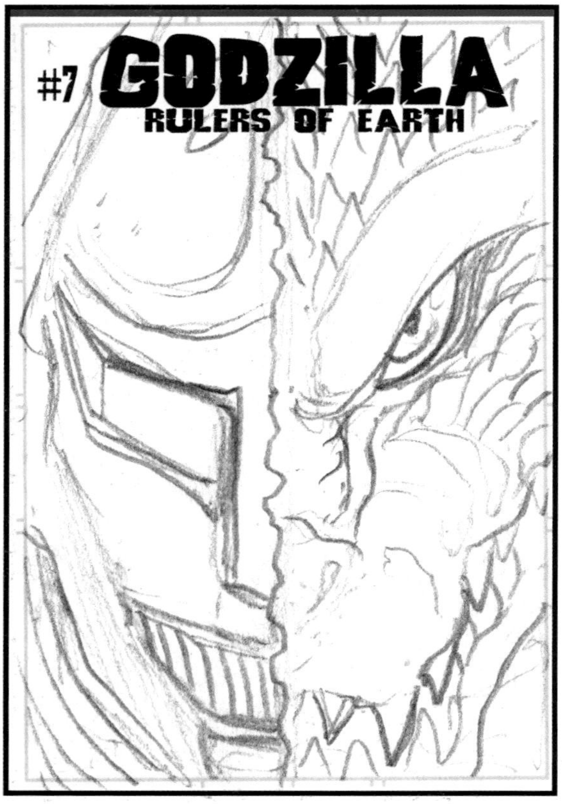
#7
GODZILLA
RULERS OF EARTH

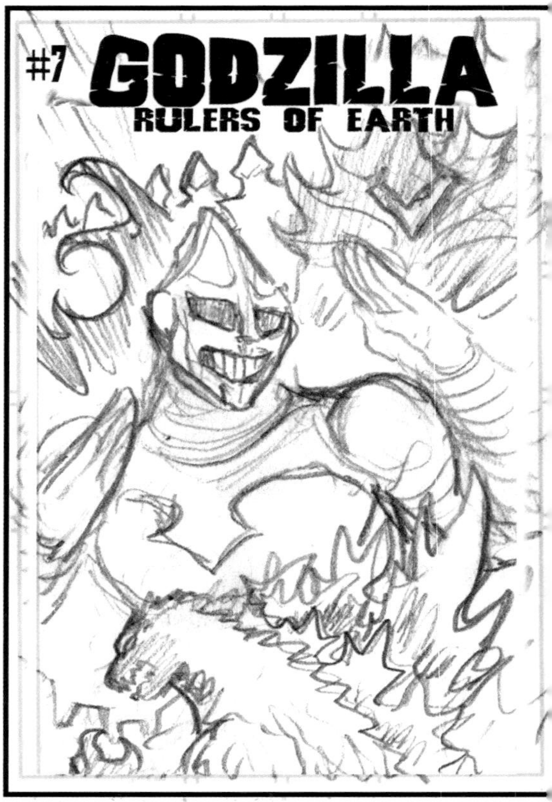
#7
GODZILLA
RULERS OF EARTH

COVER CONCEPTS
BY JEFF ZORNOW

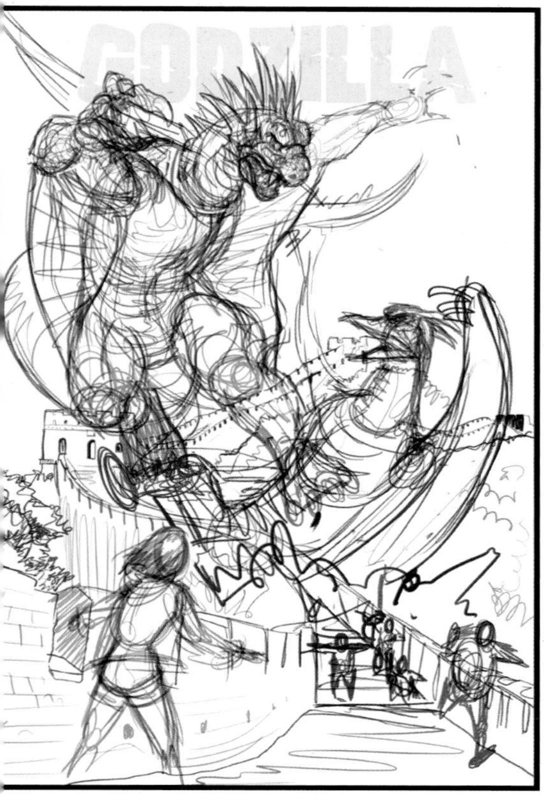
GODZILLA

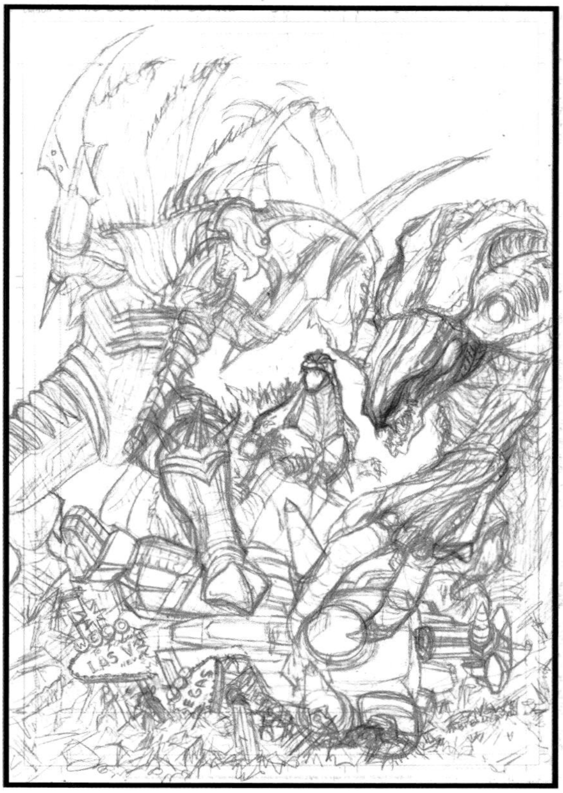

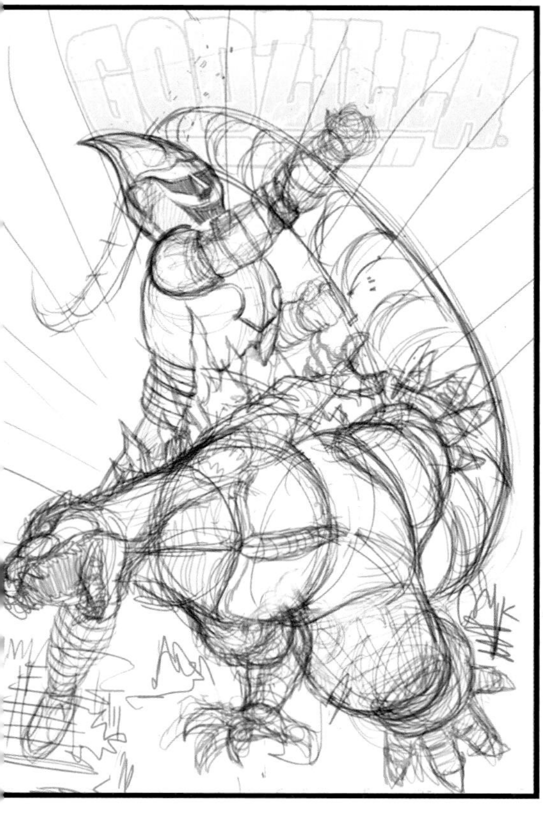
GODZILLA

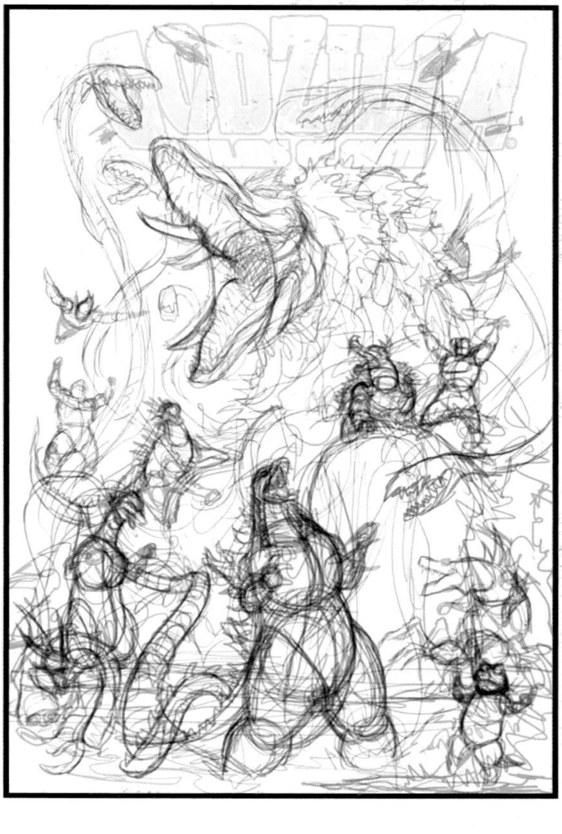

GODZILLA

MORE MONSTER ACTION AND EXCITEMENT FROM IDW PUBLISHING!

GODZILLA, VOL. 1
ISBN: 978-1-61377-413-7

GODZILLA, VOL. 2
ISBN: 978-1-61377-584-4

GODZILLA, VOL. 3
ISBN: 978-1-61377-658-2

THE HALF-CENTURY WAR
ISBN: 978-1-61377-595-C

KINGDOM OF MONSTERS, VOL. 1
ISBN: 978-1-61377-016-0

KINGDOM OF MONSTERS, VOL. 2
ISBN: 978-1-61377-122-8

KINGDOM OF MONSTERS, VOL. 3
ISBN: 978-1-61377-205-8

GANGSTERS & GOLIATHS
ISBN: 978-1-61377-033-T

LEGENDS
ISBN: 978-1-61377-223-2

RULERS OF EARTH, VOL. 1
ISBN: 978-1-61377-749-7

RULERS OF EARTH, VOL. 2
ISBN: 978-1-61377-933-0

WWW.IDWPUBLISHING.CO